Understanding Bioethics and the Law

Understanding Bioethics and the Law

The Promises and Perils of the Brave New World of Biotechnology

Barry R. Schaller

Foreword by Todd Brewster

Westport, Connecticut
London

Library of Congress Cataloging-in-Publication Data

Schaller, Barry R., 1938—
    Understanding bioethics and the law: the promises and perils of the brave new world of
    biotechnology / Barry R. Schaller ; foreword by Todd Brewster.
        p. cm.
    Includes bibliographical references and index.
    ISBN 978–0–275–99918–6 (alk. paper)
1. Medical laws and legislation—United States. 2. Bioethics—United States. 3. Medical
jurisprudence—United States. I. Title.
KF3821.S33   2008
344.7304'1—dc22   2007030213

British Library Cataloguing in Publication Data is available.

Library of Congress Catalog Card Number: 2007030213
ISBN: 978–0–275–99918–6

First published in 2008

Praeger Publishers, 88 Post Road West, Westport, CT 06881
An imprint of Greenwood Publishing Group, Inc.
www.praeger.com

Printed in the United States of America

The paper used in this book complies with the
Permanent Paper Standard issued by the National
Information Standards Organization (Z39.48-1984).

10 9 8 7 6 5 4 3 2 1

For Carol V.C. Schaller

Contents

Preface

The idea for *Understanding Bioethics and the Law* arose from my interest in the conjunction of ethical and legal decision making. Throughout my judicial career, the role of law and judicial decision making in American culture has been a major interest. My first book, *A Vision of American Law: Judging Law, Literature, and the Stories We Tell,* explored the interaction of law with American literature and culture. After that project, I became increasingly aware that the field of bioethics, which involves the intersection of science, medicine, ethics, politics, and law, raised compelling issues in American society.

In the months after *A Vision of American Law* was published, I began an intensive study of bioethics at the same time as I engaged in discussions about law, literature, and American culture. This period of study, reflection, and discussion led to my writing a lengthy article entitled *A Legal Prescription for Bioethical Ills,* for publication in the Quinnipiac Law Review just before the turn of the century. In that article, I discussed the complex relationship of law and bioethics, defining bioethics in a broad sense. I focused on key legal fields, including health care, privacy and Megan's Law, free speech and violence, religion and public life, and biotechnology. My interest in bioethics and law grew as I began regular teaching of bioethics and public health ethics. I became fascinated by the relationship between legal, ethical, and public policy analysis.

My increasing awareness—and concern—that the integrity of solving bioethical dilemmas on an ethical level is jeopardized when participants turn too readily to litigation led me to study the impact of court decisions on the field. I found many ways to acquire the practical experience needed to fully appreciate ethical decision making. Serving on a hospital ethics committee and a hospital Institutional Review Board has provided me with hands-on experience at addressing ethical problems. Collegial work with members from medical, scientific, pastoral, and social work disciplines has been enriching. At the same time, study and writing at Yale University's Interdisciplinary Center for Bioethics has provided opportunities to expand my knowledge of medicine, scientific research, and ethical problem-solving. My classrooms over the years at Trinity College and Wesleyan University have been laboratories of ethical and legal decision making. The eagerness of my students to study *bioethics, public health policy, and ethics* has been a catalyst for my future work in addressing public health problems. The breadth of the students' interests has drawn me to areas that might otherwise have gone unexplored. All of these pursuits have significantly enriched my work as an appellate judge. Legal analysis and decision making are illuminated by the study of ethical analysis and decision making.

The result of this experience is *Understanding Bioethics and the Law,* in which I attempt to demonstrate how the resort to *law* for resolution of what are basically ethical issues has great impact on those issues. While litigating is necessary at times, lawsuits have an impact that reaches far beyond what is envisioned by the litigants or the decision makers. I remain committed to the idea that, in bioethical contexts, people are better-off resolving issues without adversarial strife. Courts, however, have played a prominent role in our society and doubtless will do so in the future. I will, accordingly, suggest ways to minimize the adverse impact of resolving issues by means of litigation and judicial decision making.

This book represents another aspect of my continuing study of the role of courts in American society. Bioethics and biotechnology will continue to hold center stage among domestic issues. It is likely that courts and lawyers will become increasingly involved in the problem solving in these areas. While some governance by statute, regulation, and lawsuit is necessary, all forms of regulation should permit and guide individuals to resolve most issues independently in ways that preserve rather than harm the relationships that are so crucial to family, community, and society.

Foreword

Almost thirty years have passed since Lesley Brown, a young working-class woman from England whose blocked fallopian tubes made it impossible for her to conceive the "natural" way, underwent a highly experimental technique in which one of her eggs was extracted and fertilized by her husband's sperm in a petri dish, then implanted in her uterus, the first successful IVF (in vitro fertilization). The resulting new life, Louise Joy Brown, was the first "test-tube" baby, a phrase, popular at the time for its mad scientist overtones, which has thankfully vanished as the in vitro procedure has become more common. Louise Brown is now a grown woman and a mother in her own right (through the age-old method, not the laboratory version). But back when the news of Brown's birth was released in 1978, it stuck many as the harbinger of a scary new age.

The fear was not only that science was doing work reserved for God; many believed that in creating life in a dish, physicians risked chromosomal damage that could result in a catastrophe. "Everyone had the impression she was going to be nine feet tall and a quarter-inch wide," recalled John Brown, Louise's father. "...[like] something out of a comic strip and they were very, very surprised when they seen her." Indeed, while Patrick Steptoe and Robert Edwards, the British physicians who performed Brown's procedure, are credited with having been the first to cross this frontier, that may only be because the work of Landrum Shettles, an American doctor at New York's Columbia Presbyterian Hospital, was sabotaged by a colleague who worried that cooking up life in a glass vial was a moral breach that had to be stopped. While a test tube holding the sperm and egg of a Florida couple was incubated, Shettles's superior broke into the lab and removed it from its warm environment, effectively ending the experiment and beginning, as you might imagine, a lawsuit (which, by the way, the couple won.)

The Catholic Church still condemns IVF as a gravely evil act, but more than 400,000 Americans have been conceived in this way, enough to populate a city the size of Hartford, Connecticut, while roughly two million "in vitro" babies have been delivered worldwide. By all accounts, Louise Brown has lived a healthy thirty years and there is no evidence that there is a higher percentage of birth defects among in vitro babies. Like so many scientific advancements before it, IVF, by itself, has proved to be scarier in concept than it is in reality.

Still, historians looking back at this event may see it as the moment when the twenty-first century "began." There are other competing events for this honor, like the 1989 fall of the Berlin Wall and the 1983 introduction of the personal computer and there is even a roughly contemporaneous event that should be given serious consideration. While Louise Brown was still in diapers, the Islamic Revolution in Iran, which overthrew the Shah Mohammad Reza Pahlavi and led to Islam's ongoing confrontation with the West, was taking shape. But by the measure that defines the twentieth century as the physicist's century and the twenty-first as the century of biological discovery, the birth of Louise Brown has the undeniable mark of a beginning.

The trading of one science for another is too simple a way of describing this dramatic shift in human history. Physics is cold, the description of how forces act upon each other. Biology is hot, intimate, the stuff of life itself. The physicist's era was defined by Albert Einstein, the atom, and, of course, the bomb. It started in the lab, proceeded to the battlefield, and then landed in the human imagination in the form of the late twentieth century's contemplation of Armageddon. Biology's era started in the lab and moved to the doctor's office and the bedroom and, finally, to the creative imagination. If the logo of the physicist's era is the mushroom cloud, the biologist's is the map of the human genome.

The decisions that pushed the questions of the physicist's epoch were those of governments and leaders and it required mammoth defense budgets and research grants to navigate. We could only watch and cower from the threat that it might be misused. By contrast, our own biology-driven era has a domestic experience with science. Assisted reproductive technology has more in common with the technological individuality of the iPod and the home page; it is wrapped up with the private nature of identity, and the decisions are those of ordinary men and women and their doctors. Who were John and Lesley Brown but a couple who wanted a baby and used science's help to get one?

Much of applied technology starts with such claims on virtue. But it rarely stops there. All technologies create unintended consequences, some beneficent, others regrettable. Edison thought the phonograph's main purpose would be the recording of wills, not the agent of popular culture that it became. Henry Ford fashioned the Model T as a way to make the farmer's life less arduous (the "T" had the ability to double as a tractor) and give him a respectable way to go to town on Sundays. Instead, it destroyed rural America by inviting the traveler out. Sometimes, it is technology's critics who are wrong: those who feared that the computer and Internet would lead to greater centralization and control by Big Brother could not have been more wrong. The Internet has decentralized society and led to the democratization of information.

Steptoe and Edwards were helping an infertile couple, but as at least some critics of IVF pointed out at the time, it was not pregnancies like the Brown's that they feared as much as the questions that IVF raised, first to the imagination, and then in reality. The harvesting of eggs, the freezing of embryos, the screening of embryos for desirable (and undesirable) characteristics, the use of stem cells extracted from embryos, and the destruction of unwanted embryos all raised new and thorny ethical, moral, and religious questions that we have not yet come to terms with as a society. It is one thing to revel in the scientific achievement of a baby girl born to an otherwise infertile couple, but how will we adapt to the advent of cloning, or to more frivolous uses of biotechnology like those that physicist Freeman Dyson predicts: an explosion of genetic experimentation delivered by do-it-yourself kits that will allow the amateur biological tinkerer to create all sorts of new plant and animal varieties at the whim of his or her imagination. Think of the old rural contest for growing the largest tomato transformed now into a contest to create the biggest or most colorful dog.

Reproductive medicine focuses on the beginning of life, but there are as many maintenance-of-life issues and end-of-life issues posed by advances in the life sciences. Just as we are contemplating new definitions of when life begins and how it is conceived, so we are considering new definitions of when it ends and just how much human agency can or should be tolerated in the process.

As Barry Schaller demonstrates in this superb and important book, law is perhaps the central place where these and other questions posed by modern biology come to be answered, where there is no option to leave them to the realm of metaphysical uncertainty. In the United States, where we practice the common law we inherited from our English ancestors, law seeks answers not in abstraction, but in response to real "cases or controversies." Working from precedent, the judge determines that a new case resembles this other already-decided case, or some constellation of principles established by a series of already-decided cases, and should therefore be decided on principles long recognized by the law as just. That is the common law tradition.

Like the common law, statutory law also reacts to a changing world, but it does so in the legislature, where forward-thinking politicians determined to assist one outcome or prevent another, write new laws for scenarios that old laws had not anticipated. Both common law and statutory law, then, attempt to come to terms with how past certainties are to be re-understood according to present predicaments. The question that Justice Schaller raises is whether our legal traditions are up to the challenge.

Consider, for instance, how the life sciences challenge old definitions of property when determining the dispensation of a divorcing couple's stash of frozen embryos. If property in the old sense, are the embryos to be divided between husband and wife like real estate or money? If they are not property, but potential children, should custody be granted as it would if they were indeed children, and if granted, is it only the custody of the embryos or the custody of the resulting child, too, that must be determined?

In an advanced biological age, what constitutes injury? Justice Schaller's discussion here of "wrongful life" (in which genetic testing revealed or might have revealed signals of a debilitating and chronic condition) and "wrongful living" (in which, in cases of medical futility, life is perpetuated contrary to the wishes of the patient or loved ones acting in the patient's behalf) puts us into new territory as well. The notion in the first is that had the couple known that their child would be disabled at birth, they might have chosen to abort; in the second, that the pain and suffering of a life continued by medical instrumentation against the will of the patient is itself an injury requiring compensation.

As difficult as these issues are to resolve according to traditional legal concepts, they become more difficult when one realizes the implications that can be derived from one resolution or another. If the frozen embryos are incipient children and not property, does that mean that they are indeed "living matter" and if so, how does that square with *Roe v. Wade,* the landmark 1973 Supreme Court ruling on abortion, which saw the state's interest as only emerging at the point of viability, suggesting that before that it could not be considered a "life"? Like many states with a strong antiabortion sentiment, Illinois recently passed legislation preparing for the day when *Roe* is overturned. It defined human life as occurring from conception, not viability, and as a result a local state judge cited this definition in ruling on a "wrongful-death" suit brought by a couple whose frozen embryo was accidentally destroyed. Of course, the Supreme Court does not recognize this definition. But if it did—and who knows where the Court will go in the next couple of decades as bioethical issues come before it?—then stem cell researchers would be liable for murder.

What, too, are the implications of deciding injury cases according to the idea that no life would have been preferable to a life of disability? As Justice Schaller points out, so far courts have resisted the call to place a value on "no life at all" and to the degree that injuries have been awarded by judges, they have been according to the monetary value of coping with the unanticipated result. Judges have found it hard to quantify the absence of something and, to the degree that they must consider real-world consequences of their decision, they would have to worry about the message conveyed by the decision that disability is a condition so horrific that it would have been better for there to have been no life at all. Naturally, lobbyists for the disabled have found grave problems with even the suggestion of such a conclusion. And how far do we have to travel from such logic to determine that disabled means less capable, not incapable, opening the path for lawsuits generated by couples who thought they had programmed their pregnancy for a tall, athletic child with brown eyes and olive skin but got something "less" than they bargained for?

Justice Schaller wisely raises political questions here, too. The issues of bioethics resound with moral and religious overtones and, as with abortion, politicians have been loath to accept the responsibility for drawing the lines of the law where so much passion controls the attitudes of the voting public. However, that punts the difficult work on this subject to the courtroom, not always advisable in a democracy. Many judicial scholars, no matter where they may stand on the issue of abortion, regret the Court's decision in *Roe* as unfounded, representing faulty constitutional reasoning, and usurping a political question that would have better been decided in the legislatures than the unelected judiciary. One might even argue that by deciding *Roe,* the Court helped to fuel the social turmoil over this subject which would have been less stirred if the legislative body had been the arena of decision. When the legislative branch decides, it provides a stamp of democratic legitimacy that the Court lacks.

Similarly, by leaving the bioethical questions to the courts, we risk spurring more social upset, particularly since judges will be hard-pressed to assume an activist profile. So much of existing law is inadequate to the demands of the bioethical question, and thus it leaves it to judges to make grand leaps of reasoning for which they will no doubt be criticized.

Do we have a choice? If there is a single message to this book, it is that we most certainly do. In many ways, Justice Schaller is making a call to attention. When it comes to modern issues like bioethics, we tend, understandably, to not fully comprehend the nature of the questions we are being asked and it is about time that we sat up and took notice of that fact. Despite the earnest attempts of many to devolve life science issues into ones of personal autonomy, usually invoking *Roe*, these issues do not fall cleanly into old political divisions of the individual and the state, Left and Right, privacy and surveillance, "choice" and "right to life." Think, for instance, about some of the implications of gender selection. When it becomes easy to determine the sex of a baby in the petri dish, or at least before the transfer of the embryo, will the traditional preference for boys over girls create a worldwide gender imbalance? If so, many who call themselves feminists and supporters of abortion rights might demand some manner of regulation, yet if they did, they would clearly run up against *Roe*, which protects the mother from the interference of the state in the interest of personal autonomy.

As in most issues, we need the courage to make hard decisions and, even more important, to abide by the results, whether we agree with them or not. Democracy does not sit well with the purist or the self-righteous. While it considers moral questions, it values compromise over purity, practicality over ideology. Moral convictions are not something that we usually see with gray tones, yet until we advance this conversation, as Justice Schaller does here, we risk making mistakes about matters of grave importance.

Todd Brewster
Director, The Peter Jennings Project for Journalists and the Constitution

Acknowledgments

The inspiration to write this book came from many sources. My work as a trial and appellate judge during the past three decades fostered my profound interest in the role that judges and lawyers play in American society. The teaching of bioethics and public health law, policy, and ethics to undergraduate, graduate, and law students, and judges during the past decade inspired my interest in the fascinating ethical, legal, and cultural issues presented by developments in science and biotechnology. My participation in working and writing groups in bioethics and public health ethics with so many talented professionals at the Yale University's Interdisciplinary Center for Bioethics, the Yale Center for Public Health Preparedness, and the State of Connecticut Department of Public Health has contributed immensely to my understanding of critical issues facing our society and the global community.

I extend my special appreciation to Christopher Heller for his interest and enthusiastic support in preliminary research and editing. I am deeply grateful to Katherine Engelman, Editor-in-Chief of the Quinnipiac Health Law Journal, for her untiring contributions to research and editing as well as for her many superb suggestions to improve this book. I also thank her colleagues, Jennifer Roth, Ari Schneider, Michael Schweitzer, and Christopher Williams for their editing and research help. I am particularly grateful to Julius Landwirth, M.D., J.D., Associate Director of Yale University's Interdisciplinary Center for Bioethics, for his helpful and reassuring comments on an earlier draft of the manuscript, and to Geoffrey Hazard, Distinguished Professor of Law at UC Hastings College of the

Law, for generously applying his ethics expertise to a thorough review of the book. My wife, Carol V.C. Schaller, not only supported and encouraged me as I pursued this project through countless weekends and more than one summer vacation, but also has offered me over the years the benefit of her illuminating observations and insights on human behavior and ethics.

Chapter 1

Introduction—Bioethics on Trial

Scarcely any political question arises in the United States that is not resolved, sooner or later, into a judicial question. Hence all parties are obliged to borrow, in their daily controversies, the ideas, and even the language, peculiar to judicial proceedings.... The language of the law thus becomes, in some measure, a vulgar tongue; the spirit of the law, which is produced in the schools and courts of justice, gradually penetrates beyond their walls into the bosom of society, where it descends to the lowest classes, so that at last the whole people contract the habits and the tastes of the judicial magistrate.[1]

Alexis de Tocqueville

O brave new world, that has such people in't.[2]

William Shakespeare

BIOETHICS *IS* ON TRIAL

Bioethics, a discipline concerned with studying and resolving life-changing biomedical problems using ethical principles, is recently threatened by court intervention and by the unwise and excessive use of lawsuits. Because the situation is complex, it is important to be clear about where fault lies.

I do not claim that the current predicament has been caused by lawyers or by judges acting improperly. Nor do I argue, by any means, that litigation is never suitable to decide bioethical problems. As I see it, the present condition results from the combination of three forces: a failure, in some respects, of private ethical decision-making, lack of adequate legislative regulation in certain crucial areas, and the deeply rooted American habit of turning to litigating disputes rather than resolving them by other means, such as negotiation or mediation. In those methods of alternative dispute resolution, the parties attempt to resolve disputes by discussing the issues by themselves or with facilitators who assist in the process. In too many situations, *forfeiture* of legitimate private ethical decision-making power is followed by the parties turning to litigation. Although bringing a lawsuit often looks like the easiest and most efficient way to resolve a dispute, it rarely turns out to be the case. The consequences, intended and unintended, of litigation frequently extract a severe price, not only from the parties, but from society as well.

The discovery of an impasse or a breakdown in private ethical decision-making, as demonstrated in the chaotic events surrounding the Terri Schiavo end-of-life fiasco, is often followed by an abrupt and ill-considered attempt at government intervention. That kind of hasty intrusion is rarely effective to forestall private litigation. Since every field of medicine and science and, therefore, of bioethics, is configured differently, the interaction of law and bioethics produces different results in different situations. We will see in Chapter 3, however, that the field of biomedical research using human subjects provides a classic example of how law and ethics intersect.

Biotechnology Defined

The impact of biotechnology is central to the issues and problems to be considered in this book. Virtually all of the developments to be discussed in the following chapters have arisen because of biotechnology. Before beginning, therefore, we should understand what we mean by biotechnology and what it encompasses. I will be using the term in the broadest sense, similar to the way the President's Council on Bioethics used it in its report entitled "Beyond Therapy: Biotechnology and the Pursuit of Happiness," published in 2003.[3]

Although the term has been given a wide variety of definitions, in its broadest sense it is "the processes and products...offering the potential to alter and, to a degree, to control the phenomena of life—in plants, in... animals, and, increasingly, in human beings...."[4] An even more basic definition is "the use of living things, especially cells and bacteria, in industrial processes."[5] In this broad sense, the term would include older technologies as common as fermentation and plant and animal hybridization.[6] In the contemporary context, the term is commonly applied to a wide variety of topics, including genetic engineering for all purposes, development of new drugs and biomechanical devices, improving biological capacities of humans, developing tissues derived from stem cells—in short, "any industrially developed, useful agent that can alter the workings of the body or the mind."[7] In this sense, biotechnology reaches and affects all the subjects discussed in this book, from beginning of life to end of life, from embryonic stem cell research to transplant of organs and tissues, and medical and biological research involving human subjects. Every subject area has been profoundly changed by the dramatic developments in biotechnology. Every field has been altered by biotechnology and, with it, new ethical and legal issues have arisen. The focus of the book is on the ethical problems and how they are affected by litigation and judicial decision-making. Although I will not interrupt the narrative with reminders about the impact of biotechnology, the presence of biotechnology is a constant throughout. In a real sense, the implications of the *biotechnology revolution* are a central subject of our study.

Vital Relationships

Other fields of bioethics, beyond human research, that have been directly affected both by developments in biotechnology and in litigation include traditional medical care, new reproductive technologies, medical futility and end-of-life matters, and the quasi-public allocation of scarce resources such as organs and other bodily materials. Each field centers on one or more vital relationships that depend on trust, many of which are legal fiduciary relationships. Fiduciary relationships, in which one party holds a position of trust, invoke a high standard of care. Among them are researcher/subject; physician/patient; health care provider/ patient; and donor/distributor/recipient (in the case of resource allocation). Each professional relationship is well worth preserving. The relationships, however, do not survive intact when adversarial conflict (leading to victory or defeat) supplants ethical decision-making (leading to resolution and closure). The relationships also cannot long survive repeated violations of trust. Parties often resort to litigation because the fiduciary relationship fails on some level. We will see how transforming ethical problems into legal issues alters the very nature of the issues and problems. Further, because legal concepts and language have a way of *permeating* other institutions in society, the issues that are litigated have usually been altered by the time they return to public discussion.[8] We often discover that what once were purely ethical issues have mutated into legal issues by virtue of the powerful impact of law and legal institutions.

We will discover how various external factors also come into play to change decision making from *private ethical* to *public adversarial.* One such factor is economic change. For example, the dramatic increase in use of prescription medications as a way of dealing with medical conditions, as opposed to alternative methods of health care, has deeply affected the field of human research. Research dollars have been poured into the field, and new pressures have been placed on researchers, sponsors, institutional review board members, and subjects alike. The economics of health care changed the traditional physician/patient relationship in a way that made litigation more likely. Other factors include scientific and biotechnological developments, which have further transformed the field of medicine, particularly in reproductive and end-of-life matters. These transformations have led to litigation of questions such as who owns frozen eggs and whether a constitutional right to die exists.

Ethinomics Revisited

Although the term *ethinomics* has recently been coined to describe the convergence of ethics and economics in public policy fields,[9] I use the term to mean the (often unspoken) economic infrastructure of ethical issues and arguments. That is to say that many issues are governed by the underlying economics of the situation. And yet, because of some peculiar sensibility (some might call it hypocrisy) of American public discourse, economic considerations often remain unspoken out of concern that the discussion might sound as though it is advocating dehumanization of people. Any talk that appears to support the idea of commodifying humans is not acceptable, even when that is exactly what is happening. In reality, public policy decisions that are made legitimately for economic reasons are often clothed in other garb. In legal decisions, it is not uncommon for vital concerns that actually drive the dispute to be unspoken and unacknowledged. The fact is, ethical and legal controversies do not exist in the abstract. Such disputes (whether bioethical or legal) exist in both a factual and a complex social context, which give meaning to the particular facts of a situation. Those contexts are often only selectively acknowledged. It would be far better for the underlying backgrounds to be openly disclosed and discussed during the public debate rather than concealed.

Reluctance to rethink and reformulate traditional ethical concepts, as needed, can lead to breakdown in relationships and, eventually, litigation. For example, the steadfast refusal to allow payment for certain types of scarce resources (organs for example) while at the same time allowing it for others (eggs and sperm) may well cause some needy patients to bypass traditional ethical methods of securing the resources. Whether the steadfast refusal to allow payment is good or not is not the issue. When technology and science produce a change, a willingness to reexamine openly and publicly the traditional relationships and ideas is crucial. If that does not take place in a public arena with public discussion, it may occur privately in ways that undermine public policy. Another example is the continuing erosion in the physician/patient relationship, caused first by the shift to managed care. Additionally, the fact that more and more physicians act not only in the therapeutic role, but as clinical researchers as well, contributes to further confusion, if not erosion.

Each field of bioethics is governed by particular principles, and subject to various pressures. In reality, however, a balance must be struck among private ethical decision-making, public government regulation, and court intervention, when it is necessary to compensate for serious abuses and injuries. Dedicated private ethical decision-making and faithful adherence to respected standards will lessen the need for government regulation. When necessary, strong government regulation, followed by honest and effective enforcement, will reduce the need for private enforcement by way of litigation. Litigation, while essential to protect vital interests, too often benefits only a few, while adding economic cost to many.

Law and Bioethics

Many books have been written about the emerging, but still undeveloped, *law of bioethics*. Few have been written about how law impacts bioethics. What happens when bioethical issues are decided by courts rather than by private individuals and ethical communities of interest? The answer is essential for private decision makers and for those who conduct ethical decision-making. If the law of bioethics is not yet fully formed, can we say that it is nonetheless self-evident? The short answer is that the law of bioethics is really an evolving compilation of traditional jurisprudence from a wide variety of legal categories, including tort, contract, property, fiduciary, constitutional, and family. There is no law of bioethics, as such, although at some time in the future, the existing law will have evolved and be sufficiently integrated to deserve the name.

While a great deal has been written about the evolving law of bioethics, not nearly enough has been written to explain the way litigation and court-applied law (judicial decision-making) transforms issues that arise in both private and public health care, and raises conflicts between the ethical approaches and legal approaches to the difficult choices that people have to make.

In the course of the book, I will generally use the term law to mean decisions of courts and judges and the term social policy or policy to mean actions and enactments of the other branches of government, the legislative and the executive. There are certain types of cases in which courts are directed by existing law to take into account public policy. One such area is in state constitutional analysis; another is in determining whether a particular civil duty exists. Ordinarily, however, courts state what the law is rather than what public policy is. Official actions of the legislative and executive branches of government create law by enacting statutes and regulations and by issuing rules and orders. Courts must then interpret, apply, and enforce these actions. In their essence, however, they represent expressions of policy and the distinction is important for our purposes. Constitutions, both federal and state, are fundamental policy statements of society that control the actions of all the branches of government as well as individual citizens. Actions of courts, as well as legislatures and executive branch officers, can bring about individual and social changes, but courts have distinct limits in that regard.

THE BEGINNING OF BIOETHICS

About forty years ago, in the mid-1960s, bioethics began as a recognized discipline in the general field of philosophy or, more precisely, applied ethics. Although the term is still used in reference to ecology, it is more commonly used to mean the study of ethical issues arising from the biological and medical sciences. It is linked closely to the disclosure of abuses in research involving human subjects in both the United States and abroad. In the United States, the name *Tuskegee*[10] has become a *metaphor* for human experimentation abuse. The names *Willowbrook*[11] and *Jewish Hospital*[12] bring to mind similar connotations. When the Tuskegee abuses were disclosed, ethical attention focused with renewed vigor on the use of human subjects in medical research. Abroad, the Nuremberg war crimes tribunals, followed by promulgation of the Nuremberg Code[13] and later, the Declaration of Helsinki,[14] were major components of the development of bioethics as well.

It can be said that human subject research may be the central issue in the field of bioethics with respect to both private and public health. At its essence, bioethics involves fundamental concerns about respecting human dignity and avoiding using humans as means to an end—as mere instruments or raw material for experimentation. Under the glare of intense public scrutiny, leading scholars, scientists, and ethicists have established the importance of voluntary and informed consent. Institutional procedures were developed to protect vulnerable patients against the potential abuses of both well-meaning but misguided researchers and clinicians and those who have forsaken their ethical and moral duties.

At nearly the same time, rapid advances in biomedical science and biotechnology began to raise far-reaching challenges to existing ways of thinking about human existence and human nature. The beginning of these advances stems from the discovery of DNA by a team of researchers led by Watson and Crick in the 1950s. The very meaning of what it is to be human began to be debated with new significance. Defining *personhood* (a crucial issue in bioethics) for various purposes had renewed importance. By the late 1960s and early 1970s, what has been called the revolution in biology and the life sciences, the development of molecular biology, was beginning to make itself felt. The pharmaceutical industry was expanding exponentially, making oral contraceptives, tranquilizers, and other high-impact drugs. Cardiac pacemakers, kidney dialysis machines, and respirators were in use. In vitro fertilization of the human egg had just been achieved, and the first human heart transplant had occurred. Medical scholars were developing what was then a radical new definition of death, relying on brain activity rather than heart or lung activity as the dispositive sign of life.

Changes were also occurring in behavior therapy based on new technology. Genetic screening, especially in the field of prenatal diagnosis, was underway, less than two decades after the discovery by Watson and Crick. Scientists were beginning to discuss the future implications of genetic testing and gene therapy including genetically engineered enhancement of human beings. The exciting potential for using new knowledge and techniques to cure devastating and chronic diseases, infertility, and mental illness became apparent. At the same time, a growing awareness of the implications of intervening so drastically into the human body and mind arose. What are the consequences for human freedom, dignity, privacy, and self-understanding as well as for the future of human life individually and collectively? Another of the central issues in bioethics, with implications for public policy, came to the fore: What, exactly, is—and should be—the interest of society (the state) in bioethics issues involving individuals?

As of yet, no one had given the name "bioethics" to this vast field of inquiry. That time was to come shortly. The term *bioethics* was coined in 1971 by the biologist Van Rensselaer Potter, who used it to describe his theory that we need an ethic to incorporate our obligations, not just to other humans, but to the entire biosphere.[15] His goal was to create a new discipline of applied ethics based on principles applicable to the field of modern science rather than a purely philosophical or religious inquiry. The concept evolved into a field of inquiry that looks at the ethical questions raised in medicine, biomedical science, and biotechnology for purposes of everyday decision-making as well as for public policy, law, and social institutions.

Since its inception, the subject matter of bioethics has expanded to include discussions on ethical and policy aspects of reproductive issues such as abortion, assisted reproduction, genetic screening and testing, embryo and stem cell research, cloning, gene therapy, and genetic enhancement. It encompasses issues of death and dying such as living wills and "Do Not Resuscitate (DNR) Orders," assisted suicide, euthanasia, and medical futility. It further involves clinical practice issues of informed consent, pharmacology and genetics, organ allocation and transplants, performance-enhancing drugs, and the use of artificial or animal organs for humans, along with other biotechnology issues such as artificial intelligence and robotics. This listing is far from all-inclusive. Some scholars have proposed definitions that encompass the whole range of human activities and endeavors involving the body, mind, and spirit of individual humans.[16] Despite the occasional use of these broad definitions, bioethics is mainly thought of as dealing with ethical problems in the medical and biological sciences. I will use the term in that sense. The three major principles on which bioethics is based are well known to Western political culture as well as philosophy. They are (1) respect for persons; (2) beneficence (or doing good) and the reverse, non-maleficence (or doing no harm); and (3) justice (or distributive justice). The third plays a role in some, but not all bioethical problems. It is rarely mentioned in connection with terminating life support or limiting medical resources for an individual.

Bioethicists

Over time, the need for bioethicists has grown dramatically. Hospitals, medical schools, universities, governmental agencies, and private biotechnology companies all employ bioethicists to offer guidance and assistance in deciding difficult ethical questions. Despite the developments in the field, no formal and binding standards or principles govern bioethics or the practice of bioethics. This remains so despite the fact that bioethicists operate in environments in which most of their peers—health care executives, lawyers, physicians, and nurses—are bound by professional ethics codes. Calls for a code of ethics for bioethicists are periodically made. Most bioethicists follow a principalist approach governed by the three basic ethical principles (respect for persons, beneficence and non-maleficence, and justice) promoted in the Belmont Report, with grounding in the earlier Nuremberg Code and Declaration of Helsinki. That is not the only approach to ethical problems. In recent years, an approach advocating more focus on social context and experience and less on the basic principles has emerged.[17] It may be inevitable, and probably beneficial, that the paradigms in bioethics and health law are shifting to favor a new pragmatism.[18]

Bioethicists as a profession have emerged during the past few decades to fill the ethical void that often exists in private and public biomedical decision-making. Bioethicists, however, do not speak with a single voice and cannot always claim to be objective and neutral. While they are usually employed by health care organizations or biotechnology companies to advise and consult on biomedical issues, they may be expected, in fact, to support a particular interest. The diversity of perspectives and opinions of bioethicists may be as broad as those of the citizenry as a whole. No particular training or licensing is required, and no uniform code of ethics has been settled on. The same degree of scrutiny that applies to other experts must be brought to bear here.

The bioethics enterprise is booming in every walk of life even in the absence of firm standards or ethical codes to assure the public of integrity and consistency in bioethical opinions. Bioethicists may have received training and advanced education in such disciplines as philosophy, science, medicine, law, or any number of other varied backgrounds. As noted, although most bioethicists recognize and base their opinions on the authority of the three major principles of bioethics, those principles are not legally binding in and of themselves (except to the extent they are independently incorporated in the law, of course).

How the three principles are weighed or prioritized is up to each individual decision maker. Privacy and confidentiality are sometimes added together as a fourth principle and, in the case of public health ethics, the factor of the common good or public well-being is crucial, as well. In standard bioethics, there is no weighing of individual autonomy against the common good except when the primary issue is distributive justice. The main focus for most purposes is on the individual. But in the case of public health matters, all actions related to the individual must be measured against the impact on everyone else, as a collective group of individuals or as a collective unit in its own right.

Medical Ethics

Medical ethics, as old as the Hippocratic Oath, provides a natural foundation for the relatively young discipline of bioethics, a branch of ethics, or more specifically, of applied ethics. A basic understanding of ethics, the study of moral duty and obligation, is essential to an understanding of bioethics. The problem is that there are many different schools of ethics. There is no universal agreement as to the ethical foundation from which bioethics should derive its principles. Even when bioethicists are acting independently there can be a wide range of ethical opinions on any given issue or problem.

With the revolution in life science development in its fourth, or at most, fifth decade of development, it is obvious that American society is still in the early years of a period of revolutionary change involving the life sciences, health care, and information technology. The potential for change due to rapid advances in understanding the genetic basis of life is significant enough. When combined with developments in information technology, making biology an information science, the change becomes truly revolutionary. Our national philosophical and cultural commitment to basic principles of human dignity causes us to believe that we must impose ethical control upon change of any kind. The difficulty of imposing such control on the breathtaking advances in biotechnology is a serious challenge to our principles and institutions.

Biotechnological Change

As exciting discoveries and new applications in biotechnology and information technology are reported every day, it becomes increasingly difficult for anyone, whether ordinary citizen or professional decision maker, to stay informed about, much less absorb and comprehend, the rapid changes in all the related fields. Although the media's attention tends to be focused on the most controversial developments, such as genetic engineering, stem cell research, or human cloning, the impact of discoveries and developments upon other issues, such as criminal identification, patenting, organ transplants, and genetic screening, is just as vital in the long run. The developments in all these fields are important even when they proceed incrementally and modestly. Changes can be produced by incremental developments on a scale far smaller than the most dramatic events.

Not only do these advances in knowledge and creative applications pose numerous challenges to individuals in their personal ethical decision-making, but they also affect every sector, public and private, of American society. That includes the diverse, but increasingly interrelated fields of law, medicine, media, education, economics, politics, religion, and, of course, science and technology. The impact of change is global. We cannot insulate ourselves against the effects of events occurring beyond the reach of our regulatory powers.

Value of Bioethics

The value of bioethics is that it can provide a practical framework for ethical decision-making by examining present scientific and medical problems in the context of a variety of sources that include philosophy, religion, history, and law.

Bioethics can suggest how to go about deciding vital issues although it cannot tell us what the decisions should be. Bioethics, like philosophy itself, is a discipline that has no single set of qualifying standards and multiple sources upon which opinions are based. We must judge bioethical opinions based on how we evaluate their philosophical consistency and integrity, their analytical soundness, and the workability of their recommendations.

Framing vital issues in bioethical terms can elevate discussion to a rational level. It can provide building blocks and methods for reaching agreement among people who hold diverse viewpoints and who cling to fundamental belief systems. Bioethics is at its best when it addresses issues in their full factual and social context. Although some problems seem to be irreducibly complex and unsolvable dilemmas, true conundrums, the reality is that a resolution is *always* possible based on the factual context. A resolution in a given case need not produce a *final* resolution of the underlying issues under all circumstances. On a case by case basis, however, *all* bioethical problems are capable of solution. One difficulty with our ongoing, virulent national arguments about vital issues, are that the parties seek—or demand—an *ultimate* answer to the abstract issue involved that is consistent with their particular religious or moral belief. Resolution is not possible under those circumstances. No single belief can triumph over all others in our system of government and, so long as solutions are demanded that involve dominance of one and capitulation by the rest, the debate will continue to be as strident as ever.

RELIGION

Leaders of the Roman Catholic Church once imprisoned Copernicus for stating correctly that the Earth revolved around the sun. Centuries passed before the error was acknowledged.[19] Although religious institutions in the United States cannot legitimately claim to exercise direct authority over the world of science, they continue to play a powerful role by attempting to shape the viewpoints of public officials and private citizens. In fact, in the past decade or so, religious groups have made a renewed effort to interject religious doctrine in social and foreign policy and to control the teaching of science in American public schools. Although the focus of this effort has been to promote the teaching of intelligent design as an alternative to evolution, they have attempted to influence public policy on reproduction and end-of-life issues as well. No single religion, or religious belief system, can presume to represent moral authority in our type of society. It remains to be seen how long the success of religious institutions in driving U.S. politics as much as it has in the past decade can be sustained. Regardless, few would quarrel with the proposition that religious beliefs can and should guide individuals in their personal moral decision-making. It seems safe to say that as much of bioethical decision-making as possible should be left in the realm of personal ethical choice. Moreover, religious leaders have a major role to play in contributing religious views to the public debate. Because there are so many different versions of religious views, even within established belief systems, and because we have no national religion, religion cannot be the formal basis of our national policy on such matters. Religious beliefs and values, because they are so diverse, cannot produce consensus, especially the consensus needed to create effective policy on bioethical matters. Religious views injected into political debate can also lead to further conflict as the focus of discussion shifts from the issue under discussion to differences in religious belief systems. Fundamentalist-type views tend to hamper political and social debate rather than illuminate it.

LAW

This is a book about the impact of law on bioethics. What happens when bioethics is *on trial?* What is the impact when courts are asked to make decisions on questions that would otherwise be made by individuals or groups of individuals according to ethical procedures or standards? How does law enter the equation? What is the impact when courts decide, not only who should decide the issue, but how the issue should be decided? Law and policy constitute the ordering system of American society. Regardless of one's theory of law (and there are as many as there are theories of ethics), law is America's preferred means of regulating individual behavior, of resolving disputes, and of ensuring that society functions in a fair and orderly way.

It may be fair to say that generally, in a legal dispute, at least half of the litigants would rather have chosen another forum for decision making. In the absence of a jurisdictional problem, however, the choice of decision by lawsuit—or, if you prefer, combat by lawsuit—by one party binds the other parties. Like it or not, the party sued is in the contest for the duration and, perhaps worst of all, the cost. There is no escape from litigation other than settlement, of course. Many people feel that lawsuits, or even mere threats of lawsuits, are much overused and abused.

Nonetheless, by the sheer number of times that litigation is chosen, it does appear to be America's forum of preference. A factor that contributes to the proliferation of lawsuits is the failure (whether refusal or neglect) of legislatures, both federal and state, to address fundamental public policy issues. A litigant, it seems, can always find a common law, statutory or constitutional ground for a claim. Once a court is presented with a lawsuit, the court is bound to decide the case although not necessarily on the merits if, for example, the court determines that it does not have jurisdiction. The fact that it might involve issues that ought to be addressed by other branches of government is irrelevant.

A determined litigant, armed with constitutional access to the courts, will always be able to use litigation in an attempt to achieve his or her goals. Litigation is nearly always an unsatisfactory way of resolving disputes over bioethical issues. A lawsuit and the resulting decision also create precedent, which shapes the results in other cases. This has both advantages and disadvantages depending on the circumstances. I do not, of course, advocate policies that would interfere with the exercise of the right to bring lawsuits. Not only would that be futile, but it would also prevent legitimate claimants from gaining access to the courts. I do, however, advocate adopting policies that would appropriately minimize the number and the scope of lawsuits. To this end, it is vital that ethical supervision and resolution of bioethical issues must proceed with the utmost skill and determination in order to minimize the need for intervention by regulators and by lawyers.

Genetics and the new biology, combined with information technology, have many fascinating and important implications for the medical and the scientific research community. My emphasis, however, is not on these subjects, but on the implications of these technologies for law and public policy and, most important, for the ethical decisions faced by ordinary people in everyday life.

The format of each chapter will be to provide ethical and legal background for the particular topic before discussing the way law impacts bioethical decision-making. After a discussion of some of the major examples of litigation in the field, I will demonstrate, through analysis, how law operates on the claims litigated and how that will impact the underlying ethical issues as they become the subject of further public policy discussions.

CHAPTER TWO, THE CONTEXT OF BIOETHICS, LAW, AND SOCIETY

I will establish my formula for evaluating the way law operates. The questions for analysis will be explained here, as well as the context for our inquiry into the impact of law on bioethics. We will review the social, legal, cultural, scientific, and political features of our society as they affect the discussion of bioethical issues on trial. Issues do not arise in a cultural vacuum, but rather, have rich and detailed historical origins and contexts. I will describe the broad social context in which our discussion of bioethical issues is situated. This process will entail a brief description of the major factors that bring us to our present societal situation. I will identify the central policy objectives that we share as a society and to which we consent, as well as the disagreement on their implementation and meaning. The religious and ethical foundation of these policies is important. Fundamental ethical principles of human dignity will be discussed. Some general observations about the way courts operate and the impact court decisions have on other institutions in society will be included. We will examine the cultural factors that have defined the role of our court system.

CHAPTER THREE, THE LEGAL LANDSCAPE OF HUMAN RESEARCH LITIGATION

We begin the substantive discussion with a core field of bioethics, clinical research involving human subjects. Early abuses in human research gave rise to the basic principles in bioethics. Legislative and administrative regulation has dominated the field. Until recently, courts have intruded less than in other fields of bioethics. That situation is changing, however, with the advent of negligence claims based on principles of medical malpractice. To date, plaintiffs have had limited success with their lawsuits but the mere existence of litigation has caused the regulatory practices to change. Liability is very much a concern of institutional review boards and medical and pharmaceutical researchers. The discussion of human research will also serve to define the scope and principles of bioethics in general. After providing background information concerning clinical research protections, I will describe and analyze recent instances of litigation dealing with claimed violations of research standards.

CHAPTER FOUR, BETTER OFF DEAD? CAN JUDGES BE METAPHYSICIANS?

We are concerned here with issues in the clinical relationship of physician and patient in the context of reproductive medicine. This area of bioethics, involving the very definition and evaluation of life itself, has been widely litigated and, in fact, dominated by court decisions. Within the ambit of this area are wrongful birth and wrongful life actions for improper genetic engineering or failure to detect genetic mutations as well as controversies involving reproductive technology. Developments in medical technology and biotechnology have probably had a greater impact in the field of reproductive medicine than any other, with the possible exception of genetic screening, testing, and engineering. Reproductive medicine has been transformed by new technology and, in turn, has produced more social changes than any other field of bioethics.

CHAPTER FIVE, BODY PARTS: ALLOCATING ORGANS

This chapter addresses problems that develop when human organs and other body parts or products such as eggs or sperm, are commodified that is, are considered as property. I refer to situations in which humans are treated as instruments for some purpose, rather than simply as ends in themselves. We will examine questions including whether parts of the human body should be considered property for some purposes and how such unique resources should ethically and legally be allocated within society. The subject of cloning for embryonic stem cell research as well as reproductive purposes is relevant as well. Genetic engineering, including stem cell development and cloning and germ line engineering, carries with it immense potential for disease control and life enhancement but also the most frightening potential for species changing developments. Short of the ultimate scenarios, however, even small developments in this area can bring about immense changes. While courts have not had extensive involvement in biotechnology issues, they have been called upon to resolve many issues involving reproductive rights, including the disposition of frozen embryos in marital disputes. These decisions, which have little consistency or coherence, will be the foundation for later decisions on genetic engineering. In a society in which virtually everything else is commodified and commercialized, do valid reasons exist for maintaining the integrity of human personhood in this field? What is the impact on the bioethical issues of litigation by donors and recipients of human resources?

CHAPTER SIX, STEM CELLS: PROMISE AND POLITICS

This chapter concerns research on embryonic stem cells, a major pursuit of biotechnology. This subject has generated vigorous political and ethical controversy since 1998 when researchers at the University of Wisconsin reported in *Science* that they had isolated human embryonic cells from leftover embryos and created self-perpetuating colonies in culture. The news of that breakthrough caused a public stir in view of the potential of the cells to differentiate into a wide variety of human tissues. Hopes ran high that stem cells had the potential to revolutionize medicine and ultimately cure many diseases. The scientific triumph was tempered immediately by the recognition that human embryos had to be destroyed in the process. The Wisconsin research involved human embryos that had been obtained by the consent of donors from several IVF (in vitro fertilization) clinics.

CHAPTER SEVEN, BOUNDARIES AT THE END OF LIFE: THE STRANGE CASE OF TERRI SCHIAVO

The inquiry here focuses on controversial end-of-life issues. This field has been dramatically impacted by biotechnology during the past few decades. This area of litigation has witnessed the most publicized emblematic cases. The names Quinlan, Cruzan, and Schiavo are widely known in legal culture if not in popular culture. The questions concerning when life ends—and when life should end—continue to be the most problematic for physicians and health care institutions as well as for the courts. We ask why end-of-life decisions are so difficult for individuals, families, and courts. The dangers in allowing bioethical choices to be controlled by courts are most evident in this field. The Schiavo controversy, which consumed more than a decade with numerous court proceedings, state and federal, generated more attention on end-of-life issues than the important cases that preceded it. Whether it was an anomaly, mainly an intrafamily battle, or a significant legal and ethical controversy, remains to be seen. I will suggest why it was so problematical and what its legacy is.

CHAPTER EIGHT, NEW FRONTIERS

The concluding chapter will refer to the framework for analysis as it was applied to the five basic topics. In the course of discussion, I will comment on the future implications of our present legal decision-making and bioethical policy discussion in addition to suggesting how we can address future issues more effectively while maintaining our *societal equilibrium*. I will discuss some of the bioethics issues that are likely to generate litigation in the future.

I will recommend some considerations and judicial policies that may help to produce more effective judicial decision-making concerning bioethical issues. Although it is impossible to anticipate every new problem and issue, an informed approach, recognizing the underlying ethical issues, can be designed to provide a method for judicial decision-making that does not undermine or displace ethical decision-making as well as policymaking. Ethical and policy decision-making must be viewed as an ongoing process of applying solutions and adapting to change in order to achieve equilibrium, a state that accommodates both stability and change. The combination of decision-making processes—public policy, legal, scientific, and ethical—must occur within the political realities of our system of government.

The proper combination is difficult to achieve if too much emphasis is placed on court intervention in bioethical situations. Judicial intervention can operate consistently with legislative and regulatory intervention on a policy level if it guides personal decision-making, assists in setting the boundaries for private decision-making, and reinforces the basic principles to be weighed. My basic premise is that individualized decision-making is appropriate and most effective. When judicial intervention is prescriptive and consistent with fundamental, established ethical principles, it can be useful as a guide for personal decision-making. When it attempts to restrict or impede personal autonomy for the sake of judicial or political *agendas* that are not related to the issues themselves, court action bears the risk of interfering with the legitimacy of personal choice.

Chapter 2

The Context of Bioethics, Law, and Society

[M] an, proud man, Dressed in a little brief authority,
Most ignorant of what he's most assured. His glassy
essence, like an angry ape, Plays such fantastic tricks
Before high Heaven, As make the angels weep.[1]

William Shakespeare

Ethical issues arising from the revolutionary developments in the life sciences occupy center stage in the American media. The social and political importance of these issues is grounded in a complex relationship involving science, law, ethics, and culture. What levels and methods of accountability are appropriate for the research enterprise? How should choice and control, autonomy and oversight, risk and responsibility be balanced? What public forums are available for discussion and debate about the ethics and values of research? To what extent are existing governmental institutions capable of creating social policy to guide and control the novel developments in medicine and science? Can polarized positions on controversial issues be reconciled to allow pragmatic decision-making for the whole society? If legislatures avoid these difficult issues, are courts equipped to deal with them competently? Can court decisions fill the gaps in public policy if legislative action is absent?

BACKGROUND CONCEPTS

Social Contract

During the latter part of the twentieth century, courts in the United States acquired, in part because of legislative inaction, the authority to decide critical issues in bioethics. This gave courts the opportunity, in many cases, to formulate principles and rules that became, by default, the only policy in the field. The life science revolution has proceeded in a virtual legislative vacuum, leaving courts to define the problems and the norms governing bioethical issues of life and death.[2] All this has taken place during a period in which, according to some commentators, a new social contract for science was in the process of being negotiated between the scientific research community and the state, a contract that requires new standards and new forms of accountability.[3] The progress in science and technology has led to an uncertain relationship between science and society. The new developments have occurred in an atmosphere of tension and conflict about the status of such controversial topics as abortion and stem cell research, particularly in light of scientific and medical research that bears on the issue.

Public Forum

Despite the obvious need for ethical debate and policy discussion of important bioethics issues, no satisfactory forum for these discussions has emerged. Politically appointed bioethics commissions and councils come and go without providing more than predictable restatements of the conflicting arguments and points of view. Individuals in other forums in the private sector (nongovernmental institutions such as universities and foundations) take positions but can offer no means for resolution. Although the work of some private institutions helps to advance the discussion, it has little persuasive impact on people who remain entrenched in fundamentally uncompromising positions. We must look to the institutions of government to shed light on the subject. The executive and legislative branches have offered little guidance. They seem, in fact, uncertain or incapable of knowing how to go about formulating public policy that reconciles the competing interests in a meaningful way. It may be that the political process, on which they are firmly dependent, inhibits rational discussion and action on controversial issues. Although several states have taken the initiative in some areas, they are far from securing consensus on workable solutions. It has been observed that in the United States ''a unique constellation of structural and political factors—federalism, a presidential electoral system, a powerful judiciary, a vigorous science lobby, and a spectacularly divisive politics of abortion—has all but negated the possibility of systematic national legislation of pivotal issues."[4]

Role of Courts

Some experts have suggested that America has led the way in the bio-medical revolution because of our unique policy of public funding for private research. Executive and legislative action withholding public funding for certain types of controversial, but essential, stem cell research has recently occurred. Besides creating a situation in which the United States is at risk of surrendering its scientific leadership and falling behind the rest of the world in development of new technologies, legislative inaction has thrust the most critical issues into the courts.

While law has an important role in most societies, it has consistently been an unusually dominant force in American society. This may be so, in part, because of the absence of other prevailing systems of moral or ethical values in the United States, and thus the need for a substitute ordering system. It may even be said that law, in all its dimensions—as a code of rules, as an institution, and as a process— is *the* binding value. Law is the force that holds our political, social, and economic structure together.[5]

Barry R. Schaller

No discussion of the role of law in American society is complete without reference to Tocqueville's remark, quoted as an epigraph to this book. One critic, Sheila Jasanoff, has pointed out that, in the case of science, many issues arose first in the courts and only later in political arenas. "Only after a court ruling, and not invariably even then, were the issues taken up by state or federal legislatures and given the imprimatur of social policy. This has given American courts extraordinary latitude to rule on normative issues at the frontiers of biotechnological development."[6]

By this means, courts, by virtue of their legal and policy development, have acquired a *de facto* policymaking authority beyond the contemplation of the founders of our country. This unprecedented influence gives rise to urgent questions concerning how courts exercise their power and what is the impact of court-made law on policymaking by other branches and on the underlying bioethical issues, themselves.

Certain fundamentals are important to an understanding of the American judicial system. Since the system is based on common law, decisions serve as precedents that must be considered in future cases involving similar issues. Courts must follow previous decisions or distinguish them if they do not apply. Both state and federal systems are structured in tiers, consisting of trial, intermediate appellate, and supreme courts. Decisions of higher courts in a particular state or federal jurisdiction are binding on the lower courts. The doctrine of stare decisis, the binding effect of a judicial decision, applies to all courts. The concept of federalism allows state courts, subject to rulings by the U.S. Supreme Court, to experiment with different theories and to reach different conclusions from the federal courts. In addition, courts of one state are not bound to follow decisions of other state courts, but they may find them persuasive.

Courts are bound to decide only actual cases and controversies. They are not supposed to issue advisory opinions about the law, and they should not routinely issue purely policy decisions (except for the U.S. Supreme Court, which has latitude since it is not subject to review by any other court). Courts do legitimately contribute to public policy, however, in many ways other than pure judicial activism.[7] Courts are constitutionally prohibited from intruding on the authority of the other branches of government, just as the other branches are likewise prohibited. Separation of powers disputes, however, can be complicated to unravel. Courts base their decisions on applying existing law to specific facts. The facts are usually in dispute and, therefore, need to be determined by judges or juries. Courts, unlike legislatures or executive agencies, generally do not have unfettered discretion to avoid deciding issues or to defer decisions indefinitely; they must decide the cases that are presented. Appellate courts, however, may decide cases on narrow grounds, thereby leaving broader and controversial issues for another day. Many appellate courts, including the U.S. Supreme Court, are able to control their annual caseload by exercising their authority to select or reject particular appeals, a process called certification or certiorari.

Given these constraints on how courts operate and the fact-based incremental way the common law is designed to develop, it does not seem obvious that courts would influence policy development in cutting edge ethical issues as much as they do. We realize, however, that, in the absence of effective legislative guidance on critical issues, courts take over and do the defining, the boundary setting, and the decision making. When they do so in a legislative vacuum, the other branches yield to courts the authority to *occupy the field*, in a sense. Not only do courts assume the role of gatekeeper but that of ultimate decision maker as well. It is realistic to recognize that, ordinarily, it may be far easier for an interested party to hire a lawyer and initiate a lawsuit than to lobby a legislature and await legislative action. While lawsuits can be expensive and time consuming, they offer a more immediate response, for the most part.

Gate Keeping Authority

In America, judges are traditionally empowered with *gate keeping* authority which they exercise either to grant or to refuse access by individuals and other entities (such as corporations, associations, and partnerships) to the decision-making process. This authority determines who is entitled to invoke the authority of government. Because this occurs in the course of judicial decision-making, it is not always apparent. By enabling judges to make both threshold and final decisions concerning the broadest possible range of matters, judges hold the keys to the enforcement power of the state and to lawful enforcement by nongovernmental parties. Because all of the legal issues before courts are meaningful to someone, even in matters that have little public policy significance, the parties have high expectations and standards for what they demand of judges. In that sense, authority is extended with one hand; criticism is readily delivered with the other.

Ethical Foundation

American law clearly has an ethical foundation, and virtually all sources of law embody ethical principles derived from the Western philosophical tradition. These familiar principles in their most basic form are well-being (individual utility), autonomy (self-determination), and procedural justice (fairness).[8] Although this list is not exclusive, these principles coincide with bioethical principles. Ethical decision-making precedes the law and, to have moral authority within society, an essential ingredient of law is that it must be consistent with the governing (traditional and prevailing) ethical standards of society. That is not to say that every specific statute or judicial decision is made to serve one or more identifiable ethical purposes. Statutes or regulations are often adopted to address a particular political, economic, or social problem, and court decisions are supposed to be based on application of existing law to particular facts.

Considered as a whole, however, a statutory scheme or a body of case law will inevitably be seen to serve one or more of the ethical principles. This will commonly be so, because constitutional principles govern other types of law. As a result, principles of due process and equal protection, along with other fundamental concepts, are embedded in particular laws and decisions. In the case of bioethical issues, society must engage in some regulation to protect the autonomy of individual choices and to protect individuals from undue harm. For these reasons, I will be looking at the ethical dimensions as well as the legal dimensions of the issues covered in this book.

How courts deal and should deal with these bioethical issues is my principal focus. In our society, people have unrealistically high expectations about what they think law should be able to accomplish, both in general terms and in specific situations.[9] I include, in this sense, both the policy that becomes *law* when enacted by our legislatures and the common law.

For example, law in general and court decisions, in particular, are expected to be consistent with the traditional ethical principles from which our present society is derived. Law is also expected to accommodate change when circumstances and conditions require it. One of the primary qualities of law, as applied, is that it must be adaptable to changed circumstances. There is, of course, a familiar tension here. Legal and political scholars disagree strongly about whether the original historical intent of constitutional principles should be faithfully followed and applied or whether the principles should be more or less free of that intent, and thus applied with more flexibility to contemporary issues. In addition, law must be effective and fair to both the majority and the minority views.

HOW COURTS OPERATE

Court decisions must meet a broad array of standards. They must be fair to all sides, principled, correct, and realistic.[10] In many situations, where *old* law and procedures are being applied to *new* situations, as is the case with biotechnology issues, judges are functioning without proper legal tools, as they attempt to reason and analogize from one body of case law to issues that could not have been foreseen. In some respects, it is not that difficult since some bodies of case law are readily adaptable to new facts. The leap from fingerprint or blood grouping identification to DNA identification is not monumental. In other situations, such as dividing up frozen embryos in a marriage dissolution (in contrast to dividing up furniture or other belongings), the leap is immense for the old principles and techniques.

One of my purposes is to discuss how courts have dealt with bioethical issues to date and how they should do so in the future. A major concern is how effective courts can be in dealing with bioethical issues. Another is how society ought to regulate developments in the fields of biotechnology and what is often called the new medicine, medicine related to genetics, as they merge with information technology in the genetic revolution. This leads me to consider broader questions as well, such as what is the impact on our culture—socially, politically, legally, and ethically—of developments in bioethics? How should society address these issues? Who should decide? To what extent should decisions be left to individuals, to the market, or to professionals? Should government regulation be modest or extensive? What is the global impact on our own societal attempts to regulate?

Both stability and change are inherent in the governing principles of our democratic republic.[11] This book addresses how courts function when they attempt to address the challenges of the life science revolution, including the genetic and information technology revolution. Specifically, I will identify and analyze how law presently addresses issues of science and medicine, and attempt to forecast what will happen in the future. Although part of the analysis involves looking at statutory law, I will be examining mainly what courts do when they are forced to grapple with biotechnology and the new medicine. We need to engage fully our skills of analysis and our ethical capacity to harness and direct the process of change. We should avoid being unduly anxious about biotechnical change; neither can we afford to be complacent and negligent about our most basic human responsibilities. It may be that the most fundamental responsibility we have is to preserve what is basic to human nature in the face of the threat of change to our common humanity.[12]

Critics could argue that judges are ineffective as gatekeepers in medicine and science issues because of their excessive deference to physicians and scientists.[13] I would suggest that, despite the limitations on courts in these cases, well-trained and suitably restrained judges have an important role to play in determining these vital issues. Legislatures, federal and state, have a major role in terms of establishing broad principles to guide the developments in bioethical fields. Despite the shortcomings of our judicial system, we are not likely to establish an entirely new system of decision making for cases involving bioethical issues and we cannot rely entirely on industry-wide or professional self-regulation. The profit motive is too powerful for that. It is easy to call for more regulation; it is more difficult to propose specific and effective means that can actually be adopted. That is not to say that we should not try. We must, in fact, because some bioethical issues entail potentially harmful consequences, intended and unintended, to individuals, communities, and society as a whole. Rather than reject the existing system of regulation, decision, and enforcement, however, we should concentrate on improving it where needed. Part of the problem is the difficulty of defining accurately and insightfully the real issues and consequences. Too often, political or legal rhetoric blurs the meaning of issues and arguments.

The developments of our time are not confined to single industries, societies, or cultures. In the vast society of today, with global networks and multinational private enterprises, no society can remain isolated from developments occurring in other parts of the world. Advances and changes in technology are instantly exported by the media, for good or ill, throughout the global community. This reality creates an additional dimension of problems and issues to be resolved within our own society. To what extent should we take into account that our own legal and ethical decision-making, once translated into public policy, can readily be undermined by developments abroad?

It is well understood that science and biotechnology are not value-free; they are quickly put to the service of ideology, private or public. No society in fact, not even our own, is powerful enough to hold back the changes that occur daily. Since we believe in a (regulated) free market economic system, we have chosen not to micromanage the activities of the private sector. We can, however, shape our public policy in order to regulate the direction of those activities. The interplay of science, information technology, ethics, morality and religion, medicine, law, economics, and politics that is involved when bioethical issues arise is formidable because it is so complex. A well-defined and wisely ordered public policy is essential.

We have noted that law as a social ordering force has traditionally dealt with the vital problems of our society, including those that we now call bioethical issues. Because law reacts to events and developments in society, rather than initiating change, it is common for courts to deal with issues and disputes using procedures and techniques, as well as substantive law that any other discipline would consider to be obsolete. The problems and issues produced by the recent developments in biotechnology have now developed to the point at which we are in need of public policy decisions specifically directed to these problems. If legislatures do not adopt the public policy, courts will do so with the authority they have.

I have pointed out that, in our society, courts have customarily been *gatekeepers* for the purpose of determining whether the authority and power of society can be applied in particular situations and, if so, how it should be applied. Judges are *generalists* and lack expertise on subjects beyond law. It is noted that, for a variety of reasons, judges tend to defer excessively to science and, in particular, medical science, when issues involving those topics are involved.[14] If that is so, the question arises whether judges can be effective gatekeepers with respect to the intensely complex and powerful issues of biotechnology and the new medicine. If not courts and judges, then who could serve as gatekeepers? I submit that there is no other likely source. The solution is to equip courts and judges to be more effective gatekeepers. In the final chapter, I will offer suggestions for more effective regulation by courts as well as other policy institutions of society.

My purpose is to demonstrate how courts are called on to perform a variety of functions as gatekeepers (to the power and authority of the state) when scientific, medical, and bioethical issues need to be decided.

Given the present state of the law and the procedural limitations that inhibit courts, our courts are not fully equipped to perform these functions effectively. Litigation can be a blunt instrument when it comes to resolving vital bioethical issues consistently and completely. Too often, bringing lawsuits to address ethical disagreements and controversies may have unexpected social consequences and may compound the problems by adding expense and delay to an already troubled situation.[15]

I believe that *bioethics is on trial* in a real sense because so many decisions that are best made on a personal level by individuals and their families or by patients with their physicians are being usurped by courts. I use the word usurped advisedly, knowing that courts and judges do not bring the lawsuits, themselves. In many public and private situations, the privilege of self-regulation has been forfeited by glaring failures to formulate and maintain high ethical standards. The Tuskegee, Willowbrook, and Jewish Hospital abuses should not have been allowed to happen. I realize also that even the government regulation that began in the 1970s to supplement or supplant self-regulation by the professions did not adequately enforce ethical standards.

Courts, whether acting through judges alone or judges in concert with juries, decide cases brought by people or entities that invoke their authority. Courts decide cases retrospectively, for the most part. Cases involve events that have already happened or, at least, are underway. Exceptions exist, of course. For example, in a right to die case, although a person may have become ill and hospitalized, court action may be sought from a prospective view point when permission to end life is sought. The term "usurped applies," not necessarily because courts handle these disputes improperly, although that is sometimes the case, but often simply because of the institutional limitations of law. On some occasions, of course, courts fail to dismiss actions that should not be allowed to go to trial. A strong institutional bias exists in favor of allowing lawsuits to continue once they are on the threshold—in defiance of the true *gatekeeper* role. Most often, the gate is just left open or even opened more widely. Courts sometimes overstep their proper bounds and convert issues of choice, priority and discretion to issues of rights, duties, and power, thereby changing the basic nature of the issues.

In other instances, courts are bound by preexisting law to apply wrong, unwise, or outdated precedents or statutes to problems that need new or innovative solutions. In all instances, courts are bound to apply the accepted legal language, thereby changing dramatically the nature of the issues and the problems. Because courts do not have the luxury of postponing decision to await future developments or more evidence, but rather are bound by what the parties present, they must decide based on what they know at the time. What they know is, for the most part, what the parties tell them—according to evidence and procedural rules that are designed to aid in the goal of finality and closure as well as to guarantee that the procedure is fair for all participants. The more courts are put in control of bioethical issues, the less individual choice and autonomy individuals will have. It has been said that another reason for ineffectiveness and lack of credibility of the court system is the hyperlegalizing of issues that are basically ethical issues. Lawyers and judges speak their own language and convert issues into concepts that are different from those in use outside the legal community. Legal reasoning, although sharing some common features with scientific or medical reasoning, is different from other forms of knowledge-acquiring and decision making. It is a powerful and *transforming* tool and can produce foolish or absurd results as well as sensible results. Legal reasoning is not suitable for resolving all types of issues. Because of the accessibility of courts to the public and the public's fascination with courts, lawyers, and lawsuits, the power of legal decision-making has extended beyond sensible limits.

ANALYZING LAW'S IMPACT ON BIOETHICS

What follows is a framework to serve as a guide to analysis and discussion concerning the impact of court decisions—adjudication—on bioethical issues. With regard to each bioethical and legal topic, only the questions that are pertinent will be used in the analysis. Minor rephrasing of questions may occur, but the basic format will remain constant. The issues and cases that I will analyze are not necessarily the *paradigm cases* in the field. My intent, rather, is to look at cases and issues that are timely and on the *cutting edge* of law and bioethics.

The Idiom of the Law (Language and Concepts)

a. What is the effect of translating bioethics issues into traditional legal language and concepts?
b. How are bioethics issues transformed by law?
c. What is the effect of the fact that legal discourse and decision is restricted because it is initiated by individual parties and limited to their interests?

Discussion: Two major problems with litigation, especially constitutional litigation, are relevant to controversies in bioethics. First, lawyers and judges narrow the scope of debate on the issues by framing them in terms of rights, duties, and authority. Those terms are the language of the law.

The broader meaning of the issues (which could be fully described in non-legal language) must conform to the sometimes awkward and artificial categories of legal analysis. Lawyers and courts limit the discussion of issues by conforming them to well-defined, traditional legal categories.

Second, litigation is usually inimical to democratic discourse. It removes issues from the realm of individual citizens and arrogates them to lawyers, judges, and the few interested parties who participate in the litigation. Individual choice and discretion are not considered unless the party has the type of interest that is legally recognized and authorized to bring an action seeking (or defending) court intervention. Only interests specifically brought into the lawsuit are considered although someone not a party to the case can seek court permission to file an amicus curiae (friend of the court) brief. The interests of other parties or of society's common good or public well-being are generally irrelevant to a legal proceeding except insofar as the common good may be a basic part of constitutional doctrine or statutory law. Courts must limit participation to parties represented in the action. Examining the pattern of legal decisions may reveal that courts develop the law in a piecemeal way. Limiting parties and language is part and parcel of the law, serving worthwhile purposes (for example, limiting the jurisdiction and authority of courts) but it is unduly restrictive in cases in which full democratic discourse is called for.

Additional comments about the way law operates are pertinent to this category of the analysis. I adopt the idea that the ultimate purpose, role, and function of law is to serve as social regulation, although the specific purpose of adjudication is to resolve the controversy among the parties, consistent with existing law. Cases are resolved using existing law and precedent, often giving a false impression that existing law is adequate. That process can discourage new legislation because of the assumption that existing law is adequate to the task.

Courts set the agenda for legal resolution and, in the process, determine what constitutes law and what constitutes policy. Law generally is expressed in terms of minimums for social behavior, not maximums. Moreover, law is oriented toward distrust of human behavior rather than optimism. Law is often framed as rule-based to limit discretion. That works for law but not for ethics or bioethics. Law defines sharply its own context, which is limited to the relevant facts, according to legal relevance. Bioethics problems have a broad and deep social context. They do not exist outside of a factual and social context.

Legal standards and tests are frequently satisfied by outward signs—by form—rather than substance. Gaps and spaces exist in any body of case law because court decisions depend on participants who invoke court involvement. Court decisions, therefore, are issued to apply only to the particular controversies litigated. Court decisions are based on the evidence that the parties produce in court, even if it happens to be incomplete or inaccurate.

The Adversarial Process

   a. What is the effect of adversarial adjudication as the decision-making format: is winning the only thing?

   b. How do evidence rules affect decision on the issues: is truth relevant?

   c. How do burdens of proof and other procedural rules control decision making: is there a place for uncertainty and ambiguity?

Discussion: Issues are polarized based on traditional adversarial process, thus denying the natural complexity and ambiguity of issues and the fact that not all issues can be framed in either/or terms. Legal cases involve winning and losing. There is no authorized middle ground allowing for a compromised decision or a complex or innovative weighing and balancing of interests and positions. Law is a binary process, a fact that does not reflect the realities of complex, or even simple, situations and controversies.

The legal decision maker ordinarily is limited to choosing from a limited number of options. Once the last decision is made in a case, whether by a trial or appellate court, it is final and cannot be second-guessed tomorrow or the day after tomorrow when circumstances may be altered. Adversarial process is natural to the judicial system. That is our chosen means of resolving disputes, but it does not serve some problems and issues well.

Courts do not seek the truth but rather determine which of the parties has prevailed based on the evidence presented. Even if the evidence proves a patently erroneous proposition, courts are not supposed to substitute their own knowledge to decide the case. Even when information is known to exist beyond what is brought in, the decision is made based on the limited evidence presented. The truth of a controversy is not pertinent. Courts must decide based on the evidence presented even if not sufficient by normal standards to make an accurate decision.

Courtroom proceedings are highly ritualized and subject to a series of conceptual and rhetorical filters that affect the substance. A complex set of rules tells courts how to decide when uncertainty exists (burdens and standards of proof), a process that is good for closure but not for the normal ambiguity that colors bioethical issues. Without a legitimate process for gathering evidence, courts must rely on the parties. An entirely different mechanism would have to be established if courts themselves were to be required to produce the evidence. Courts may appoint experts to advise them, but that option is rarely used. The favored procedure is to allow the parties to control the production of evidence.

Many legal concepts, including procedural rules, are merely judicial constructs and yet they are meant to be dispositive. Even the concept of due process is a judicial construct to be determined in judges' discretion. Procedural rules can be lenient or burdensome and can greatly affect the outcome.

Evidence rules, as interpreted within judges' discretion, determine the relevant admissible evidence based on standards not applicable in the real world but for purposes of convenience and courtroom reliability, given the limitations of the trial format. Issues are frequently oversimplified, and trials are limited in time, scope, and depth to suit legal convenience and the need to handle other business.

Closure, Finality, and the Retrospective View: Revisiting the Past

    a. What is the effect of the requirement that a court must decide the case presently rather than leaving it unresolved for the time being or indefinitely?

    b. What significance attaches to fixing the facts of the controversy at a moment in the past?

Discussion: Courts must decide the cases presented and cannot postpone or forego decision because facts or convincing arguments are lacking. Courts must decide once and for all and not retain jurisdiction except in special cases. The finality required has generated burdens of proof, evidence rules, and procedural rules that assist in making a decision but do not necessarily reflect the complexity of the facts. There is, of course, an advantage to finality and closure; that is why the concepts are used. But it does not serve well the kind of ongoing, dynamic, complex choices of a bioethical nature. Closure is essential for a well-functioning court system. Although the concept does not serve bioethical issues well, it often is necessary when a dilemma or dispute has no end in sight.

Decisions are made retrospectively and, once made, are not revisited or revised except under very limited circumstances. Appeals do not involve presenting new facts but are based on trial evidence. With rare exceptions, no mechanism exists to bring the situation up to date. Courts, therefore, generally lack the capacity to use an ongoing prescriptive approach on a continuum, but rather limit the resolution to adjudicating fixed interests at a particular time, thus denying natural change. Only *completed* controversies that have reached a certain stage of closure or finality can be adjudicated, resulting in a contrived or artificial state of facts.

A related problem is the use of precedent and analogies from prior cases in deciding present cases. Despite the value of precedent based on an appellate decision, the actual decision binds only the particular parties to the court proceeding. Courts apply by way of analogy, case law and other legal material whether or not it was designed to apply to the present subject matter. In cases of first impression, courts must analogize from past opinions, some of which may have little to do with the present issues. In applying law, courts do not usually look specifically at the basic ethical foundations of legal principles; rather they favor a superficial approach resulting in application of law as somehow *detached* from an ethical base. Courts are not free to analyze bioethical issues using the widely accepted ethical principles that should govern their resolution: respect for persons, doing no harm, doing good, and distributive justice; rather, they must apply law, even when it has little bearing on the issues.

Institutional Biases, Assumptions, and Deficiencies: Unspoken Factors in Shaping the Decision

a. What interests do courts favor over others? Do courts favor economic interests rather than non-pecuniary interests (such as ethical or moral)? Are some interests, such as ethical and moral interests, systematically disfavored?

b. How well do courts give adequate access to affected parties? Do legal decisions illuminate or undermine distinctive issues of ethics and social responsibility?

c. Do courts naturalize human intervention by applying an uninformed, uncritical receptiveness to medical science and biotechnology?

d. Do courts unduly elevate individualism rather than collective interests and rights over responsibility—especially rights of the individual in opposition to society?

e. Do courts use a rights analysis rather than responsibility analysis, thereby enabling a less complicated but less realistic result? Do courts thereby oversimplify controversies? Is there room for ambiguity, ambivalence, or uncertainty, or is the subject shorn of the imprecision that characterizes human response to changes in biological science and technology? What, if any, consideration can be given to public opinion or the political nature of courts?

f. Do courts elect to preserve life at any cost because it is the safest course of action, even when it may not be the wisest?

g. Is there an irrational bias in favor of neutrality: the ignorance of the clean slate? What is the impact of lack of expertise and limited use of experts except in the adversarial process?

Discussion: Courts have certain institutional biases. For one, they have a strong reluctance to terminate life and so, in life and death situations, they tend to favor the sustaining of life in bioethical situations even when allowing death to occur may be the wise choice. They tend to *normalize* change, even when that may be unwise and unwarranted. An institutional bias also exists in favor of economic interests, which are palpable and politically acceptable. That often results in undermining and ignoring other interests that are not as easy to define, such as moral or ethical ones. Courts also generally deny the existence of a strong element of politics embedded in statutory law. They promote the legal fiction that court-made law is somehow purely nonpolitical, even when they engage in political decision-making.

Although no justification exists for institutional biases, they are a fact of life. Paradoxically, it is not uncommon for the real issues, for example, economic considerations, to be undisclosed and for the case to be decided on grounds that are legally permissible or acceptable. The real issue may not even be mentioned during the proceeding. One reason for institutional biases is lack of knowledge and expertise. Courts and judges, for example, have only limited knowledge and understanding of medical and scientific concepts and often misuse technical and scientific terms. Courts often give a false elevation in the courtroom to medicine and medical experts, thus overly deferring to prevailing medical views of certain issues. Judges could become more knowledgeable, but the demands of judicial work and the policy that favor judges being generalists rather than specialists discourages that. Judges are supposed to be neutral and open to the evidence produced by the parties, so judicial expertise is not favored.

What Impact Does Judicial Decision-Making Have on Future Controversies?

a. Since our law provides that appellate decisions are binding precedent for future cases, is that process unfair to litigants in later cases because they had no role in the earlier decisions? Do the court decisions unfairly impact the *interests* of people who were not involved at all in cases past or present?

b. Do courts *naturalize* the unnatural thereby defining the terms in which future controversies will be considered? Do courts illuminate distinctive issues? How well do courts do in defining controversies? What is the effect of shaping facts to fit well-defined categories of law?

c. Do courts encourage or discourage legislative policymaking? Do courts give a false impression that existing precedent is adequate to the task?

d. Concerning the future, how capable are courts in exercising their boundary making power to distinguish law from policy? Because courts have the authority to determine boundaries between law and policy, even while they purport to defer to legislative prerogatives, can they mute discussion of new and different issues? What normative impact do courts have while they appear to emphasize deference to legislative policymaking? How accountable are courts for their actions?

Discussion: Precedent limits future litigants and future cases. A court decision, while resolving only the immediate case, creates precedent value that is used to resolve other cases. The effect of precedent, with the exception of a U.S. Supreme Court decision, is limited to the state or Circuit in which the decision is rendered, and offers only persuasive authority to sibling states and Circuits. This is so whether it is an appellate decision (that must be followed) or a trial decision (that may be followed). In this way, the reach of court decisions extends to other people's choices. Once individual court decisions become the law with regard to a particular subject, they directly impact on individual choices and options, thus assuming the role of public policy. In this way, public policy is created without the deliberative discussion of policy that ordinarily occurs in the legislative process, where the impact would be weighed against other alternatives. The particularized, fact-based decision of a single (appellate) court can reduce the flexibility and freedom of individuals who have no relationship whatsoever to that litigation.

When legally actionable interests are involved, individuals and legal entities, like corporations and partnerships, have the right to go to court. Sometimes they go to court to seek compensation for real or perceived injuries. Sometimes they do so to get help in making decisions that are not being resolved otherwise. I do not say that such lawsuits are inappropriate, but I do say that, in general terms, they do not serve well the process of bioethical decision-making. Even when necessary for one reason or another, they produce a change that always limits or reduces the area for personal ethical decision-making. Lawsuits can operate to limit the exercise of personal bioethical choice in several ways. For example, by changing the language, by creating new rules, and by changing the issues involved, they tend to have a serious impact on ethical decision-making.

This impact can be especially harmful in the area of bioethical decision-making, which involves complex, personal issues and choices that rightfully involve an often undecipherable and unfathomable mix of economic, moral, legal, interpersonal, and medical factors and values. Ideally, the people involved in a crucial bioethical controversy should work the problem out by selecting one of many options available—all of which may be *somewhat right* and *somewhat wrong*[16]—and then review and revise as needed.

Statutory and regulatory policy-generated law can produce similar consequences. Ordinarily, however, legislatures generate policy to establish guidelines to guide conduct rather than creating specific rules of law. Criminal statutes operate differently, however, because they proscribe specific behavior and impose consequences for violation. Statutes or regulations that are *too case-specific,* either by intention or by inadvertence, are not favored. The law passed in connection with the Schiavo case[17] by the Florida legislature, *Terri's Law,* is an example of a case-specific statute that violated the separation of powers provision in the Florida constitution and was declared unconstitutional by the Florida Supreme Court.[18] Terri's Law gave the Governor of Florida the authority to issue a onetime stay to prevent the withholding of nutrition and hydration from a patient in a PVS (persistent vegetative state). The law was adopted specifically to address the Terri Schiavo situation.

Not every lawsuit or court decision embodies or illustrates all of the above characteristics. In each case that I will describe, however, some of these factors are visible and prominent. Every bioethical problem involves complex choices and alternatives, none of which is perfect. That is the reality of hard choices. A wise decision involves discussion, analysis, negotiation, and soul searching to find the combination of choices—the order of priorities in an ongoing dynamic process that allows for change, new ideas, and new beliefs. A court decision cannot accommodate that process. My point is that courts and judges—and juries—are restricted by legal concepts as they attempt to decide most bioethical controversies.

The discussion of pertinent legal cases will demonstrate my thesis. Often what happens is ongoing, relentless litigation, resulting in immobilization in some cases or unwise and precipitous action in others. Courts have no follow-up capacity unless parties invoke further court involvement so there is no way of knowing how often court decisions may be thwarted by consent or by inaction.

It is not far-fetched to apply existing law—old law—to new problems when the underlying principles remain the same. When the technology produces fundamental change, however, it is not enough to adapt old law, old procedures, and old expertise. In these instances, we need change not only in substantive law but also in court procedures and expertise in order to deal effectively with the new problems and to carry out the role of gatekeeper.

In the course of discussion, I will suggest realistic changes in law and court procedures that will allow courts to keep pace with the speed of bioethical developments so they can be more effective gatekeepers and decision makers. These measures may include mechanisms for dismissing lawsuits that involve matters that should be privately resolved, mechanisms for speeding the process of litigation including establishment of specialized courts, procedures for appellate courts to decide cases without sending them back for retrials, procedures for bringing in parties whose interests ought to be represented when public policy implications are obvious and important, expanding provisions for court-appointed experts to avoid the dependence on the parties' experts, and judicial education and training. There is no legitimate reason why courts should not be able to adapt to the new situations presented by developments in science and technology and, in the process, deal more effectively with new issues.

Even recognizing that courts are by nature conservative, *reactive* institutions and not essentially policy-initiating institutions, litigation does serve an important and legitimate role in terms of social regulation. There is no denying that what courts do in terms of establishing rules, categories, and tests often becomes policy. Courts should not have to rely on devices such as *legal fictions* in order to promote the illusion that they are keeping pace. If courts are expected to adjudicate future issues involving science and technology that are beyond our present imagining, they need the tools to become more effective decision makers.

Chapter 3

The Legal Landscape of Human Research Litigation

One day in 1984, Jesse Gelsinger, a Tucson, Arizona boy then nearly three years of age, fell asleep while watching cartoons. After his parents were unable to wake him, they rushed him to a local hospital. Upon examination, Jesse responded to stimuli but did not awaken. Physicians classified him as being in a coma. Several days and many laboratory tests later, Jesse was diagnosed as having ornithine transcarbamylase deficiency, known as OTC.[1]

OTC is a rare genetic disorder in which an important enzyme is missing or in short supply. This enzyme deficiency means that the body is unable to break down ammonia, a by-product of protein metabolism. As a result, ammonia gradually accumulates in the blood and eventually causes coma, brain damage, and death. Females are carriers of the gene, which they pass on to their sons. The disorder occurs in approximately one of every forty thousand births. Infants with the disorder usually die within seventy-two hours of their birth. Half die within a month of birth, and half of those who survive die before age five.

No one else in Jesse's family or known ancestry had ever been diagnosed with this genetic disease. Jesse suffered from a relatively mild form of OTC because his body contained both normal and mutated cells. He had the potential of remaining healthy if he followed a low-protein diet and took his medications. At age ten, however, after an episode of consuming too much protein, he again fell into a coma and was hospitalized.

He returned home after five days and remained healthy by getting careful monitoring by a metabolic clinic.

In 1998, when Jesse was seventeen, his father heard from a doctor at the clinic about a gene therapy clinical trial at the Institute for Human Gene Therapy at the University of Pennsylvania. Researchers at the Institute intended to use gene therapy to supply the gene that would assist in producing the enzyme needed to prevent OTC. If they were successful, a treatment could result that would prevent brain damage to babies in comas. In the following year, Jesse and his father traveled to Pennsylvania and met with researchers. Arthur Caplan, a prominent bioethicist at the university, had advised the researchers that they could not ethically use infants born with OTC as participants in a gene therapy trial. Caplan reasoned that, because parents would be desperate to find a way to save their children's lives, any consent they might give would not be voluntary. The only permissible subjects, in his view, would be women who were carriers or men in stable health who had a mild form of the disease.

In June of 1999, Jesse and his father met with Dr. Steven Raper to review consent forms and discuss Jesse's possible involvement in the study. Dr. Raper would be the researcher performing the gene-therapy procedure. Jesse was warned that the procedure would lead to him developing flu-like symptoms. Further he was told he might develop hepatitis, could require a liver transplant, and that death was a possible outcome. The risk of death from the biopsy was stated as one in ten thousand. Dr. Raper also explained that Jesse could not expect any personal medical benefit from participating in the trial. Jesse was tested to determine how well his body removed ammonia in his blood. A month later, when Jesse was informed that he did qualify, he responded that he wished to participate. Dr. Mark Bratshaw informed Jesse's father of the success with animal studies and a recent treatment of a human patient in a subsequent conversation.

The researchers were operating with a modified protocol that had been approved by the FDA (Food and Drug Administration), as well as the federal Recombinant-DNA Advisory Committee. The researchers were supported by a grant from the National Institutes of Health. The study was a Phase I Clinical Trial, the purpose of which was to determine the maximum tolerated dose of the genetically altered virus. Phase I trials are concerned with determining toxic effects, safe levels of doses, and potential side effects.

On Thursday, September 9, 1999, Jesse, having reached the age of majority, checked in alone at the hospital. The level of ammonia in his blood was high, and he was put on IV-medication to lower it. Four days later, on September 13, he became the eighteenth subject to be treated in the trial. Dr. Raper injected thirty milliliters of the genetically modified virus into Jessie's artery. This equaled the highest dose given to any participant. Another subject had gotten an equivalent dose from a different batch of the virus and had done satisfactorily. Later, in the evening, Jesse began developing flu-like symptoms. He was feverish and feeling ill when he spoke by telephone for the last time to his father and stepmother. His fever escalated, and he began to develop signs of jaundice, something that had not been encountered with the other volunteers. By Tuesday afternoon, Jesse's blood-ammonia level had soared and he slipped into a coma. He was placed on a ventilator. Although he needed a liver transplant, he was not a good candidate for transplant surgery. Within days, he sustained multiple organ-system failure and irreversible brain damage. After a family religious service by his bedside, his father gave the signal to switch off the ventilator. Moments after Jesse's actual death, Dr. Raper pronounced him dead and said "Goodbye Jesse" and "We'll figure this out."

What caused Jesse Gelsinger's death? The answer is not clear, even after an autopsy. The most likely suspect appears to have been an immunological response to the viral injection. What is clear is that this death, occurring in a clinical trial at a highly respected medical research center, brought about a substantial change in the way the law regulates human research experiments in the United States. The Institute for Human Gene Therapy was put out of business by the FDA and a year later ceased to exist. The OPHRS (Office for the Protection of Human Research Subjects) committed itself to a major effort to educate researchers in the requirements for protecting participants in clinical trials and to stress the importance of IRBs (Institutional Review Boards) in seeing to the safety of volunteers. But the major development following Jesse's death was the beginning of a new kind of oversight of human research trials in the form of tort litigation and the wrongful death lawsuit. On September 18, 2000, a year and a day after Jesse's death, the Gelsinger family filed a wrongful death lawsuit against the researchers conducting the clinical trial and the University of Pennsylvania. The defendants included, among others, the university bioethicist, Arthur Caplan, who had ruled on the ethics of the clinical trial. Caplan was eventually dropped from the lawsuit.

Although the lawsuit was settled out of court in November of 2000 for an undisclosed, but reportedly substantial amount,[2] this case may prove to be a major event in extending the reach of medical malpractice litigation in the human research field. We will return to the Gelsinger case later, especially to look at the allegations that were made in the complaint filed by the lawyers to initiate the lawsuit. We will also examine what has happened with other pending lawsuits involving researchers, including a lawsuit against Johns Hopkins Medical Institutions by the family of Ellen

Roche, another volunteer who died during a clinical research study. Our goal is to assess and analyze the positive and negative effects of the intervention of litigation into the field of research using human subjects according to the five analytical categories set forth in Chapter 1: introduction. While our focus is on evaluating the intervention of courts, some background is necessary to set the stage.

BACKGROUND OF REGULATION

Prior to the advent around the turn of this century of malpractice litigation in this field, the enterprise of human research was supervised almost exclusively by the federal regulatory system, along with a network of local IRBs, following several dramatic disclosures of major ethical lapses in the United States that had occurred decades earlier. The most famous of those ethical lapses, the Tuskegee Syphilis Study, a name that has become a symbol for gross ethical breaches in the United States, preceded the War Crimes trials following World War II and the Nuremberg Code, which was promulgated in 1947.[3] The Tuskegee Study was designed by the PHS (U.S. Public Health Service), which later became the CDC (Centers for Disease Control and Prevention). The purpose was to demonstrate the need for establishing syphilis treatment programs by studying the effects of untreated disease. Macon County, Alabama, was selected as the site for the project. In 1932, black male subjects who had syphilis were recruited with offers of free examinations and medical care. They were not informed about their disease or told that the study would not benefit them. At the inception of the study, the prevailing medical information, including medical textbooks, strongly advocated treating syphilis even in its latent stages so, in that sense, the study was flawed from the start.[4] Moreover, even though penicillin became the widely available treatment for syphilis by 1951, it was withheld from the men. Not until 1972 was the story of Tuskegee revealed to the public by a Washington newspaper. Eventually, this disgraceful chapter in human subjects research resulted in a formal apology from the U.S. government and payments to survivors and their families.[5]

The Nuremberg Code required, in brief, (1) informed consent of volunteers without coercion, (2) prior animal experimentation before human experimentation, (3) anticipated scientific results to justify any experiment, (4) qualified scientists, (5) avoidance of physical and mental suffering, and (6) no expectation of death or disabling injury from the experiment.[6] During this era of egregious breaches, ethical standards of researchers and their colleagues governed the conduct of studies.

In 1953, the World Medical Association began work on a new document that would apply the Nuremberg principles to the practice of medical research. This document was eventually published in 1964 as the Declaration of Helsinki. The Declaration provided rules for both therapeutic and nontherapeutic research, a distinction that has questionable significance.[7] Helsinki modified some of the rules for informed consent for therapeutic research and allowed legal guardians to grant consent. The third publication that contributed to the ethical framework of Belmont was not a formal statement but, rather, an article by Dr. Henry K. Beecher, published in 1966 in the *New England Journal of Medicine* reporting on twenty-two studies that had serious ethical problems. Beecher reported various deficiencies in study design and informed consent.[8] This article contributed greatly to stimulating debate and action on ethical principles relating to research in the United States.

History of Human Research Regulation

The Belmont Report described three basic principles relevant to the ethics of human subject research: respect for persons, beneficence (and the reverse, non-maleficence), and justice. The first, respect for persons, incorporates at least two ethical convictions: first, individuals should be treated as autonomous agents; and second, that persons with diminished autonomy are entitled to protection. This principle functions mainly through informed consent, which is a process of information exchange. This began the legal oversight of research involving human subjects, a process that had previously been dependent on the evolving and usually fluctuating ethical standards of both the researchers and their professional colleagues and associations.

The Belmont Report led to adoption of Human Subject Regulations by the DHHS (Department of Health and Human Services) and the FDA in 1980 and the adoption of what is known as the Common Rule. In 1991, seventeen federal departments and agencies adopted a common set of regulations, known as "the Common Rule" to govern human subject research sponsored by the federal government.[9] The Common Rule was extracted from the first of four subparts of the DHHS regulations for the protection of human subjects. These regulations were first approved in 1981, when they were published along with FDA human subject protection regulations. It is significant that the Common Rule regulates research conducted or supported by federal agencies. The equivalent FDA regulations govern all research with drugs, biologics, and devices, whether or not sponsored by the government. The supervision of human research pursuant to legal standards, therefore, is a mere three decades old.

The Common Rule provides for three main protective mechanisms: review of research by an IRB, required informed consent of subjects, and institutional assurances of compliance. Virtually every institution that engages in or sponsors research involving human subjects has its own IRB and, in addition, some regional IRBs cover research conducted by multiple researchers. The purpose of an IRB is to review proposed research to determine whether the rights and welfare of human subjects involved are adequately protected. Institutions establish policies that provide for peer scientific review, another key component of research monitoring and IRB review. It is not uncommon for institutions to require review and verification of projects that are exempt from federal regulation.

Standards evolve and change in all fields, including medical research and human rights. The process of identifying and correcting human rights abuses is not static. Rather the process is one of revelation, recognition and comprehension and, eventually, change. I would argue, however, that reliance on self-regulation alone has been forfeited given the number of severe human rights abuses that occurred in the United States prior to any government regulation. Even considering the evolution of ethical standards and the cultural context, the extreme abuses of Tuskegee, Willowbrook, Jewish Hospital, and various government sponsored experiments, such as the Manhattan Project,[10] are unacceptable. Government oversight and regulation are necessities, but we also must conclude that even the combination of self-regulation plus government regulation was not stringent enough to prevent some obvious deficiencies that were acknowledged by the institutions involved in the Gelsinger and Roche cases.

Several important features of medical research must be kept in mind in order to establish the proper context. One obvious point is that research involving human subjects is an important part of modern medicine. Given the heavy reliance in health care today on drugs and technology, ongoing development in the field is of vital importance to the medical profession as well as the public. New technologies and drugs must be routinely tested on animals and humans before physicians are allowed to use them in clinical practice. Another important feature of research is the crucial distinction between medical research and medical treatment or therapy. Research is not therapy and is not evaluated ethically in the same way as the medical practice. Although researchers commonly are physicians who also practice therapeutic medicine on patients, they act in a different capacity when they conduct research on human subjects. When patients are subjects, ethical standards of medical practice are applied differently to the researcher–subject relationship in contrast to the physician–patient relationship.

The basic set of ethical principles is the same, but the configuration in each case is distinct. Despite a common misapprehension on the part of subjects as well as the public in general (aptly called the therapeutic misconception) that subjects may expect to benefit from their participation that is not the case. Benefit to research subjects is not part of the equation. In the process of informed consent, subjects—who of course may also be patients of a referring physician or even the researcher himself or herself —are informed that there is no expectation of benefit to them and, certainly, no promise is made that they will benefit. Incidental benefit could occur during the study if a new medication proves effective but there is no guarantee that the patient will even get the new medication (as opposed to placebo or an existing medication). Further, usually no guarantee is offered that the medication will be available to the patient after the study is concluded. Ambiguities in the informed consent materials or in accompanying oral representations can cloud the situation. If researchers are dealing with seriously ill subjects who have little hope except through experimental drugs, the subjects may hear what they want to hear. Researchers often confuse the situation themselves in their eagerness to recruit subjects by implying that benefits may occur. Informed consent is a critical element of research studies, and the IRBs that protect subjects focus their attention on the consent forms used as part of the protocols.

Patient autonomy and informed consent lie at the heart of both the clinical relationship and the researcher–subject relationship. Doing no harm (non-maleficence) is an essential ingredient of both but doing good (beneficence) is part of the clinical relationship but not the research relationship, except in the sense of doing good for humanity. Fairness in the way benefit and harm are distributed (distributive justice) is relevant to both enterprises in an overall sense. While (wisely or unwisely) justice is not an essential element of the standard physician–patient relationship, it is a factor in selecting research subjects in a particular and general sense and is, therefore, a core part of the relationship. Justice is a fundamental element in the case of many bioethical issues, such as determining the proper allocation of scarce resources, e.g., organ transplants and societal health care in general, among many others.

Before federal regulation of research, researchers and their colleagues governed the conduct of studies. Although a great deal of research was conducted without negative consequences or, at least, without *known* negative consequences, a number of studies were recognized, often after the fact, to involve significant abuses of human dignity. Three events in particular are generally thought to have led to the push for federal regulation in the United States. These are, in chronological order, the 1946 Nuremberg Doctors Trial (for conduct occurring in Nazi Germany from

1942 to 1945), the 1960s Thalidomide Tragedy in Europe, and the 1972 Tuskegee Syphilis Study expose. Tuskegee, the only U.S. contribution to this particular *parade of horrors,* extended for more than four decades, from 1932 to 1972. Although other events such as the Willowbrook Hepatitis Studies (1956–1970),[11] the Wichita Jury Study (1955),[12] the Jewish Chronic Disease Hospital Study (1963),[13] the Stanley Milgram Study (1963),[14] and the San Antonio Contraceptive Study (1971)[15] were highly controversial, the first three events listed had the most direct impact on shaping federal regulation in the United States.

Belmont Report and IRB Review

The publication of the Belmont Report in 1974 established the fundamental ethical principles that should apply to all research involving human subjects in the United States. Two presidential commissions, the National Bioethics Advisory Commission, and the President's Council on Bioethics, were appointed, for different political reasons, to keep the subject of ethical standards prominently before Congress and the public.

The CIOMS (Council for the International Organization of Medical Sciences) published the International Ethics Guidelines for Biomedical Research Involving Human Subjects in 1982. The CIOMS Guidelines, as they are known, were designed to guide researchers from technologically advanced countries when they are doing research in less developed countries. The CIOMS Guidelines, like the Helsinki Declaration, have been revised to stay current with new developments and thinking.

An IRB has authority to approve (with or without conditions), disapprove, or require modification of research. Continuing review is also a part of the process. IRBs must consider the risks to the subjects, anticipated benefits to subjects and others, importance of the knowledge that may result, and the informed consent process to be used. IRBs must report promptly to appropriate institutional officials, OHRP (Office of Human Research Protection), FDA, and any sponsoring federal agency the following: injuries to human subjects or other problems, serious or continuing noncompliance with regulations of IRB requirements, and suspension or termination of IRB approval for research. Among other procedures, research investigators must present requests for proposed changes in previously approved studies to the IRB and changes may not be implemented without approval. The IRB pays special attention to the research protocol as a whole and the consent form, in particular.

Before a federal grant or contract can be awarded, the research institution must file an *Assurance of Compliance* with the government. The document is called an FWA (Federal-Wide Assurance). The institution must

agree to apply the federal regulations and to adhere to the ethical principles of the Belmont Report. The OHRP (Office for Human Research
Protection) is the federal office that negotiates assurances for DHHS and
oversees compliance. Although an FWA is required only for federally
sponsored research, most institutions voluntarily extend the protections
to all research conducted at the institution. The OHRP has employed
a variety of sanctions including limiting or withdrawing the FWA or
suspending federal research. Violation of the obligations of an FWA can
result in termination or suspension of the institution's FWA, suspension
of or restrictions on the projects, departmental restrictions, or individual
restrictions.

Advent of Litigation

The federally regulated system, which is complex, has been in place and
operating satisfactorily since the adoption of the Common Rule in 1991.
As far as we know, all problems, complaints, and grievances had been
handled within the ethical community and the regulatory framework
until 2000, when the family of Jesse Gelsinger brought suit against the
University of Pennsylvania and other defendants. That introduced a new,
controversial, and highly problematic approach to complaints about
research involving humans—tort litigation. Since the Gelsinger action,
other lawsuits have followed but, so far, without securing a court judgment in favor of the plaintiffs. Other lawsuits include an action against
the University of Pennsylvania on behalf of Dolores Aderman, who allegedly suffered temporary liver toxicity;[16] a class action against the Fred
Hutchinson Cancer Research Center in Seattle for alleged harm in a study
aimed at making bone marrow transplantation safer;[17] a suit against Ohio
State University on behalf of a patient and her husband who claim they
were harmed by experimental medication to aid nerve regeneration;[18]
and an action against four University of Oklahoma scientists that alleges
that the subjects were injured in a melanoma vaccine trial.[19]

Since the research system appears to have worked successfully for more
than a decade, what accounts for the emergence of lawsuits claiming
improper action on the part of well-known and respected institutions
and other researchers? One suggestion is that the complexion of medical
research has changed dramatically during that period of time. Modest
studies dealing with questions of a straightforward nature have given
way to large, complex projects with challenging social and ethical dimensions, such as studies dealing with reproductive technology or genetic
predispositions. The problems reveal that many important issues relating
to the ethics of human research are unresolved despite the regulations, at

a time when U.S. medical and pharmaceutical research is expanding. Another possible answer is that public interest in these studies has increased tremendously during the past few decades with potential advances in research involving cancer, AIDS, and other serious diseases. Patients expect and demand access to experimental drugs as the best, and perhaps only, hope for their survival. The technology of the information age, including cable TV and the Internet, have contributed to produce a public that is better informed (although not always accurately) about medical science, the health care industry, and pharmaceuticals. This field, moreover, appears to have attracted the attention of the trial bar, perhaps based on successes in other fields with similar features. The increased exposure, especially through extensive direct-to-consumer drug advertising, may have contributed to eliminating the mystique of the medical profession, if not decreasing respect for health care professionals.

There is no question that human clinical research trials, by means of which pharmaceutical and other companies bring new drugs, devices, and procedures into the practice of medicine, and the marketplace of medicine, have become part of a huge growth industry.[20] The National Institutes of Health doubled its spending during the five-year period from 1998 to 2003, reaching a total of about $27 billion in the 2003 fiscal year.[21] The largest pharmaceutical companies, which spend billions on research and development every year, are continually expanding their expenditures. In order to maintain their current levels of profit, they must engage in aggressive efforts to bring new drugs to the market, through an approval process involving human clinical trials.[22] A 2002 estimate indicates that the number of Americans who have participated in clinical trials to be approximately twenty million. As the numbers expand, so do the number of trial sites. Whereas previously most trials occurred in academic medical centers, more and more physicians have entered the realm of clinical research to become physician-investigators and many of their patients have become patient-subjects.[23]

In recent years, the federal government, notably the OHRP, has become more aggressive about disciplining researchers for rules violations.[24] In addition, the Justice Department has pursued research violations in situations where federal funds have been misused.[25] The Gelsinger case, however, seemed to be the catalyst for the latest surge of tort litigation. Some observers predict that the continuing growth of medical research, particularly in the pharmaceutical field, will produce burgeoning litigation.[26] It is important to note that, following the settlement of the Gelsinger case, a related settlement was announced, this one between the federal government and the researchers and research institutions involved. [27]

Both institutions, the University of Pennsylvania and Children's National Medical Center in Washington, DC, agreed to pay substantial sums of money to resolve the government's allegations of improper conduct. The institutions also agreed to changes in the way they administer human subject protection programs. In addition, the government placed restrictions of several years duration on the clinical research of the three institutional research investigators who were named in the enforcement action.[28] Additionally, another instance of the imposition of administrative sanctions occurred following the death of a volunteer participant in a study conducted at Johns Hopkins.[29] I will return to discuss regulatory and legislative measures because more stringent ethical and regulatory action could serve to minimize the amount of, and the need for, private litigation, which has disruptive effects on the entire process of medical research as it serves to compensate occasional victims of injury.

While the malpractice model has so far been used in the early stages of tort litigation in the medical research field, there has been little recognition in the tort field of the fundamental differences between medical practice and medical research. As noted above, ordinary medical treatment is geared solely to helping individual patients. Medical research is geared solely to developing new or revised drugs, devices, or procedures that may help future patients and, by the very nature of research, is not geared to help the particular research subjects. Research protocols and informed consent documents typically specify that no benefit is promised to the subject.

Several points of clarification are useful here. One is that clinical trials typically are in four phases, each having a different purpose and each having different implications for the subjects. Maximizing the effectiveness of a drug may or may not be the goal of the particular phase in which the subject is participating. Phase 1 trials mark the first test of a drug (or medical device or procedure, of course, but I will refer generally to drugs since they are the principal use of trials) in humans and are limited to very few subjects (twenty to eighty). This phase is used to investigate dosage and toxicity, not to test efficacy. Patients are sometimes used as volunteers in addition to healthy subjects. Phase 2 trials are used to test efficacy and to obtain additional data on the safety of drugs. A limited number of subjects are used, perhaps two to three hundred. Phase 3 trials constitute expanded efficacy testing. Several thousand subjects are used. Phase 4 trials are generally post-marketing studies of FDA-approved drugs that are aimed at gathering more information, such as concerning a specific adverse reaction.[30]

Another point is that, although some research literature makes a distinction between therapeutic and nontherapeutic trials, that terminology seems to stem from a confusion between experimental treatment and research trials. It is obvious that a volunteer subject could benefit from the drug or device being investigated but no such benefit could be promised. Subjects are usually randomly assigned to one treatment level or another. No commitment is made as to how long a trial will last and whether the treatment will be available after its termination. Research trials are not therapeutic, that is, with direct participant benefit being foremost. On the contrary, unlike treatment, the goal is to produce future benefit provided the drug passes investigation. In short, research on human subjects does not constitute "therapy" even when a subject happens to be a patient of a physician who referred the subject to the researcher or when the physician himself or herself is the principal investigator.

Trials can be conducted with healthy volunteers or patients, depending on the purpose of the trial and the need for subjects. Healthy subjects have nothing whatever to gain whereas critically ill patients might cling to the hope that they will receive beneficial doses for the time being on an experimental drug even when they are informed that no benefit is promised. Finally, peer review done in the course of evaluating the scientific merit of research proposals is generally (and always should be) a vital part of IRB review responsibilities. Ordinarily, each research proposal is subjected to close scrutiny and evaluation by at least one IRB member who has expertise in the field.

All these factors combine to complicate—or clarify, as the case may be—the issues in human research. Several other features of research help to define its character. Risk is an ingredient of research as is the possibility of an adverse event. The purpose of informed consent is to alert the subject to the potential dangers. The protocol should be structured to minimize risk and to protect against adverse events. The intent is to catch adverse events early and report them immediately to the IRB. Effective clinical trials help to insure that drugs and devices, when approved by the FDA and placed on the market, will not carry undue risks. If drugs are rushed to the market, without effective trials, they may result in injury and increased lawsuits at the other end of the process.

Also involved here are two underlying issues that are not always discussed in the context of research issues. One is the relationship among researchers, researching institutions, sponsors (usually a drug company which is funding the study), and the subjects. These relationships may have personal, professional, social, and economic aspects, depending on the situation. The relationship of physician to patient and researcher to subject is vital and must be preserved. Another issue involves profits. Everyone is assured some benefit from the research except the subjects.

This problem is worth reconsidering even in light of the usual argument against compensation for subjects because of the danger of creating a coercive situation. Why should subjects not be free to accept risks for compensation in addition to other reasons? Why is compensation considered so potentially coercive that subjects should not be compensated? I do not necessarily advocate compensation but suggest that the relationships should be reexamined along with all other aspects of the problems.

Historical Antecedents of Lawsuits

As we begin to examine the new wave of medical research lawsuits that followed the Gelsinger case, it is well to keep in mind that there are historical antecedents for these lawsuits. The antecedents come from two sources. One is research conducted by the government involving both military personnel and citizens. Those cases concerned subjects including exposure to radiation, LSD, and experimental medical treatments. Litigation concerning these practices did not occur until several years after the events and presented procedural obstacles, such as statutes of limitation, that often were dispositive. Governmental immunity was also a problem.[31]

The second antecedent arose from a situation in which the human research was conducted by a private entity rather than by the government.[32] This was the subject of a well-known case, *Grimes v. Kennedy Krieger*.[33] This case, prominent in every bioethics casebook, concerned a study by public health researchers into lead abatement techniques. In the action, the plaintiffs alleged that the researchers improperly allowed children to remain in housing that contained varying amounts of lead paint. Basically, the ground for complaint was unconsented research rather than failure to disclose particular information that would have given the subjects a basis for deciding whether to participate. The decision of the court was what some consider an aberration, that is, that children cannot be research subjects in any nontherapeutic studies involving any risk at all. Since all studies involve some risk, the court's decision would bar children from research studies, thus severely restricting the development of devices or drugs that could benefit children.[34]

The wave of recent cases that began with Gelsinger represents a new phenomenon in the field of research litigation. Although most have not progressed far enough in the court system to warrant any sweeping conclusions about their ultimate success, some observations are possible. First, they cover a wide span of events, claims, and theories of law. Second, although they encompass many liability theories, neither the lawyers nor the courts have formulated an adequate approach to this type of lawsuit.

There is still no discernible law of bioethics as such but, rather, a variety of hybrid combinations of existing law adapted to fit specific types of lawsuits. In short, many problems exist with respect to this new brand of litigation. The problems inherent in attempting to apply existing law from one field to a field that has fundamental distinctions are accentuated by a lack of understanding on the part of lawyers and judges of the fundamental features of medical research.

The question of what standard of care researchers should be held to has not been fully resolved. Further, policy makers in health care and pharmacology should be concerned, even if lawyers and judges are not, about the impact that tort litigation could have on the development of new drugs and other medical technologies. I make that comment realizing that researchers and drug companies, which work hand in hand in this development process, are engaged, not in charitable work, but in a highly profitable enterprise—profitable in sales dollars for drug companies, profitable in research dollars, and profitable in terms of notoriety for researchers and their sponsoring institutions.

Another observation is that, based on the pleadings and the literature about the cases, they reflect the fundamental misunderstanding referred to above about the distinct nature of medical research involving human subjects. That misunderstanding may be real or, as regarding the lawyers, contrived for the purpose of finding and applying existing malpractice doctrine to these cases. So far, the spate of litigation has not met with success in court but at least two cases have accomplished an important goal—settlements for substantial sums. The claims in Gelsinger and Roche have reportedly been settled for sums in the millions.[35] Both have had a role in bringing about notable administrative sanctions by federal agencies and have resulted in sweeping internal changes at the two major research institutions involved, the University of Pennsylvania and Johns Hopkins Medical Center. As far as development of the law of human research liability is concerned, however, neither case advanced the law because, presumably, both death cases were settled based on the risk of damage awards.

THE LAWSUITS

Before analyzing and evaluating the implications of the substantial intervention of litigation in this important field of bioethics, we first return to look closely at the Gelsinger case and then examine the Roche case along with other recent lawsuits. Although the Gelsinger litigation is complicated, we will examine several features for the purpose of analysis. Critical information will include the nature of the participants (which defendants were sued), what factual context was considered important to the plaintiffs, what theories of liability were claimed, what institutional biases and lack of expertise were revealed, and, finally, the impact of the case as far as we can predict at the present time.

The Case of Jesse Gelsinger

The family of Jesse Gelsinger initially named as defendants the trustees of the University of Pennsylvania (the research institution where the study was done), Children's Hospital of Philadelphia, and Children's National Medical Center (which were the other research institutions involved), James Wilson, M.D. (coinvestigator), and Genovo, Inc., a biotechnology company, which had a financial interest in the genetically altered virus being tested. Wilson was the founder of Genovo as well as a stock holder and the University also had an equity interest. Other defendants included Steven Raper, M.D. (the principal investigator), William Kelley, M.D. (former medical dean who had patents involved in the procedure), Mark Batshaw, M.D. (coprincipal investigator, from Children's National Medical Center), and Arthur Caplan, Ph.D. (director of bioethics at the University of Pennsylvania and the bioethicist who advised the researchers).

Although numerous legal theories were alleged in the multi-count complaint, the plaintiff's lawyer focused on several aspects of the events that led to Jesse's death. A major focus was the alleged inadequacy of the informed consent form which, the lawyer asserted, underestimated the risk and left out crucial information about adverse events involving earlier human volunteers and animal subjects. Another major focus was on the claim that Jesse should not have been deemed qualified for the experiment because, according to the FDA, his blood ammonia levels were too high just before he underwent the infusion of genetic material. Finally, the attorney alleged various conflicts of interest that affected the judgment of the University, the medical dean, and Dr. Wilson. The allegations were that the University and Wilson had stakes in Genovo which, in turn, had a financial interest in the genetically altered virus, and that Wilson and Kelley had patents on some aspects of the procedure.

In view of the principal theories of negligence alleged in the complaint, it is fair to say that the factual context on which the plaintiff relied was one that portrayed the defendants as violating the most fundamental and sacred, human right of a research subject—the subject's autonomy, his knowing and informed consent to participation. All three major theories of wrongdoing portrayed the defendants as taking advantage of a seriously ill subject by using him in the study without informing him fully and candidly of crucial facts, in particular, their undisclosed constellation of interests beyond research, his unsuitability for the study, and the actual risks of participating in the research. It is difficult to think of a stronger set of allegations that strike at the heart of ethical conduct concerning research with human subjects.

Because the case was settled rather than decided by a court, it is not possible to identify particular institutional biases or lack of expertise on the part of a court. It is fair to say, however, that by framing the major issues in terms of lack of respect for the subject's individual autonomy, the plaintiff's lawyer appealed to prominent and favored themes in the law. We can see how *the idiom of the law* played a role in the Gelsinger case. The story of Jesse Gelsinger's life and decline in the course of the research trial is a complicated human story. The entire narrative was transformed by the legal documents until it fit within the structure of several theories of legal liability.

In the case of Jesse Gelsinger, the informed consent process, which took place over the course of numerous conversations, did not appear to be a clear violation of the rules of informed consent but, at worst, was ambiguous. Many risks were pointed out and information was offered concerning past studies. The conflicts of interest were not sufficiently explained although, of course, they would not be a causative factor in Jesse's death. Although the FDA found violations of research guidelines, it cannot be said with certainty what caused his death. The participants in the lawsuit were limited to those whom the plaintiff sued although, of course, the defendant institutions initially selected the research subjects. The fact that market forces drive priorities, production and profit in drug development complicates such matters because it adds economic factors to the ethical mix.

Although Arthur Caplan, who was dropped as a defendant prior to settlement, characterized the regulatory response to Gelsinger as "a lot of hand waving and handwringing," and asserted that "not a single regulatory change has happened post-Gelsinger,"[36] it did have considerable impact in terms of administrative sanctions and, equally important, self-regulatory changes. The FDA placed prohibitions on the University's research involving human subjects, including a temporary ban on its Institute for Human Gene Therapy, and a permanent prohibition on Wilson.[37] In addition, the other researchers involved, Batshaw and Raper also had restrictions placed on their clinical research for several years. Additionally, the University and Children's National Medical Center each agreed to pay more than half a million dollars to the federal government.[38] The University agreed in a settlement with the federal government to make changes in the conduct of its human subjects protection programs, including increasing IRB oversight of clinical research, mandatory training for investigators and staff, using an independent contract research organization to monitor research, and creating an Office of Human Research to focus on participant safety. The National Medical Center agreed to similar administrative protections.[39]

Jesse Gelsinger's father did not support the federal settlement because it did not involve an acknowledgment of wrongdoing or an apology. He contended that the improvements should have occurred long ago. It was said that Jesse's father "would like to see changes outlined in the Institute of Medicine's book, 'Responsible Research,' applied to the oversight of clinical research, in particular recommendations to address conflicts of interest."[40] He also said, "[i]t will take legislation with severe financial and criminal repercussions to actually get all of research to pay attention and upgrade their oversight systems."[41] The University president appointed a special independent panel chaired by Dr. William H. Danforth, to review the policies of the Institute for Human Gene Therapy. Based on the recommendations of the panel, the University established the administrative changes outlined above. Gelsinger was probably correct; the changes made after Jesse's death should have been made long ago. Who could argue against the proposition that the "Standard Operating Procedures for research" and "clear standards that will guide the review and monitoring of clinical trials" should have been in place for any human research conducted at the University?[42]

Caplan correctly pointed out that no federal regulatory changes of general applicability are directly attributable to the Gelsinger matter. The federal government did take a hand in the aftermath, however, and, equally important in this field of bioethics, the research institution strengthened its own self-regulatory process. The FDA did note numerous violations of its guidelines, thus leading to a federal initiative to cause the institutions to agree to changes in their procedures. Specifically, the FDA found that the University had failed to notify the FDA that four patients who had enrolled ahead of Jesse suffered reactions to the treatment so serious as to require that the study be halted and the FDA notified, pursuant to rules the University had agreed to in advance. The FDA also found that informed consent forms that were supposed to tell volunteers about the potential risks of participation were changed, without informing the FDA, to eliminate all reference to monkeys that had died after getting a similar treatment.

If the economic and social impact of the Gelsinger litigation produced the administrative action to improve the human research regulation, we could conclude that the tort litigation was worthwhile. Since the purpose of the litigation was to compensate Jesse's family for his death and since that was accomplished without any judicial decisions, we cannot say for sure what factor brought about the changes. As a result of the publicity surrounding the litigation and settlement, the public is better informed about the process and risks of human research. Surely, no one would discount the impact of public sanctions against well-known researchers and a prominent institution. We cannot discount the possibility that the threat of that alone would have caused the institutional changes. The case for regulatory impact of tort litigation remains unfulfilled. Nothing detracts from the argument that adequate self-regulation, bolstered by strong and effective federal regulation, is the best policy. In fact, what is needed is policy and ethical self-regulation in order to preserve the vital but fragile relationships within the research field. Courts cannot adopt or promulgate policy in the framework of tort litigation as they award money damages to particular injured parties. We cannot discount, of course, the value that such risk warnings may have.

Courts are not primarily policymaking institutions; legislatures, the executive branch, and regulatory agencies have that function. The fact that a settlement occurred does not directly produce *policy* on which future lawsuits can rely. Can a lawsuit or threat of a lawsuit produce leverage and persuasive impact? Of course it can. Can it produce policy that will guide future activities? Only on a limited basis does that happen.

The Case of Ellen Roche

I want to turn now to a *case* that did not become a lawsuit because it settled before litigation—the matter of Ellen Roche, a healthy volunteer in a clinical trial at another prestigious research institution, Johns Hopkins Medical Institutions. Ellen Roche, a woman in her 20s, was participating in a study designed to understand the body's natural defenses against asthma.[43] The study, which was funded by the National Institutes of Health, was not a clinical trial to test a specific therapy but, rather, a "baseline psychological test." The purpose was to assist physicians in understanding how the body fights asthma.[44] Roche was the third subject to participate in the study. She signed an informed consent and was to receive up to $365, $25 for each visit in the first phase and $60 for each visit in the second phase. She was a technician in the Johns Hopkins Asthma and Allergy Center and was recruited by an Associate Professor of Clinical Immunology, Dr. Alkis Togias.

Serious illness or death was not listed among the risks of participating in the study. The first subject reported coughing a day after participating, but the cough disappeared after a few days. The second subject did not experience any ill effects. Prior to Roche's acceptance, she had undergone a series of tests, including lung function tests, and was reported healthy and eligible for the study. During the study, she was given a drug called hexamethonium by inhalation. Twenty-four hours after receiving the drug, she developed a dry cough, difficulty breathing during exertion, and muscle aches. Two days later, the researchers informed the IRB that the symptoms had not abated and she was asked to return for evaluation. When her oxygen level dropped to a critical level, she was hospitalized and her condition was considered a "serious adverse event."[45] She was treated over the course of many weeks to determine the cause of her condition but died on June 2, 2001, about a month after the event, after her condition proceeded to ARDS (adult respiratory distress syndrome).[46]

The study was suspended upon Roche's death, and investigation was undertaken by the FDA, the OHRP and Hopkins, itself. As a preliminary action, the OHRP suspended all federally supported medical research projects involving human subjects at almost all of Hopkins' institutions. Hopkins called the action "draconian."[47] Hopkins initiated its own internal investigation of the highly unusual occurrence of death of a healthy research subject. The report found several violations of procedure but concluded that the "tragic outcome may have been unavoidable" although "the policies, practices, and institutional culture made its occurrence more likely."[48]

The violations included the following:

As to the principal investigator :

a. He did not report an adverse event in the first patient.
b. The information contained in the informed consent was misleading.
c. The protocol was changed without informing the IRB.
d. Inhalant preparation was not sterile, not analyzed, and not appropriately prepared.
e. The toxicology literature review was adequate but not outstanding.

The Department/Research Center failed to have expert internal peer review at the level of the Asthma and Allergy Center.

The IRB review process was inadequate.

As to the University: Subtle coercion existed in the recruitment of volunteers to the Asthma Center studies. Many people believed that oversight and the regulatory process were a barrier to research and were reduced to the minimum.

As to regulatory agencies: There was an adversary relationship with OHRP, and the FDA refused to answer whether an application for investigational new drugs was required for a nontherapeutic inhalant.

The panel made some general recommendations about reorganizing, strengthening, and raising the quality and integrity of the entire research and review process. In particular, the panel made some general recommendations and a few specific ones.

The general recommendations included (1) oversight of clinical research at Johns Hopkins must be significantly strengthened; (2) expert internal review and discussion of every protocol at the department or research level is needed before a proposal is forwarded to the IRB; (3) special care is needed to ensure the safety of volunteers in studies having no therapeutic potential; (4) encourage the Institute Of Medicine or other appropriate body to convene representatives of various regulatory agency members with those from academic medicine and the National Institutes of Health to develop appropriate standards for nonpharmaceutical substances to be given to humans; (5) reorganize the IRB as necessary so that each proposal is given full discussion by the entire board; and (6) web-based training of investigators.

The recommendations specific to the Roche study were (1) the quality of the substance and its preparation should be ensured by an institutional research pharmacy or equivalent; (2) greater sensitivity is needed to prevent subtle coercion of volunteers; and (3) the staff should be prohibited from participating in studies within academic units and separate time spent in any study from regular working hours. Johns Hopkins submitted a corrective plan to the OHRP, and OHRP accepted it.

The case was ultimately settled for an undisclosed amount of money, without a lawsuit being initiated. The settlement specifically precluded a lawsuit and included a statement by the Roche family attorney that "the family is confident that what happened to Ellen won't ever be repeated and understands the need for medical experiments on human subjects to advance science."[49] Hopkins published a long list of administrative improvements and no evident action resulted on the part of federal agencies against the University. After the Roche controversy, however, the Maryland state legislature passed a law in 2002 that extends the federal protection requirements to all research involving human subjects conducted in the state, regardless of the funding source or FDA jurisdiction.[50]

What conclusions can be drawn from the Roche situation and the aftermath of a claim by the Roche family? Both parties in Roche made positive public remarks following the settlement that was reached before the adversarial process actually began. The fact that Roche worked for Hopkins and that she shared an interest in the goals of human research may have contributed to an amicable settlement. Perhaps because the case was settled before the parties entered into full confrontational positions, Hopkins announced significant changes and improvements and implicitly, at least, admitted deficiencies, in its human research procedures. In contrast, the University of Pennsylvania announced changes in policy as well but in a much more guarded tone and the family of Jesse Gelsinger maintained an adversarial tone, consistent with the context of the situation.

In both cases, the institutions strengthened their self-regulatory processes and complied willingly with regulatory oversight measures. Clearly, the key to effective human research protection procedures lies in public openness, scrutiny, and regulatory oversight coupled with strong internal self-regulatory measures consistent with the other factors. Creating an atmosphere in which IRB members are viewed, not as antagonists or obstructionists, but rather, as participants in a process designed to facilitate productive research with adequate protections for the subjects is crucial. It is evident that the adversarial nature of litigation can permanently alter relationships within the human research field. Research depends on a trusting and responsible relationship of researcher to subject. If researchers fail to protect subjects, the relationship is betrayed. When litigation pervades the field, this crucial relationship is lost. Without willing subjects, who enter into the studies without promise of benefit, research is impeded. While pharmaceutical companies lose only profits when that happens, humanity loses the benefits of productive research and development. In litigation, subtle ethical questions have no place. Rather the important questions demand all or nothing decisions. The subtleties and complexities of ethics are surrendered to the enterprise of winning.

Other Litigation

Several unresolved cases may eventually shed some light on the impact of litigation in this field. For the most part, we know only the allegations at this point. None of the cases have been fully decided, although a few decisions on preliminary issues have been rendered. Some of the cases involve claims that appear to be straightforward, that is, they deal directly with alleged lapses in the conduct of research. Some appear to reflect clearly the distinction between treatment and research. Others appear to have broader allegations. It will be illuminating to see how courts address these cases in their gatekeeping roles.

Two federal cases, *Abney v. Amgen*[51] and *Suthers and Martin v. Amgen*[52] are noteworthy. Both cases arise out of similar circumstances. The defendant Amgen, a large pharmaceutical company, sponsored research involving the delivery of a drug to help with Parkinson's disease. The plaintiffs in *Suthers* were Parkinson's disease patients who served as research subjects in a series of trials conducted by researchers at NYU (New York University Medical Center). As the trial court in *Suthers* put it, "[t]he decision to participate in the trial was no small matter. It was accompanied by invasive surgery to implant a pump in the abdomen and catheters into the brain in order to deliver the treatment. Each knew that there was a 50/50 chance of receiving nothing more than a placebo through the first six months of the trial. Although plaintiffs did receive placebos for the first six months of the study, Mr. Suthers and Ms. Martin eventually received the experimental treatment"[53] during the next phase.

In the *Abney* case, the plaintiffs received the drug during the initial phase.[54] All of the plaintiffs believed that the drug relieved their symptoms, and a researcher reported improvements in their physical conditions. When the company discontinued the trial, the plaintiffs brought suit to compel the sponsor, Amgen, to resume giving them the drug. The plaintiffs asked the court for a temporary injunction, that is, an order that would prevent the company from stopping the trial while the lawsuit went forward, in addition to permanent relief. The district court, in a written ruling, denied the preliminary injunction on June 6, 2005, on the basis that the plaintiffs failed to demonstrate a likelihood of success. I will discuss the trial court's decision on the temporary relief issue. The plaintiffs relied on three theories to support their application for an injunction. First, they claimed that Amgen breached its contract with them to supply the experimental drug known as GDNF so long as it was beneficial to them, and it seemed to be beneficial. Second, they asserted a promissory estoppel cause of action, that is, a claim that Amgen made promises, which they relied on to their detriment by having the surgery necessary to deliver the GDNF. Third, they claimed breach of a fiduciary duty, that is, a duty based on a special relationship of trust. Amgen denied making such promises or agreements and denied being in a fiduciary relationship. Amgen further asserted that it discontinued the trial based on discovery that GDNF produced certain antibodies that risked worsening the subjects' condition.

The district court's decision as to all three counts turned on the absence of a contractual or fiduciary relationship between Amgen and the plaintiffs. Amgen, in its role as the sponsor, had no direct relationship with the plaintiffs, although it had a legal relationship with the researchers. The principal investigators recruited and dealt with the subjects. The consent document, the court pointed out, informed participants that the study could be terminated by its sponsor. Whether the participants or the investigators agreed with Amgen's decision to terminate the trial was irrelevant. In fact, some investigators agreed and some disagreed. The plaintiffs' attempt to establish a legally sufficient relationship with Amgen through the researchers as agents was rejected by the court. The plaintiffs' attempt to obtain an injunction in Abney was unsuccessful for the same reasons. The court observed:

While the plaintiffs assert that denying an injunction would discourage patients from participating in clinical trials, the reverse is also true of discouraging clinical trial sponsors from financially supporting clinical trials. Granting an injunction and forcing a trial sponsor to provide drugs it—and the FDA—finds unsafe, because other experts find the drugs safe and effective, would discourage sponsors from financially supporting human clinical trials. This is true because sponsors would have to continue to make and provide drugs that are potentially dangerous.[55]

The court went on to conclude that three of the four factors to be considered (likelihood of success, irreparable harm to plaintiffs, harm to defendant, and public policy concerns) weighed against a preliminary injunction.[56] The court found that it would side with the plaintiffs only concerning harm to the defendant. In discussing the public policy factor, the court added, curiously that "because the public's safety and the future of clinical trial research weigh in favor of denying the injunction, the Court finds that the public interest would not be furthered by entry of an injunction."[57]

If the court had decided that its view of the public's safety and the future of clinical research weighed in favor of granting the injunction, we are left to wonder whether it would have granted the injunction despite the lack of a legal relationship between the plaintiffs and Amgen. To what extent is the court's decision, after all, dependent on its public policy conclusions? In these cases, the merging of distinctions between researcher and sponsor did not prevail. The attempt to make claims that would override the informed consent provision acknowledging the right of the sponsor to terminate the trial did not succeed either, at this stage in the litigation. There is no question but that these cases challenge certain fundamentals in the field of human research. They are based on realigning the research relationships and duties into therapeutic relationships and duties. Depending on what action the courts take, public policy could be affected significantly through the process of litigation.

Wright v. Fred Hutchinson Cancer Research Center,[58] an action brought in the federal district court in the State of Washington, provides a rare opportunity to see far-reaching claims that were actually ruled on by the court, in this instance, adversely to the plaintiffs. This case involved a study purporting to investigate whether using eight antibodies to kill T-cells in bone marrow donated by tissue-matched siblings would eliminate GVHD (graft-versus-host-disease) following bone transplantation in leukemia patients. The plaintiffs complained that with the T-cell eradication, the rate of rejection of donated marrow and the relapse of cancer increased dramatically. The class action lawsuit was brought on behalf of the families of eighty-two patients who participated in the trial, designated Protocol

126. Eighty of the eighty-two patients died from graft failures and leukemia relapse following the experimental treatment, according to the complaint. The plaintiffs claim that twenty of those deaths are attributable to the faulty and misguided experimental treatment. The plaintiffs based their suit on claims that the Hutchinson Center and its officials misrepresented the risks of participating in the trial, improperly allowed it to continue, failed to abide by IRB recommendations, and intimidated IRB members. They also claimed that the researchers had financial conflicts of interest in the outcome of the study. In addition to the Center, the defendants included individuals who served as directors, investigators, oncologists, and officials of a company, Genetic Systems, Inc., which had financial ties to the Center.[59]

Although the complaint contained seven separate counts, each based on a different legal theory, the defendants moved successfully to dismiss the first four counts. The district court's ruling on the first four counts provides insights into disposition of the type of sweeping legal claims that fall outside the context of human research litigation. The first count alleged a claim for breach of rights created by the Nuremberg Code and the Declaration of Helsinki. Apparently recognizing no basis in American law for such direct claims, the plaintiffs argued that the count raised those claims in the context of the Fourteenth Amendment to the U.S. Constitution. The court, accordingly, dismissed the first count yet indicated that it would consider the Code and the Declaration in connection with a substantive due process claim that was brought under Section 1983 of the Civil Rights Act.[60]

The second count asserted violations of various federal regulations,[61] which regulate the manufacture and control of investigational biological drugs used in clinical trials and provide protections for human research subjects. The court's response to the motion to dismiss this count reveals the relation between government regulation and private enforcement. The plaintiffs claimed that the violation of federal regulations was privately enforceable through Section 1983. The court rejected this claim because Congress did not give the plaintiffs a statutory basis in Section 1983 for the private rights of action they sought to enforce.

The third count alleged that the plaintiffs were third-party beneficiaries of an assurance agreement between the DHHS and the Center in which certain guidelines based on the Belmont Report were included. The court rejected the notion that the plaintiffs had standing as third-party beneficiaries, based on existing authority. Finally, the fourth count, which raised a Fourteenth Amendment due process claim because of claimed violations of informed consent, was dismissed because it did not raise a Section 1983 claim. Substantive due process is not to be expanded by court fiat in view of prominent cases including *Stanley*,[62] *Heinrich*,[63] *Stadt*[64], and the radiation litigation.[65] Violations during the studies in the present case are not similar to the scale of the violations in those prominent cases, according to the court. As the court said, "Plaintiff has not identified, and the Court has not found any case which has equated lack of informed consent in the medical context with a constitutional violation."[66] The plaintiffs are left to pursue their attempts to prove traditional type legal claims and do not have available the kind of sweeping federal claims asserted in the first four counts. Two interesting sidelights exist with respect to the *Wright* case. First, the incidents at the Center attracted the press; the *Seattle Times* did investigative reporting and an explosive series of articles about the studies. Second, the OHRP undertook its own investigation of the incidents. Whether administrative sanctions will result remains to be seen. The case proceeded with the three remaining counts: (1) Assault, Battery, and Violation of the Health Care Provider Act, (2) Strict Products Liability, and (3) Violation of the Consumer Protection Act. [67]

ANALYSIS

An analysis of the impact of litigation in the field of human research is useful at this point. We will look at each major area of concern in turn in the context of the lawsuits.

The Idiom of the Law

What is the effect of translating issues into legal language and concepts?

Plaintiffs' lawyers appear to take one or both of two alternate routes in their efforts to secure favorable verdicts in this relatively new and potentially fertile territory for litigants who claim to be injured through research negligence. The first route is to attempt to fit the claims into existing legal frameworks, the most common being medical malpractice (negligence), assault and battery (lack of informed consent), fraud and misrepresentation (intentional and negligent), breach of fiduciary duty, infliction of emotional distress, products liability, strict tort liability, and violation of specific state statutes (consumer protection, health care provider acts). The second route is to assert claims as general, broad claims based on human rights, usually within the context of constitutional claims. As we have seen, the broad human rights-type claims have failed, even when posing as Fourteenth Amendment violations. It is likely, however, that a claim of egregious conduct on the scale of the government radiation experiments would gain entry through the constitutional route.

When medical research claims are dressed in the garb of traditional legal theories, they get over the threshold but, of course, they may face additional challenges on route to a verdict. Malpractice likely has the best chance of success. The problem is, however, that the researcher–subject relationship is not the same as the physician–patient relationship. In cases in which a physician conducts research involving his own patients, however, the duty as a physician would appear to prevail over the research role. In that situation, the emerging relationship would contain elements of the original physician–patient connection. There is as yet no precise equivalent in the law for the ethical relationship of researcher to subject although the fiduciary relationship may be the closest. In a fiduciary relationship, the researcher would be considered to owe a duty to the subject.

As I indicated earlier, the subject is the only person who cannot expect, or at least is not assured of, any benefit at all from the research. No legal equivalent to the ethical relationship of researcher and subject has yet been clearly established by either courts or legislators. Judges, in fact, should not attempt to create new legal relationships out of whole cloth, at least not in the exercise of proper judicial restraint. Courts and lawyers, therefore, are bound to do their best to adapt existing legal concepts and relationships. They must fit new factual situations into existing well-defined categories. The result, ironically, is often to discourage new legislation because the result suggests that new law is not needed. In the course of deferring to legislative policymaking authority, which may be unexercised, courts sometimes proceed to fill the void with their own policymaking by judicial decision. The settlements in Gelsinger and Roche avoided having courts grapple with the obstacle posed by the fact that the language of law confines controversies to well-defined legal categories.

What is the effect of restricting the interests that are allowed to participate in court?

The only interests represented in lawsuits are those of the particular participants who can claim to have legally cognizable relationships. "Legally cognizable" is a term that courts often use. It means recognized as a matter of law, that is, authorized by cases or statutes. In the cases that we have examined, plaintiffs will attempt to sue parties from whom they wish to collect damages if they can prove liability. They must be able to allege a recognized legal claim against a party in order to join the party in a lawsuit. In every scenario that leads to a legal claim, using the Gelsinger case for example, dozens of people were doubtlessly involved at one stage or another. Many people not named in the lawsuit probably had some role in the chain of events that led to Jesse's death. They may have included family members, hospital staff members and medical professionals, social support staff, and IRB members. Not all of those people, however, played a role that would give rise to a legal relationship with or legal duty to the subject. A lawsuit is based on a snapshot in time governed by strict rules.

Adversarial Process

What is the effect on ethical decision-making of adversarial adjudication?

By relying on existing legal causes of action, plaintiffs must conform the factual situation to the legal framework. Allegations are limited to claimed facts that are relevant to allowable causes of action. The defendants are those whom plaintiffs have chosen, even when other potential responsible parties exist. The situations being litigated are expressed in legal language, that is, the language approved by statutes, cases, or regulations, even when that language does not serve to explain accurately the underlying facts. The complexity of the real situation, with its ethical overlay and its unique circumstances, becomes oversimplified and even altered to fit specific causes of action, all of which are separately stated in the complaint. Defendants are similarly restricted when they respond. Pleading rules do not allow for explanation beyond the traditional form. Discovery, depositions, and even trial testimony are not allowed to range free of evidentiary and procedural restrictions.

A complex and ambiguous situation is transformed into the language of winning and losing, right and wrong, proper and improper. No middle ground is officially recognized in the usual case. Courts and juries, however, do find middle ground, as a practical matter, in various ways. For example, a trial judge in a court trial may find for a plaintiff, but limit damages, perhaps even substantially. The flexibility of damage awards provides opportunities for compromise and consensus, especially when juries are involved. When the time of trial arrives, sides are clearly delineated even when, realistically speaking, the relationships are complex and subtle. When evidence is offered, it must not range beyond permissible boundaries. Burdens of proof determine who wins, rather than operating as an ethical assessment of which party may be more right than others or which may be more wrong.[68] Only people or entities that have established claims can gain access to courts. Individuals who are floundering in ambivalence, uncertainty, or confusion do not bring claims. That means that many issues arising from developments in various fields of bioethics, which are still in a state of uncertainty, ambiguity, and complexity, are left out. The concept of standing (the constitutional and legal right to bring a lawsuit) excludes from litigation many people who have serious interests in the outcome based on the ordinary understanding of the term interest. For example, in a situation that we will address later on, the Schiavo case, Terri Schiavo's parents were denied the right to participate in various proceedings once her husband was firmly established as guardian and decision maker even though they had a vital interest in the ordinary sense of the word.

The binary nature of adversarial process forces every situation into a confrontational format. Relationships and events are complex and have many aspects, both cooperative and confrontational. In Gelsinger, the relationship of Jesse with the researchers was far from confrontational and adversarial but, as described in the complaint, the relationship was characterized by those features. Many aspects of the situation do not see the *light of day*. For example, why did Jesse participate, for no benefit, in the first place? Why did the researchers study the gene transfer? What caused Jesse's death? Surely the answers to these questions are not simple but, in the context of a complaint, the inquiry is strictly limited.

How would evidence rules and burdens of proof have affected decision-making in the Gelsinger case?

Since this case did not go to a final adjudication but rather was settled, we do not know precisely what would have happened. We do know, however, that the rules of evidence severely restrict the facts that can be placed before a fact finder, whether jury or trial judge. Courts control the admissibility of evidence, but the parties decide what evidence will be presented to the court. Courts must then decide the case based on the admissible evidence, whether complete and adequate or not. In the event of confusion, ambiguity, or uncertainty, after evaluating evidence, burdens of proof aid the trier of fact in determining who wins and loses. Since indecision based on uncertainty or ambiguity is not allowed, the party who has the burden of proof loses unless the burden is satisfied.

Finality, Closure, and the Retrospective View

What is the effect of the requirement that the court must decide the case?

We have noted that one of the virtues of judicial decision-making is that courts can decide only actual cases and controversies, rather than issuing advisory opinions about hypothetical situations. Another is that courts must decide cases based on whatever is presented, rather than deferring to the future or waiting for additional information. A third is that once a case is presented in court, the court must decide the case rather than deferring decision or delaying it indefinitely. Finally, judicial decisions, once made, become precedent and thus have normative effect on the actions and conduct of citizens other than those before the court in the present controversy. In the human research litigation context, this requirement forces the parties and the court to reach a decision in a case with overriding ethical implications regardless of whether all meaningful facts are presented and whether all important interests are represented. Decisions will have far-reaching impact on decision making in the ethical context. Even settlements are reached with awareness of the implications of court decisions. That is, the parties are under pressure, in a sense, to settle because they realize that, if they fail to do so, the court will issue a decision based on the situation as presented.

What significance attaches to fixing the facts of the controversy at a moment in the past—the retrospective aspect?

Since the cases discussed in this section were either settled or remain pending, we cannot know what later developments might have affected or may affect the resolution. In general, however, adjudication is intended to resolve a narrowly restricted controversy that has concluded—insofar as legal relief is concerned—at some past moment. Given that factor, it is possible to see why future events do not affect the controversy, given the artificial environment within which the lawsuit exists. In ordinary affairs of life, however, we would hardly ever fail to consider present circumstances in deciding an important issue.[69]

Institutional Biases, Assumptions, and Deficiencies: Unspoken Factors in Shaping the Decision

Do courts favor economic interests?

In Gelsinger, the ethical or moral interests of the plaintiff and the defendants are not set out in the pleadings. Although Jesse and his family presumably undertook the risks of the trial for reasons unrelated to a contract for personal benefit, since the informed consent document rules out personal benefit to him, this fact does not appear in the legal proceedings. Nor does any interest on the part of the researchers to develop the gene transfer procedure to benefit patients appear in the pleadings. Only their economic, or at least material, interests are described.

It appears that Jesse was willing to take some risks, at least, for humanitarian purposes.

How would the law recognize interests of this sort on the part of either subjects or researchers?

In the Roche situation, the fact that, and the reasons why, a healthy volunteer subjected herself to a potentially harmful and risky study is not revealed in any information about the events. In the Wright case, it is not clear whether the volunteers who died allegedly from the GVHD would have died anyway, like so many of the other subjects of the trials. The nonmaterial aspects of the situation are not explored in the legal documents, which are confined to facts and claims pertaining specifically to legal duties and rights.

Do courts naturalize human intervention?

Although the method of gene transfer that was the subject of the clinical trials was clearly in the exploratory or investigational stages, that fact does not appear in any of the legal documents. By implication, the judicial system naturalizes this still unproven, unperfected and, thus, unnatural procedure and the events that transpired because of it. Once again, in *Roche* and *Wright,* the unnatural aspects of these clinical trials of unproven methods are not explored but are assumed. The effect is to naturalize the techniques and procedures.

Do courts elect to preserve life?

Although this issue is not directly presented by the Gelsinger controversy, it is apparent that Jesse's life was in jeopardy and that he was willing to undergo serious risks with no gain to himself. The court documents do not convey this reality. All the volunteers in *Wright* were leukemia patients who needed bone marrow transplants. Their poor prognosis is not explored in the legal documents, as not relevant to the controversy. The realities of life and death are not part of the legal proceedings, although they may well be part of the proof when the plaintiffs attempt to prove causation of death.

Do courts oversimplify controversies?

We can see in the above discussion how the abbreviated and abridged nature of legal proceedings forces oversimplification. The decision maker addresses only well-defined legal issues and interests. All others are relegated to the extra-judicial discussions. In this regard, it is striking how public discussion of legal controversies often confines itself to the legal definitions and terms when there is no obligation to do so. Legal language and concepts have a way of influencing public discussion of issues beyond their normal and expected impact.

Do courts unduly elevate individualism?

Because lawsuits are decided with respect to particular parties, no representation is allowed for the public interest or the common good. Issues affecting human research have powerful impact on the public in general. The rights and responsibilities that arise, however, are decided only in terms of the participants. The right of informed consent is, for example, not a general right to be exercised by members of the public but only by particular research subjects. The interest of the public is basically unrepresented insofar as the impact of the adjudication is concerned. To the extent that a settlement has persuasive or normative impact—which it does—clearly the public interest has no role.

What Impact Does Judicial Decision-Making Have on Future Controversies?

Since none of the research cases have gone to judgment, we are limited to addressing the impact of the initiation of litigation itself and the partial resolutions to date.

What is the role of courts in defining controversies, thereby contributing to defining the terms of future controversies?

Many ethical controversies have arisen in the field of medical research involving human subjects. Prior to the extensive network of federal regulation that is now in place, such controversies arose, for the most part, after the research was concluded. Investigations occurred and disciplinary action was taken against researchers and institutions alike. No one could reasonably claim that method of regulation to be adequate. The abuses led to stricter controls to monitor research from the outset, including the extensive approval process using IRBs. Left to self-regulation or non-binding ethical review, an unsatisfactory number of violations occurred. The present system of mandatory ethical regulation is justified. The system of regulation addresses the ethical relationships and conduct of the participants vis-a-vis subjects using the ethical framework based on the Belmont Report. The system of regulation respects the various established roles of researchers, sponsors, and subjects.

The litigation that has occurred since Gelsinger reveals a number of alleged legal violations in the field. Traditional malpractice law, along with other bodies of law, has been adapted to encompass violations in the research field. Since the duties and rights of individuals in this field were not previously delineated, lawyers and courts have attempted to analyze the researcher–subject relationship using language and concepts that apply to the physician–patient relationship. A number of other legal theories have been applied as well, including fiduciary, contract, and general human rights law, among them. Even though no plaintiff has yet received a successful verdict or judgment from a court, the research field has been transformed. The impact has been felt. Given the potential legal liability, researchers and research institutions have already begun to evaluate their potential liability and, in the process, review and change their rules, to protect against claims. To the extent that improvements have been made in procedures and regulations, the benefits are obvious.

To the extent that legitimate research has been impeded or prevented, the changes are not so salutary. Once law enters a field of endeavor in American society, changes occur. The impact of law in transforming the rules and transforming the discussion is unmistakable and permanent. Relationships that were once considered in purely ethical terms are now seen in legal terms. Law, which has its own imperatives, has transformed an area of ethical decision-making into a legal domain. Law's idioms govern our conduct in ways not always grasped fully, and they have limits that extend from the ends for which they were created. We cannot blame individuals who believe that they have been injured as a result of negligence in the human research system from seeking remedies. The consequences of litigation as a form of redress, however, reaches beyond the expectations of the individuals involved.

How well do courts illuminate and address controversies of ethical significance?

Because courts intervene essentially at the behest of parties, rather than on their own initiative, they are limited, for the most part, by the facts, issues, and parties brought into the case. The way issues are presented and what issues are presented in the first place are within the control of the parties. In the research tort cases, for example, courts are not free to determine exactly what the relationship between researcher and subject is. Rather, the courts' role is to adjudicate the viability of the alleged relationship and its implications. Courts are within their rights, of course, to determine what the applicable law is, but they are not free to reframe or reconfigure the issues or to introduce additional parties. Exceptions exist, of course, but we are speaking in broad terms here. Issues of ethical significance may or may not be presented for determination. The outcome may or may not address all the issues of importance to people within the research community. How well courts illuminate and address important controversies is dependent on how the parties have framed a particular case. In some of the research cases, it is apparent that important and traditional relationships are manipulated to some extent to fit within the liability framework of the legal allegations.

Since legal proceedings often do not recognize nonmaterial interests, if they are not included within legal definitions or categories, courts are not free to adjudicate such ethical issues and controversies. In *Gelsinger, Roche,* and *Wright,* for example, the interests of all parties were complex, a mix of self-interest and humanitarian interests. No lawsuit was filed in *Roche.* The noneconomic or nonmaterial interests are not reflected in pleadings because they are not recognized in the law or at least have no bearing on the particular causes of action. Medical researchers surely are not motivated only by pecuniary gain. All current subjects are not victims. All subjects have their own particular reasons for participating in studies. We can say for certain that monetary gain is not a principal motivating force since subjects are rarely paid more than nominal sums. Risk is present in virtually all research studies and, given today's level of disclosure, risks are almost always disclosed to subjects. While lapses can occur and ambiguities can exist, deliberate misrepresentation and concealment are probably rare.

Do courts encourage or discourage legislative policymaking?

We can say with some confidence that, since traditional medical malpractice causes of action appear to be malleable enough to encompass research tort liability claims, legislatures have little motivation to design an alternate framework for these claims. The distinctions between physicians and researchers within the ethical world are vast, but many courts do not seem to appreciate the significance of the distinctive roles. Although some courts, such as the federal court in the Amgen cases, seem aware of the impact of litigation on the research community, courts focus understandably on the liability of defendants and rights of plaintiffs. They are not at liberty to reframe issues in ways that would be likely to alert legislatures to a need to change public policy. Extensive public policy already exists in the form of federal statutes and regulations. Courts are engaged to intervene for the specific purpose of redressing alleged violations of duty and providing relief to plaintiffs who prove entitlement to it.

How well do courts carry out their boundary making power?

Courts, for the most part, confine themselves to adjudicating the law rather than launching into public policy statements. Exceptions exist, however, and courts offer policy rationales in order to support or bolster their legal decisions. The court in one *Amgen* case, for example, added policy reasons gratuitously in support of its decision. Although I do not suggest that courts should totally ignore the social context of decisions and refuse to consider the consequences of decisions within the real world, they are bound to respect the boundary between law and policy. Judges who have minimal experience in the practice of law and in normal activities within society are less likely to make effective decisions. Most judges probably have considerable experience in law practice or, at least, in the general affairs of the community within which they operate. If they cannot comprehend what the effect of their decisions will be on the people involved, they are not likely to make good decisions even if they apply the law accurately. When judges talk about public policy in specific terms, however, I believe it is improper unless they identify an appropriate source of that public policy. While judges should always identify frankly the bases for their decisions and the rationale for their decisions, they should also be forthcoming about using extra-judicial sources of information when it is acceptable to reinforce legal decisions in that way. Accountability requires such explanations. Courts are bound, not only to decide cases based on the facts and the law, but also to provide a clear analysis of the reasons. Legislatures often support their decisions with policy statements; courts must always support theirs with legal analysis. Courts, of course, may, in appropriate situations, rely on policy reasons and intent that clarify legislative actions.

What is the normative impact of the court decisions?

The decisions in cases with strong, identifiable ethical components have powerful normative effect. In the absence of legislative policy, court decisions can take on policy significance. While courts properly speak in terms of deference to legislative policy, they are bound to decide cases and in doing so, may render decisions that will have the effect of filling policy gaps until legislatures take action.

Chapter 4

Better Off Dead?
Can Judges Be Metaphysicians?

Josephine and Gerard Paretta visited a fertility center to explore IVF (in vitro fertilization) with an egg donor. They decided to go forward but, unknown to them, the egg donor was a carrier of CF (cystic fibrosis), a serious genetic disorder for which a patient requires surgery, medication, and intensive care throughout life. The father and sperm donor, Gerard, turned out to be a carrier as well. Theresa, the baby who was conceived from a fertilized egg which was implanted in Josephine, was born with the disease. The parents and child brought a lawsuit against the center's doctors for failing to test Gerard for the CF gene and for failing to disclose the egg donor's status as a carrier.[1]

Advances in medical technology during the latter part of the twentieth century have drastically changed the way physicians treat patients at all stages of life. The most dramatic applications of technology apply to medical crises that occur at the beginning and end of life. Issues arising at those two defining points on the spectrum have produced the most controversy as well as some of the most notable lawsuits. At one end of the spectrum lies the relentless controversy over abortion, perhaps the most volatile and divisive issue in American culture. Other controversies include genetic mapping and screening and stem cell research, which implicate human cloning.

At the other end of the spectrum lies the multifaceted controversy surrounding the right to refuse treatment at the end of life, encompassing medical futility, right-to-die, and physician-assisted suicide. While I do not minimize the importance of ethical controversies concerning medical issues that affect intermediate stages of life, beginning and end-of-life controversies seem to cause the greatest political, ethical, and religious turmoil and strife in our society. At both end stages, however, troubling questions arise. When does life begin? When must new life be protected? When is it autonomous? Who represents, speaks for, and should decide what happens to that new life? What if protecting the new person conflicts with other vital interests, such as a mother's health or well-being or her very autonomy? When does life end? What is the proper definition of death? Can the definition of death vary according to the purpose for defining it? When can life-sustaining treatment be withheld? When must it be continued? Who speaks for an incapable person? What factors should be taken into account when these decisions are made?

These questions, which merely begin the inquiry, and many others, must be addressed in light of the two crucial features of ethical questions mentioned earlier. The first is that all bioethical issues exist only in factual context. There are no abstract bioethical questions. While philosophical questions can be abstract, bioethics is a branch of applied ethics, a study that depends upon a factual context. The second is that the statement of ethical questions or issues frequently embodies, and sometimes masks, other types of issues, such as economic factors. Because of the reluctance to frame issues of life and death in economic terms alone, thereby seeming to reduce them to material questions of cost and commodification, economic concerns are usually part of the silent agenda.

Both areas of controversy, the beginning and end of life, have at least for the time being been resolved legally by the U.S. Supreme Court.[2] Nevertheless, there are not only legal challenges to the status quo continually in process but also, more importantly, technology changes take place on a daily basis in ways that will further affect medically, legally, and politically both endpoints on the life spectrum. Medical technology develops ways to produce viable fetuses at earlier and earlier stages of development. Technology also produces new and more effective ways to prevent pregnancy, such as the morning-after pill. At the terminal stages of life, technology produces new and better ways of allowing people to live longer, at least in the physical sense. Continuing developments in medical technology will keep changing and affecting the issues.

The current ethical controversies that concern life and death choices also involve some controversial legal actions, namely, actions for *wrongful life* and *wrongful living*. Wrongful life actions concern the beginning of life, and wrongful living actions, the end of life. Both types of civil wrongs, known as torts, have arisen because of medical technology advances, which created possibilities that did not exist before. Both are controversial, although wrongful birth actions are accepted in a majority of jurisdictions. Although the ethical or metaphysical questions that arise are similar, what happens to one type of action may have little or no bearing on what should happen to the other. Both involve difficult metaphysical questions that courts (judges and juries) are ill equipped to address. Some courts decide the questions based on law alone. Others interject public policy; still others decline to enter the inquiry and defer to legislatures. However particular courts deal with these issues, they reveal to the careful observer the inner workings of the legal system. In the process, they alter the landscape of the discussion for the future since, as we noted, legal decisions tend to colonize other public policy institutions.

As to the beginning-of-life issues, tests have existed for some time now that can inform a pregnant woman about certain defects that her unborn child possesses or is likely to possess. Examples of defects include Down syndrome, Anencephaly, and Tay-Sachs disease.[3] Now that the Human Genome Project has been completed, scientific knowledge of genetic markers is vastly increased.[4] The Human Genome Project, which began in 1990, was a thirteen-year effort coordinated by the U.S. Department of Energy and the National Institutes of Health. Its goals included identifying all the genes in human DNA, determining the sequences of the three billion chemical base pairs that make up human DNA, storing the information in data bases, and addressing the relevant ethical issues. Literally hundreds of tests have been developed to give pregnant women the capacity to detect birth defects that range from severely disabling diseases to insignificant infirmities. As the number of available tests has increased, however, so too has the likelihood of lawsuits alleging negligence on the part of physicians and other health care providers.

The term wrongful life needs more explanation in the context of other causes of action that fall into the same general category of reproductive torts: wrongful birth, wrongful pregnancy, and wrongful conception. In the most basic terms, wrongful pregnancy and wrongful conception actions are based on claims by parents that by reason of a physician's negligently failing to sterilize an individual or perform an abortion, a healthy child is born. Because the birth of a healthy baby is not generally considered to be an injury, damages are limited to expenses connected with pregnancy and birth. Wrongful birth actions involve claims *by parents* that a physician negligently failed to inform parents of likely birth defects or the increased risk of defects and the negligence resulted in a child born with birth defects. Wrongful life, in contrast, is the name given to actions brought by or on behalf of *children* who claim that as a result of physician negligence they were born with defects so serious that they would be better off had they not been born at all.

Controversy concerning wrongful life and wrongful birth lawsuits has gone on for many years. Courts faced with the issues have overwhelmingly permitted wrongful birth actions, while rejecting wrongful life actions. Courts have clearly found it more palatable to deal with lost parental choice as an injury than to attempt to answer the metaphysical question of whether nonexistence is ever preferable to life impaired by disability. Experts disagree on the issue, some asserting that both torts are consistent with traditional tort principles and, therefore, both should be allowed to proceed.

On the other end of the spectrum, the widespread availability of medical technology that can be used to keep people alive together with increasing recognition of what amounts to a "right to die"[5] (an extension of the right to refuse medical treatment)[6] has given rise to another type of lawsuit. These lawsuits allege that patients who received unwanted life-sustaining treatment have suffered a compensable injury when they were given unauthorized life-sustaining treatment. The majority of suits of this nature have relied on traditional common-law tort causes of action such as battery, or infliction of emotional distress.

Some commentators, however, have called for a new type of lawsuit, wrongful living actions.[7] Plaintiffs bringing these actions would assert a rationale that their diminished quality of life, following medical treatment, makes their life not worth living. They would, therefore, be better off dead, according to this rationale. Few courts have ruled on the validity of such actions.[8] With the increasing use of living wills, durable powers of attorney, and other documents manifesting patients' right to refuse treatment, the number of wrongful living cases may well increase. These lawsuits, like wrongful life actions, will attempt to force courts to decide whether particular lives are not worth living. Both types of action may have adverse impact on people with disabilities, it has been urgently noted.[9] Although I will touch on the concept of wrongful living causes of action, this chapter is primarily concerned with ethical controversies that arise at the beginning of life.

With this background, we proceed to examine how courts address these controversial cases involving metaphysical questions that lie at the heart of bioethics and how adjudication affects public policy discussion of the issues.

THE BEGINNING OF LIFE: THE CONTEXT OF WRONGFUL LIFE ACTIONS

One of the main developments that impacts the field of reproductive technology is genetic screening, which brings with it the possibility of gene therapies, such as the therapy that was tested in the case of Jesse Gelsinger. Genetic screening is the testing of a population group to identify a subgroup of individuals at high risk for having or passing on a particular genetic disorder. I should note that the earliest cases in this general field did not involve genetic testing, but resulted from the birth of healthy children who were, for various reasons, unexpected or unwanted by parents. Those cases were usually called "wrongful conception" or "wrongful pregnancy" cases. In those early cases, the child was healthy and the claim related to medical expenses and emotional distress damages. Most states still recognize that type of action, which resembles a typical malpractice action.

Turning to wrongful life cases, one of the very first of this category, was *Zepeda v. Zepeda,*[10] a 1963 Illinois case. This case involved an action by a child, Joseph Zepeda, against his father because the child had been born out of wedlock. The father, who was married to someone else at the time he fathered the plaintiff, had promised to marry Joseph's mother. The Illinois Appeals Court rejected the action despite acknowledging that the father's actions were willful and "legally wrong and a tortious act" against the child himself. The court stated that "it may be inconsistent to say, as we do, that the plaintiff has been injured by a tortious act and then to question, as we do, his right to maintain an action to recover for this act."[11] The court, however, acknowledged that the child's claim of harm was legitimate but declined to recognize the wrongful life claim, insisting that this decision was best made by the state legislature.[12] Should we gratefully applaud the court's decision not to rule on policy matters? Perhaps so, but if the court believed that all necessary elements of a tort action had been covered, should the court have so declined? It is legitimate to ask whether the court, without specifically saying so, made a policy determination while claiming to refuse to do so?

The court did express misgivings about whether all people born into the world under conditions that they might regard as undesirable might then be entitled to sue. The court also had concerns about how this type of action might be abused by people who would bring actions lacking in merit. It seems clear that the court ventured into ethical territory in the course of denying the validity of the cause of action in these circumstances. Even though law and legal theory may be based on well-established ethical principles, courts are supposed to decide cases based on the law, not on the basis of ethical or moral judgments. One wonders whether the court could have found legitimate reasons for rejecting this action without resorting to ethical considerations. For example, the court could have determined that the plaintiff in this case failed to allege sufficiently that it was better not to have lived at all than to live as a person born out of wedlock. While the Illinois court may have overlooked some ways of rejecting the claim within legal bounds, at least it did acknowledge the ethical implications of a wrongful life claim and did leave the matter for a legislative decision based on social policy. Determining not to recognize a claim based on illegitimacy does not mean that similar claims in other contexts should also be rejected.

Another early case that encompassed both a wrongful birth and a wrongful life claim was brought following the birth of a disabled child in a 1967 New Jersey case, *Gleitman v. Cosgrove*.[13] The mother involved in the case had contracted rubella in the early stages of her pregnancy. Despite knowledge common in the medical community that rubella could result in birth defects, the physician advised the mother that no adverse effect was likely. The parents sued for wrongful birth, and the child for wrongful life on the ground that the mother would have aborted the fetus had she known of the consequences. The court easily rejected the child's claim as "not cognizable at law" on the ground that it was "logically impossible" to "measure the difference between his life with defects against the utter void of non-existence."[14] The court had more difficulty with the parents' claim but, in the end, rejected that as well. Significantly, this was a pre-*Roe v. Wade* claim and, at that time, New Jersey had a statute that criminalized abortions without lawful justification. It is well known that the U.S. Supreme Court, in its *1973 Roe v. Wade* decision, gave constitutional protection to the right of a woman to have an abortion before fetal viability without undue interference by the state. The decision also confirmed the state's authority to restrict abortions after viability so long as the law contains exceptions that protect the woman's life and health, and confirmed the scope of the state's legitimate interests.[15] Finding it "impossible" to weigh the child's "injuries" against the "complex human benefits of motherhood and fatherhood," the court declined to do so.[16] Moreover, based on the pre-*Roe* statute, the court reasoned that "[a] court cannot say what defects should prevent an embryo from being allowed life such that denial of the opportunity to terminate the existence of a defective child in embryo can support a cause for action."[17]

More than ten years later, in 1978 (five years after *Roe*) the issue resurfaced in the Court of Appeals of New York in *Becker v. Swartz*.[18] After the birth of a child with Down syndrome, the parents and child brought actions for wrongful birth and life. After Dolores and Arnold Becker learned of her pregnancy, they engaged the services of the defendants, who were obstetrics and gynecology specialists. In May 1975, Dolores gave birth to a retarded and brain-damaged infant, who suffered from Down syndrome. The parents contended that the defendants never advised them of the increased risk of Down syndrome in children born to women over age thirty-five or of the availability of testing. Like the *Gleitman* court, the court in this case noted the complexity of the wrongful life action. The court reasoned that it "casts an almost Orwellian shadow, premised as it is upon concepts of genetic predictability once foreign to the evolutionary process...and such resolution, whatever it may be, must invariably be colored by notions of public policy, the validity of which remains, as always, a matter upon which reasonable men may disagree."[19] The court refused to recognize the claim, stating that the infant plaintiff could not be shown to suffer a legally cognizable injury in the absence of a corresponding right to "be born as a whole, functional human being." [20]

In a passage that has been repeatedly quoted by those following the majority rule rejecting the wrongful life tort, the court declared, "[w]hether it is better never to have been born at all than to have been born with even gross deficiencies is a mystery more properly to be left to the philosophers and the theologians. Surely the law can assert no competence to resolve the issue, particularly in view of the very nearly uniform high value which the law and mankind have placed on human life, rather than its absence."[21]

The court accepted the wrongful birth claim of the parents, however, reasoning that this type of action was not outside the realm of tort claims. Following *Becker,* many courts accepted the wrongful birth cause of action but wrongful life actions were generally unsuccessful until 1980 when a California intermediate appeals court endorsed the claim in *Curlender v. Bio-Science Laboratories.*[22] Several examples of the reasoning of courts rejecting this type of claim follow.

The South Carolina Supreme Court decided in 2004 in *Willis v. Wu*[23] that Thomas Willis did not state a recognizable common law cause of action when claiming wrongful life. Thomas was born with a condition called Maximal Hydrocephalus, a condition in which the cerebral hemispheres of his brain were missing. According to the court, those areas of the brain control thinking, motor control, speech, voluntary movement, and the ability to interact with other people. A CT scan of Thomas' head at birth revealed a brain stem and brain tissue only in the frontal and temporal lobes. He received therapy at home and school and will never be able to care for himself independently. His physical and mental abilities are at the same level they were at birth.[24]

Thomas' mother, his primary caregiver, brought the action on his behalf against his physician, Donald S. Wu. She claimed that Dr. Wu failed to adequately diagnose his condition by prenatal testing and to inform her of the results. She was, therefore, deprived of the opportunity to terminate the pregnancy while she could legally do so.[25] She alleged specifically that Wu failed to timely perform or interpret ultrasound examinations that revealed Thomas' congenital defect which had devastating consequences. The trial court rendered summary judgment in favor of Dr. Wu, holding that South Carolina did not recognize the tort of wrongful life.

The issue on appeal, which was a matter of first impression, was whether South Carolina recognized at common law (since no statute had been enacted) a cause of action for wrongful life brought by or on behalf of a child born with a congenital defect. The court declined to recognize the claim, stating that it adopted the reasoning of a majority of other courts that had rejected it. The court concluded that "being born with a naturally occurring defect or impairment does not constitute a legally cognizable injury in such an action...We find untenable Child's argument that a child who already has been born should have the chance to prove it would have been better if he had never have been born at all."[26] The court added that a jury would have to face the "imponderable question: Is a severely impaired life is so much worse than no life at all so that a Child should recover damages."[27] Such a question is beyond human experience at present.

Wrongful life claims brought in the Kentucky courts on behalf of two children, Carlei Nacole Grubbs and Nathan Robert Bogan, met a similar fate as did wrongful birth actions brought at the same time. In both cases, the plaintiffs alleged that early diagnostic procedures revealed incurable and profound birth defects but that the physicians involved failed to correctly diagnose or inform the parents of the medical conditions in time to allow abortion decisions to be made. According to the Kentucky Supreme Court, Carlei, who was born in 1996, was diagnosed with spina bifida and hydrocephalus. She was paralyzed from the waist down and suffered from poor vision and misshapen kidneys.[28] Nathan, born in 1993, had "no eyes and no brain, although he [had] an underdeveloped brain stem that supports minimal autonomic functioning. He ha[d] a cleft palate and [could not] speak....He [was] strapped into a wheelchair to sit, and he ha[d] no control over his bowels."[29] The Bogans argued in their brief before the Kentucky Supreme Court that Nathan "cannot do anything but exist."[30]

The Kentucky Supreme Court noted that the trial courts in these cases denied the childrens' claims and that the court of appeals consolidated them to consider whether Kentucky law recognizes birth-related torts, including wrongful conception or pregnancy, wrongful birth, and wrongful life.[31] The Supreme Court stated the issue before it as "whether the claims now before this Court upon the facts presented can be decided upon existing tort principles or whether deference to legislative initiative would be more appropriate."[32] Applying traditional negligence principles, the court concluded that the causation element was problematical. The medical provider's negligence, if any, cannot be said to have caused the types of injuries alleged. The court concluded that the claims fail for lack of a "cognizable injury."[33] A life cannot be considered a legally cognizable injury. The many questions that arose reinforced the court's view that "courts should exercise great restraint in recognizing such new and complex causes of action."[34] The court was troubled by potential questions regarding the compensability of incurable birth defects left negligently undiagnosed from prenatal diagnostic procedures. Although the court did not specifically refer to being troubled about ethical issues, the court's concerns about the implications of the new torts went beyond mere legal concerns.

This chapter began with the facts from *Paretta v. Medical Offices for Human Reproduction*,[35] the New York case in which Josephine and Gerard Paretta went forward with IVF using an egg donor. The trial court ruled that the parents could proceed with their wrongful birth claim but that the child's wrongful life claim would not be permitted. The trial court based its decision on the 1978 decision of the highest court in New York, *Becker v. Schwartz*, discussed earlier.[36]

In *Taylor v. Kurapati*,[37] a Michigan case which abolished the wrongful birth tort claim in that state and rejected the wrongful life action, the appellate court gave an extended discussion of the ethical context of these claims. In that case, the plaintiff, Brandi Taylor, gave birth to the couple's daughter, Shelby, in 1994. Shelby was born with "gross anatomical deformities including missing right shoulder, fusion of left elbow, missing digits on left hand, missing femur on left leg and short femur on right."[38] The Taylors brought an action for wrongful birth and negligent infliction of emotional distress, alleging that the standard of care in performing the initial ultrasound had been breached by the radiologist when he failed to locate all four limbs at the time of the ultrasound in addition to failing to reveal the disabilities. They alleged further that the failure to reveal the disabilities deprived them of their right to make a reproductive decision regarding the pregnancy. Both counts were summarily disposed of by the trial court based on procedural defects. In the course of affirming the decision, the appellate court discussed wrongful pregnancy and wrongful conception actions, which Michigan recognizes, along with wrongful life and birth actions, both of which it determined should not be recognized.

The *Taylor* court noted that its prior 1987 decision in *Proffitt v. Bartolo*[39] rejecting wrongful life torts would stand in light of the Michigan Supreme Court's refusal to review that decision and the legislature's inaction on the point. As to the wrongful birth claim, the *Taylor* court noted that the *Proffitt* court concluded:

[we] are reluctant to resolve all of the moral and public policy arguments that others at a different or higher level have declined to address. There comes a point at which three judges on an intermediate appellate court should restrain themselves from making new law. The decision whether a life with birth defects has a greater or lesser value than no life at all is beyond such a point. Consequently we will allow the law to remain where it stands. The "wrongful birth" claim in this case must go to trial and the "wrongful life" claim will remain dismissed.[40]

The *Taylor* court decided that, while it would follow its earlier decision in *Proffitt* concerning wrongful life claims, it would discard the *Proffitt* decision on wrongful birth since "this mixed decision elevates the principle of stare decisis over all logic."[41] The *Taylor* court noted that it had previously allowed parents to bring a wrongful birth action on the same facts as the wrongful life action when neither the Supreme Court nor the state legislature had recognized either type of action. It concluded that it should not have allowed the wrongful birth claim to go forward. The court proceeded to detail an analysis of the various types of claims. What is most interesting is that the court then reinforced its decision by discussing the "slippery slope of the benefits rule," which, in turn, led it into a prolonged discussion of the danger of moving toward eugenics.

The court noted that, in wrongful birth cases, the jury must quantify the costs of bearing and raising the disabled child against the benefits to the parents of the life of that child at a point when the whole life is unknown. Any such quantification of "the unquantifiable" is impossible and improper. "How," the court inquires, "would a hypothetical Grecian jury, operating under Michigan jurisprudence, measure the benefits to the parents of the whole life of Homer, the blind singer of songs who created the Iliad and the Odyssey? Absent the ability to foretell the future and to quantify the value of the spoken and then the written word, how, exactly would the jury do that?"[42]

The court then moved quickly to address its fear about the inevitable "slide...into applied eugenics."[43] The phrase "wrongful birth" suggests that the child's birth was wrong and should have been prevented. If it should have been prevented, the court reasoned, it is a short step to the premise that the births of defective children should be prevented, not just for the parents' sake but for the protection of the "public welfare."[44]

The court launched into a discussion of positive and negative eugenics, which it described as advocating either "the reproduction of the 'fit' over the 'unfit' (positive) and discourages the birth of the 'unfit' (negative)." The court went on to discuss the Third Reich and Justice Holmes' well-known assertion in *Buck v. Bell*,[45] that "three generations of imbeciles are enough"[46] before predicting another "short half step" to the proposition that "for the benefit of...society as a whole...the existence of the child should not be allowed to continue."[47] The court cited the concept of age-based rationing of health care for elderly persons, and suggested that "if the elderly have a duty to die—indeed, to be starved to death—then why not the disabled child?"[48] To avoid this "logical end" (in its view) of the slippery slope, and to save the nation, or at least the citizens of Michigan, from this calamitous development, the court erased the wrongful birth tort from the slate of available legal actions.

Recognition of Wrongful Life Actions

In contrast, plaintiffs have been successful on common law grounds in wrongful life cases in four jurisdictions: California, Colorado, New Jersey, and Washington. The California Appellate Court in *Curlender* was the first to venture forward. The plaintiff child was born with Tay-Sachs disease, a fatal disorder which the court defined as "[a] familial [hereditary] disease affecting children...characterized by partial or complete loss of vision, mental underdevelopment, softness of the muscles, convulsions, etc." [49] The child in this case suffered from conditions including mental retardation, convulsions, loss of motor reactions, inability to sit up or hold her head up, muscle atrophy, blindness, and inability to feed orally. She had a life expectancy of about four years.

The lawsuit was premised on claims that the defendant laboratory had negligently performed tests and had failed to detect that both parents were carriers of genes known to cause the disorder. After distinguishing the rejection of wrongful life claims in the context of illegitimacy, the court acknowledged that public policy and "a deeply held belief in the sanctity of life" had caused many courts to reject this cause of action. The court, however, concluded that there was no "universal acceptance of the notion that 'metaphysics' or 'religious beliefs,' rather than law, should govern the situation."[50] The court explored other avenues of public policy such as "regard for social welfare" and the need to safeguard careful genetic testing. The court, commenting on *Roe,* noted the "present legality of, and availability of, eugenic abortion in the proper case."[51] It further commented on the "increasingly large part of the overall national health care burden" represented by children with genetic defects.[52] The court endorsed a wrongful life action because tort law should reflect the "basic changes in the way society views such matters" and was "needed to avoid genetic disaster...."[53]

This court did not find troublesome the concept of naming life as an injury. It reasoned that:

[t]he reality of the "wrongful-life" concept is that such a plaintiff both *exists* and *suffers*, due to the negligence of others. It is neither necessary nor just to retreat into meditation on the mysteries of life. We need not be concerned with the fact that had defendants not been negligent, the plaintiff might not have come into existence at all. The certainty of genetic impairment is no longer a mystery. In addition, a reverent appreciation of life compels recognition that plaintiff, however impaired she may be, has come into existence as a living person with certain rights.[54]

The court acknowledged, in passing, that its reasoning would support an action by an impaired child against its parents for choosing to give birth. The California legislature lost no time in passing legislation to insulate parents from such liability (California Civil Code, Sec. 43.6 Civ., added by Stats. 1981, Ch. 331, sec. 1). Two years later, the California Supreme Court added its endorsement of the wrongful life cause of action in California. The court also concluded that one of the functions of juries is to answer difficult questions involving damages.

Turpin v. Sortini,[55] a California Supreme Court decision, presented the issue of whether Joy Turpin, a child born with a hereditary deafness affliction, could maintain a tort action against a medical care provider who, before conception, negligently failed to advise the parents of the possibility of the condition, thereby depriving them of the choice of not conceiving a child at all. The California Supreme Court decided to hear the case to resolve a conflict in decisions by panels of the intermediate appellate court. The parents' first child, named Hope, was born with hereditary deafness condition that was misdiagnosed. The doctors advised that Hope's hearing was normal when, in reality, she was "stone deaf."[56] Before learning the correct diagnosis, the parents conceived a second child, Joy, with the same condition.

The complaint alleges that had the parents known of Hope's condition and the reasonable probability that another child would also have the condition, they would not have conceived Joy. The California Court allowed the child's action, holding that the plaintiff would be limited to extraordinary expenses of raising a deaf child but not general damages or those associated with rearing a healthy child. The court rejected an argument that the action should not be permitted because any life is better than none at all. The court further argued that a public policy placing the highest value on all human life does not lead to a conclusion, "as a matter of law—that under all circumstances 'impaired life' is 'preferable' to 'nonlife.'"[57] In support of this policy or philosophical conclusion, the court cited to a statute dealing with the individual's right of autonomy in a "terminal condition."[58] The court stated its view that "public policy supports the right of each individual to make his or her own determination as to the relative value of life and death."[59] The court also relied on reasoning that it would be an anomaly to allow parents to recover expenses of this sort but deny the same right to a child. The Washington case, *Harbeson v. Parke-Davis*,[60] relied on similar reasoning to the *Turpin* court in upholding a wrongful life action.

In New Jersey, Peter Procanik brought a wrongful life action against physicians whom he alleged negligently failed to diagnose that his mother had contracted German measles in the first trimester of her pregnancy. Peter was born with congenital rubella syndrome. His symptoms included eye lesions, heart disease, and auditory defects. Alleging that his parents had been deprived of the choice of terminating the pregnancy, he sought damages for pain and suffering and for his parents' impaired capacity to cope with his problems. After the trial court and the intermediate appellate court dismissed the action, the New Jersey Supreme Court reversed, holding that the infant plaintiff could recover special damages for the extraordinary medical expenses attributable to his affliction but not general damages for emotional distress or for an impaired childhood.[61]

Many difficult legal, ethical, and pragmatic questions are raised by the controversies underlying wrongful life and birth actions. Is it possible to compare nonexistence with living an impaired existence? Is nonexistence comparable in any meaningful way with the ending of existence? Can a court devalue the life of a disabled person? Can a court equate a genetically produced disability with a medical injury? Can a lawyer advocate that her client would be better off dead or, more accurately, still nonexistent? Is there a serious danger that allowing wrongful life claims will encourage unnecessary abortions? Will physicians advise discretionary abortions to avoid liability? What will be the impact on the practice of obstetrics as a matter of public policy? Will such claims pit children against parents?

As a matter of public policy, can a parent responsibly bring such a claim on behalf of a child? What privacy rights are involved? What is the value of life at various stages and in all its forms? Can a child who has not been conceived, and is therefore merely a possible child, have rights that create duties in others? Does any attempt to grapple in traditional legal terms of rights, duties, causation, and damage necessarily involve a gross distortion of the metaphysical concepts involved in these issues? Should difficulty in calculating damages result in nonrecognition of a cause of action? Does the lack of public policy dealing with the *Wild West* of reproductive technology from legislatures cause a serious gap, thereby legitimizing courts to make public policy, using the only tools available, that is, traditional legal theories of tort liability?

What events have brought us to the brink of this precipitous legal and judicial situation, in which courts are expected to resolve complicated questions that are ostensibly framed as legal issues but are essentially ethical questions of a profound nature? I suggest that the intricate fabric of court decisions in the field of reproductive technology serves as relevant context for the present inquiry. This consists of the main reproductive rights cases, namely, *Roe, Casey,* and their progeny and the mosaic of state court cases involving the disposition of frozen embryos, which raise issues of instrumentalization, commodification, and property interests. It also includes state court cases involving disputes among biological, gestational, and surrogate parents, such as *Baby M,* involving reproductive technology. All these cases have led us step by step to the present predicament in which dilemmas are presented and no satisfying answers are apparent.

After laying the groundwork for analysis of the rationale of the cases in this complex area of metaphysics, we will examine the cases to see how well, or poorly, they resolve the difficult issues raised and what impact they have on public discussion. Technology will likely continue its forward march without substantial guidance or direction from public policy institutions. In our democratic, free-market society, we prize individual and corporate actions and initiatives. Government does not attempt to control developments in advance of their occurring. Regulation tends to follow movement and action just as legal adjudication follows events and occurrences. If the reverse were true, we could be living in an anti-utopian *Brave New World* of the likes of Huxley's fictional work.

Reproductive technologies will be developed, and genetic diagnosing technology will be created, subject to regulations that apply to drug and medical device research involving human subjects. When the use of new technology produces bad results, a legal arsenal of negligence law stands ready to be wielded to secure compensation for those who claim to be injured. The problem with such a system is that, as we have seen, the collective welfare or the common interest is not represented in the process and damage awards benefit only the few, not the many who have a wide range of interests. The result of litigation may be, in part, to discourage the production of new pharmaceuticals, to drive health providers out of the field, and to encourage medical providers to overprescribe diagnostic tests. If that happens, the interest of the consuming public will have been adversely affected by litigation without representation in the process.

In the absence of coherent public policy formulations, is it possible to address such questions using traditional legal language and concepts without transforming the debate? If not, is the controversy adversely changed by the legal intervention? What does language of rights, duties, causation, and damage do to complex social, cultural, political, and ethical questions? How do the institutional biases of courts undermine and distort the real issues involved? If the legal resolution changes the way in which vital issues are discussed, how can proper dialogue be assured? One problem with our policymaking institutions, including legislatures, and the executive branch (as well as judges who must stand for election), is that their public policy responsibilities sometimes conflict with their political interests. Another problem, especially on the federal level, is that debate about vital issues in bioethics, especially reproduction and medical futility, that is, the beginning and the end of life, has been preempted by the obsession with the abortion agenda. When any issue is perceived by any of the participants as affecting the status of abortion rights, all bets are off and the issue is in danger of being reframed into abortion agenda terms. If legislatures fail to fulfill their duty to make policy, vital issues are left to the courts, which are forced to deal with them with a limited supply of tools. The result can be an incoherent public policy or a system of adjudication that wreaks havoc on the overall, collective interests of society.

The short history of the wrongful life and wrongful birth torts, dating back to the 1960s, sheds some light on the present situation, in which the viability of this action remains very much disputed and unresolved. Next, we consider the underlying ethical, social, and cultural issues that contribute to the present state of tension in this field, a tension that can only cause further drift toward incoherence until a public policy is developed.

For those whose interests lie primarily in tracing the development of the law, the focus of inquiry would be to determine which jurisdictions allow wrongful birth and life actions and which deny them. The rationales used by courts would indicate how decisions are made and would, to some extent, suggest where the trend would go in the future. Any consideration of the ethical ramifications of the issues or the actions of courts would be superfluous. Our inquiry is more penetrating. We want to know what courts are doing in this regard, but our primary interest lies in knowing how courts explain their actions as a way of understanding the impact on the pervasive ethical issues that confront society. Whether courts allow such actions, or not, affects those who wish to prosecute and those who must defend such actions.

American society, in many respects, will be judged by how well we address and resolve, as a matter of public policy, these important ethical issues, which reflect our deepest values and priorities as a society. If our public policy institutions fail to adopt effective policy, it may be that what courts say about the issues will be all that is said. That would be unfortunate because what courts say does not amount to policy that is based on ethical, economic, social, or political reasoning. Judicial decisions, rather, constitute many individual decisions that are confined by traditional legal constraints, in this case, elements of rights, duties, causation, and damages. It is true that courts occasionally will base results on what is called policy. In the absence of clear policy statements by the other branches of government, that policy amounts to the personal beliefs or assessments of community beliefs by particular judges.

Our inquiry leads to an analysis of the impact of court decisions on the resolution of important ethical issues. How do decisions arrived at through the adversarial process, framed in legal language and concepts, alter the ethical issues? How do court limitations and biases affect the outcome? What is the impact on later debate in other institutions, such as legislatures? Does the legal process change the way the issue reenters broader discussion? Do participants welcome the fact that the issue has been limited and restructured? Surely it is easier to discuss the status, and the human rights to be accorded to, preconceived possible children in terms of limited concepts of duty, breach, causation, and harm or damage than it is to discuss the issue in far-reaching ethical terms. It is easy to see why legislatures shy away from such issues. Not only do they risk their political capital, but also the issues threaten to occupy significant amounts of legislative time, perhaps with little to show for it. Few states allow wrongful life actions; however, in the future, undoubtedly more states will allow the cause of action by judicial decision and/or statute as the issue and its implications become clearer.

LEGAL CONTEXT OF WRONGFUL BIRTH AND LIFE CASES

We also know that the huge impact of the national abortion agenda will continue to impact this area of ethics and law. The legal issues surrounding the dissemination of genetic information, literally, the explosion of genetic information, first reached the courts in the context of wrongful birth and life cases. Various courts have decided that physicians and geneticists have duties to provide information to prospective parents concerning genetic risks to potential offspring and to provide available diagnostic procedures to identify the risks. The purpose of disclosure is to give prospective parents either an opportunity to refrain from conceiving or an opportunity to abort a fetus with a serious disorder.

A brief recap of the history of wrongful birth and life actions reveals not only the impact of the abortion divide in the United States but also the increasing impact of genetic information and medical technology. In the beginning, courts tended to resist recognizing causes of action for wrongful birth and, at the time, wrongful life cases had not yet appeared before the bench. Two problems dominated the early response. First, courts were troubled by the causation issue; nothing the provider could have done would have prevented the harm to the child. Early cases rejected liability based on failure to warn,[62] although liability for a missed diagnosis was imposed in other areas of medicine even though the physician did not cause the illness.[63] The major reason for rejecting liability, however, was that abortion was not allowed in many states until *Roe v. Wade* was decided in 1973.[64] As one court put it, "[t]he value of genetic testing programs...is based on the opportunity of parents to abort afflicted fetuses, within appropriate time limitations."[65] Potential liability includes situations in which the physician should have known about the risk because a previous child had a genetic disorder or because of the woman's advanced age. Knowing that parents belong to a particular ethnic or racial group can also trigger potential liability on the part of health care providers. Courts also find physicians liable when they fail to inform patients about genetic assessment services when specific services are available.[66] Most states, as we have seen, allow wrongful birth actions either by judicial decision or by legislation.

We have noted, however, that wrongful life actions present a different story. The fact that these actions are brought by children (usually through their parents) asserting rights that arose prior to conception poses one problem. The fact that the child does not claim that negligence caused the disability, rather that the failure to inform the parents of the risk caused the very birth of the child raises an additional obstacle when courts attempt to apply the strict legal categories. The child claims that but for the inadequate advice, it would not have been born to experience the unbearable pain and suffering produced by the disability, whatever it may be. The nature of the claim, that a person would be better off not existing than living with the impairment, is troublesome to courts even though they are not required to make an ethical judgment about the issue. Although courts are troubled primarily by the idea that nonexistence can be preferable to existence, other problems are the capacity of a child to make such a claim and the problems of quantifying the preferences. Only four states, California, Colorado, New Jersey, and Washington,[67] allow these actions to go forward and some specifically prohibit them.[68]

Ethical Questions

Whether wrongful birth or wrongful life actions should be authorized is less important for our purposes than assessing how decisional law works and impacts the way these vital issues of life are being addressed by our society. Whether they are allowed or disallowed, the rationales that courts offer inform us about the impact of judicial decisions on the larger ethical and political discussion of the issues. We must keep in mind that courts address these issues from a very limited series of concepts that make up the traditional legal elements. The ethical dimensions are much more expansive. Courts reveal that the ethical dimensions trouble them even beyond their impact on the strictly legal issues. Courts appear concerned about possible future permutations of the issues even beyond legal arenas. But, since courts are not warranted to address the ethical dimensions as such, they do so implicitly and thereby impact the issues without expressly saying so. They tend to reframe the ethical issues in legal terms that can change the way the issues are later discussed in a nonlegal forum.

The ethical issues involved in these types of actions essentially involve defining and explaining personhood. This concept is dealt with differently in legal contexts and ethical contexts. Basically, personhood, when it begins, ends, and can be diminished, raises theological and philosophical questions for which there can be no certain answers. They can be debated and explained, but without universal consensus because they are matters of moral belief. For legal purposes, however, personhood can be closely defined for different circumstances. At law, the question is not what personhood is in general but, rather, what personhood is for a specific purpose, for status at the beginning of life, the end of life, or capacity for various decision-making purposes or legal rights.

What are the major ethical dimensions of wrongful life actions that trouble courts, whether they deal with those dimensions expressly or implicitly, or not at all? Many such questions seem implicit in court decisions. One such question is whether a physician or other provider can ethically be held responsible (have a duty) to someone who did not exist at the time a violation of duty is alleged. Another is whether there is, in any sense, a right to be born free of handicaps, or a right not to be born. These questions bear on the legal issue of duty.

Can any institution of society acknowledge officially that nonexistence is preferable to existence with a disability and, if so, can those conditions be measured and compared except insofar as they can be measured in terms of predictable cost of care? In legal terms, the question is whether allowing someone to be born (to exist) can be a violation of a duty and whether it can harm someone. How can nonexistence be measured or valued under any circumstances? Is it ethical or unethical to encourage physicians to suggest abortion as a remedy to terminate risky pregnancies? This question deals with a possible consequence or implication of allowing the actions.

Still another weighty ethical question is whether devaluing the life of a person with disabilities puts at risk the security of all disabled people in society. Among the main opponents of the wrongful life tort are disabled people and those who advocate their interests. Clearly, this cause of action bears on the cultural acceptance or rejection of disability. Is recognizing that nonexistence might be preferable to living with pain or disability in any sense a normative judgment about whether someone ought to die? Are the merits of wrongful death claims implicated? What about refusal of treatment jurisprudence?

The possible variations of these questions are limitless. The answers to these questions in legal opinions and in ethical discourses are in conflict, as one might imagine. Legal commentators have taken positions both in support of and in opposition to wrongful life actions. Ethical debate is now centered on the abortion agenda with an increase of efforts by abortion opponents to persuade state legislatures to pass statutes preventing further recognition of wrongful birth actions (and wrongful life actions), which are seen as potentially encouraging the use of abortion as a way of reducing risk on the part of health care providers.[69] Opponents of legislation abolishing such actions contend that the statutes interfere with individual autonomy, the right to decide whether to have an abortion, and that malpractice liability is an essential safeguard against physician negligence. If the newly constituted U.S. Supreme Court cooperates in severely restricting a woman's federal constitutional right to choose an abortion in the future, the implications for the future of wrongful life actions will be significant. In that event, state legislatures will be free to place restrictions on abortions. Although state laws would probably still allow abortion for genetic reasons, they might well be limited to cases of serious disorders.

With the continuing progress in the evolution of genetic testing and genetic risk assessment and the increasing availability of new tests to inform people not only about risks to their potential offspring but also about future risks to themselves, there is an increasing likelihood of malpractice claims. It has been noted that physicians are often unprepared for the "onslaught of genetic information."[70] Many practicing physicians do not have an adequate understanding of genetics as it is and, with the increase in the number of genetic risks that may become predictable, it may become unreasonable to anticipate that all physicians who deal with reproductive matters will be capable of warning patients of the available tests and the potential risks. Courts are reacting already to identify what tests must be disclosed and what risks are reasonable.[71]

A FOOTNOTE AS TO END-OF-LIFE ETHICS: THE WRONGFUL LIVING CAUSE OF ACTION

The wrongful living cause of action, which lies at the other end of the spectrum of life, is far less developed and accepted as a genre of law. Few cases in this area, in fact, can be identified by that name alone at this time, but it seems likely that the increasing recognition of the right to die, in whatever terms it is cast, will change that drastically. After the case of Karen Ann Quinlan in 1967, in which a right to die was recognized in some form, most states have adopted an extended right to refuse medical treatment, in statutory or case law form. One state, Oregon, stands alone in providing, by statute, for physician-assisted suicide.[72] The practice authorized by that statute has come under review by the U.S. Supreme Court in *Gonzales v. Oregon*.[73] In that case, the Court determined that an interpretive rule of the U.S. Attorney General was not entitled to deference. The rule indicated that physicians who assist suicide of terminally ill patients pursuant to ODWDA (Oregon's Death With Dignity Act) would be violating the federal Controlled Substances Act. The decision, therefore, prevented the federal government from interfering with Oregon's practice. It may, however, receive further scrutiny in the future by opponents. As medical technology advances to keep the aged or terminally ill alive, refuge in the right to refuse treatment will become more and more important to many people, who do not care to live indefinitely in a debilitated state. In essence, the wrongful living tort grows out of the widespread recognition of a right to refuse treatment at the end of life. These are suits for damages alleging that patients who received unwanted life-sustaining treatment have suffered a compensable injury when their right to die was violated.

Advances in medical technology have drastically affected the way physicians treat patients and the circumstances under which people die. Whereas six decades ago, barely one-third of Americans died in hospitals and nursing homes, between eighty and eighty-five percent now pass away in those institutions. It is estimated that at least seventy percent of these people do so after a decision to forego life-sustaining treatment.[74] Many of these individuals die after undergoing, or refusing, treatments that did not exist sixty years ago, including cardiopulmonary resuscitation, respirators, ventilators, intravenous nutrition, feeding tubes, and others. Technological advances make it possible for people to live longer, even past the point when physical and mental capacity have been seriously diminished. Many people began questioning the quality of such lives and, starting in the 1970s, patients and families began asserting a right to die a natural death, that is, one that occurs without undue reliance on medical technology or, as it is often stated, a right to die with dignity.

The court that was in the forefront of recognizing a right to die supported its decision on the basis of a constitutional right to privacy, even though the right of privacy does not appear expressly in the Constitution.[75] The New Jersey Supreme Court, in *In re Quinlan*,[76] noted that the right to privacy recognized under the U.S. Constitution is broad enough to encompass a patient's decision to decline medical treatment. A number of courts followed *Quinlan* and based their decisions on the federal or state constitutions.[77] More recently, however, most courts rely on informed consent principles or on informed consent combined with a privacy right.[78] Most states have adopted living will statutes, which attempt to give adults the right to control decisions relating to medical care, including the decision to have life-sustaining treatment withheld or withdrawn in various circumstances. Such statutes permit the designation of a health care agent to make these types of decisions on behalf of an incapacitated individual.

Despite the proliferation of advance directives, studies have shown a fair amount of physician resistance. The reasons usually cited are fear of liability, interference with the physicians' professional duties, and undermining of physicians' judgment of what is in the patients' best interest.[79] At best, physicians are ambivalent toward advance directives. They believe that advance directives can be ignored if their professional judgment as to the best interest of the patient dictates treatment. In other words, end-of-life decisions are often driven by the physician's values rather than the patient's.[80] Financial motives have often been cited as well as playing a part in physicians' decisions to treat despite contrary indications in advance directives.[81]

Although we will examine more background information on medical futility and end-of-life issues in Chapter 7, which deals with the recent litigation involving Terri Schiavo in the context of other landmark right-to-die cases, this background is sufficient for consideration of wrongful living cases. The lack of accountability when physicians fail to follow advance directives has led to an interest in a new wrongful living tort that would allow civil liability when a health care provider violates a patient's decision to decline or stop life-sustaining treatment. Most claims that seek damages for this type of activity have, so far, been based on common-law torts such as battery or infliction of emotional distress or a violation of an individual's civil rights pursuant to Section 1983 of the Civil Rights Act. Various cases have been identified as wrongful living cases although none have yet succeeded in convincing appellate courts of the merit of this cause of action. Two such cases are *Anderson v. St. Francis-St. George Hospital*,[82] and *McGuiness v. Barnes*.[83]

Anderson was an Ohio Appeals Court case, which was affirmed by the Ohio Supreme Court. The administrator of Edward H. Winter's estate sued the hospital claiming that it was liable for resuscitating Winter despite a DNR (do-not-resuscitate) order that was in place in the hospital record. On May 25, 1988, Winter was admitted to the hospital complaining of chest pains, having lost consciousness at a local senior citizens' center. He was eighty-two and had suffered two previous heart attacks and had chronic heart disease and other health problems. In conversation with his family doctor, Winter, who was competent and alert, made clear to his doctor that he "wanted no extraordinary life-saving measures in the event of further illness." His daughter also told the doctor that he had been upset about the extreme actions, taken with respect to his wife during a hospital stay, including shocking her heart and beating her chest. Winter told his daughter "never to let anybody do that to him." As a result, the doctor entered a "No Code Blue" instruction in the hospital record.

Three days later, Winter suffered a ventricular fibrillation, a type of irregular heartbeat that could be fatal. A nurse resuscitated Winter using defibrillation, electrically shocking the heart with paddles. Winter thanked the nurse when he regained consciousness. After another episode, which ended spontaneously due to a medication prescribed by the doctor, the medicine and the heart monitor were discontinued. A day later, Winter suffered a stroke which left him paralyzed on one side. After four weeks in a rehabilitation hospital, during which he was unable to walk, incontinent, had difficulty speaking, and needed basic assistance, he returned home. During the next two years, he had nursing care at home, moved to a daughter's home, and finally to a nursing home, where he had numerous visits and outings with his family, before dying in April, 1990.

The lawsuit against the hospital claimed that the nurse's resuscitation was a battery to Winter, the nurse was negligent in resuscitating contrary to the doctor's order, and the hospital was liable for his wrongful living. The trial court granted summary judgment in favor of the hospital on all counts. Although summary judgment was reversed on the battery count, the wrongful living ruling was upheld. Winter's administrator had argued that, after the defibrillation, his life "was, for him, not worth living." The appellate court found unpersuasive an earlier Ohio unauthorized treatment case, *Estate of Leach v. Shapiro*,[84] and two cases involving wrongful pregnancy actions. The court noted that the Ohio Supreme Court had "noted with disapproval the wrongful life cause of action for children of negligently sterilized mothers, which measures 'damages on the relative merits of being versus nonbeing.'" The Ohio Supreme Court had also "referred to the joy of life as an 'intangible benefit' that [could] not be valued monetarily."[85] The Anderson court stated that "[d]amages . . . are not those things that add to life, but those that subtract from it."[86] The court rejected the analogy to the *Leach* case, which did not specifically rule on wrongful living, concluding that: "[the estate's] attempt to create a wrongful-living cause of action fails because life is not a compensable harm."

Later clarifying that statement, the court said, "[b]y that we mean that he cannot recover general damages just for finding himself still alive after unwanted resuscitative measures."[87] The Ohio Supreme Court agreed with this conclusion, stating that continued living is not a compensable injury, even if the plaintiff shows a breach of duty and resulting prolongation of life. The court characterized this type of claim as beyond "the outer bounds of liability in the American civil justice system," adding that "[t]here are some mistakes, indeed even breaches of duty or technical assaults, that people make in this life that affect the lives of others for which there simply should be no monetary damages."[88]

McGuinness v. Barnes,[89] a New Jersey appellate decision, also rejected a wrongful living claim, although it raised the possibility of future recognition of the action. Richard McGuinness, the plaintiff, was a former detective who suffered brain damage during surgery to remove a tumor. In early 1986, he noticed that he began stubbing his toe and that he had difficulty answering questions. In July, McGuinness, then 57, saw a neurologist, who diagnosed him with a possible brain tumor. In August, he had an angiogram and a frontal parietal craniotomy, which totally removed the tumor. After surgery, he was unable to move his legs and his right arm was weak. At the time of the action, he was unable to care for himself and resided in a nursing home. After his first attorney failed to file a lawsuit, he hired a new attorney and sued for medical malpractice. One of the medical malpractice claims asserted in the lawsuit was an allegation that had he been informed of the risks of surgery, he would have rejected it. He claimed that the doctor did not advise him of the possible serious risks. Since he later learned that he would have died within six months to a year without the surgery, he alleged that he would have preferred that early death to living with his present disability. His lawsuit alleged that to hold that he had no legally cognizable claim for damages would in effect license the medical profession to disregard the rights of those who have life-threatening illnesses.

In a decision based mainly on informed consent, the trial court determined that the doctors had no duty to inform him of the nontreatment option because a reasonable person would have gone forward with the surgery. The court concluded, "[g]iven that [McGuinness] had successfully undergone treatment which saved his life, this Court finds that . . . [McGuinness] . . . has no cause of action for wrongful life."[90] The appellate court affirmed on the same ground but stated in dicta that such a claim could be viable under some circumstances. Those circumstances would involve depriving a patient of his right of self-determination which, in the view of both courts in this case, did not occur.

ANALYSIS OF WRONGFUL LIFE CASES

The Idiom of the Law

What happens when courts apply the idiom of the law, both language and concepts, to cases involving bioethics issues that are presented for decision? We will examine four representative wrongful life cases, including two that reject the cause of action (*Willis*[91] and *Taylor*[92]) and two that accept it (*Turpin*[93] and *Procanik*[94]).

Referring back to the discussion of ethical issues of life and death, we can see that these cases involve questions, not about when life begins, but about the value of human life in different circumstances. In these cases, the question concerns the relative value of life with "defects" or "disabilities" to use courts' own terminology. Beyond the value of encumbered life lie issues concerning how society should consider and deal with people with disabilities. Many of the notable ethical issues in this field have, in fact, concerned how whole societies treated such people as a matter of public policy. Although the basic ethical issues in this context are challenging on a purely ethical level, they obviously concern economics as well, on both an individual and a societal level. The cost to individuals and families as well as the cost to society as a whole is a serious concern. That aspect is rarely debated seriously in public policy discussions of bioethics because we do not generally like to speak of human life in ways that sound as though we are commodifying it, that is, reducing it to matters of economic cost. Occasionally, however, provocative ideas are offered for discussion such as occasional speculation about withholding care from the elderly for the overall good of society. We openly discuss the economics of scarce resources but rarely suggest seriously that humans should be deliberately deprived of such resources for reasons of cost-savings, even if the benefit to others is obvious.

When lawsuits for wrongful life (or, for that matter, any of the other *wrongful* categories) are brought, the ethical issues are not expressly stated in the cause of action. The actions are brought pursuant to law's role in social regulation. We regulate behavior to prevent or deter harm and to compensate those who have wrongly suffered harm. In the legal context, we do not deal with the broad ethical issues involving beginning of life. We deal with specific claims for compensation based on alleged negligent or intentional misconduct of professionals. The issues are transformed, narrowed, and made specific in this context. The claims are economic; they involve the right to compensation and the burden of liability. But the valuation questions, and the implications of valuation in terms of society's duty to treat disabled persons, are involved chiefly in the valuation of damage stage. Many courts tend to be stymied at this point because they are overwhelmed by the public policy consequences, or simply lack the means to instruct juries (or themselves) how to make such a valuation.

In *Willis,* for example, the court noted that "damages were too difficult to ascertain because of the Hobson's choice between non-existence and an existence with a defective condition."[95] The court further referred to the illogic of determining that being born can be a legally cognizable injury. In *Taylor,* we saw that the court carried the thread of logic, as it perceived it, to absurd lengths—from legitimizing damage actions for wrongful birth or life all the way down a hypothetical slippery slope to the deliberate killing of the aged and the disabled. Even considering the weakness of many slippery slope arguments, it would take a remarkable stretch of thinking to arrive at that point of social policy.

These courts not only oversaw the translating of ethical questions into narrow questions of duty, damage, and liability, thereby narrowing the scope, but also revealed their fear of venturing into the creation of public policy by applying legal concepts to questions of valuation of encumbered life versus nonlife. These courts were unwilling to deal with the issues in narrow legal terms, ignoring the possible policy implications of so doing.

The treatment of these issues by courts that authorized wrongful life actions, such as *Turpin* and *Procanik,* is not substantially different, but these courts were willing to deal with the issues as legal issues alone and not worry about policy implications. These cases, while recognizing the difficulties inherent in wrongful life actions, opted to allow the injured parties access to the courts without undue concern for the ethical implications. They viewed the cases narrowly apart from their overall ethical implications. One could say that they exercised the social regulatory purpose of law as their foremost duty. They did limit recoverable damages, however, which eliminated some difficult questions for juries and courts.

We can say that each of the courts operated according to its perception and expectation of its role, either a limited role as applying the law or as an instrument of public policy. In all cases, the ethical issues were stated in the traditional terminology of social regulation by law. They were thereby transformed into specific, concrete problems rather than larger ethical issues. In carrying out the social regulation mission, some courts wrestled with whether they could properly instruct juries on distinguishing between encumbered life and no life at all and in quantifying the result. Others were willing to leave those determinations to triers of fact but did limit damages to exclude categories that were difficult to measure. Courts uniformly have addressed such issues despite the fact that many points of view or interests were not represented. They have applied traditional concepts and categories of law even when the issues to be decided arose because of new technology. Although deferring to legislatures, as some courts have done, suggests that existing categories are not adequate or authoritative, courts rarely indicate that there is no applicable law. Even when courts declare matters to be cases of first impression (a novel question that has not been decided authoritatively), they go on to make analogies based on existing law. That is difficult to avoid since courts must decide cases. If they did not apply existing law, they would have to state boldly that they were applying the personal views or opinions of the judges. Judges undoubtedly do that on occasion, but they rarely do so without embedding the views in legal precedent. By refusing to admit that some issues cannot be dealt with by applying existing law, courts give a false impression that existing law is adequate. That, in turn, discourages or at least does not alert legislatures that new legislation is needed.

Since I have noted that the courts in question gave primary emphasis to their social regulatory purpose, it is evident that courts define the boundaries between law and policy and those problems are solved by prescribing minimums for social behavior, rather than optimums. Perhaps by definition, social regulation deals with minimums and with distrust and skepticism about human behavior. That seems to be the essence of social regulation and perhaps appropriately so. Courts attempt to establish rules for dealing with future controversies as a way of confining discretion in the future. One other feature of the translation of the ethical questions into legal terms is that, by initiating actions, litigants exercise control over what courts decide. Only issues that are presented in courts are decided. Citizens and their lawyers must attempt to predict, based on existing decisions, what courts are likely to rule in other situations.

The Adversarial Process

The key inquiry here is the extent to which the adversarial nature of litigation in which parties are pitted against each other, producing winners and losers, affects the way the underlying bioethical issues are altered. In addition to the general impact of adversarial process on truth-determination, we consider the impact of the techniques of adversarial decision-making, including rules of evidence, procedure and decision making itself, burdens and standards of proof and, importantly, summary decision, the effect of which is to avoid a full-scale trial of the issues.

Each of the cases considered in this chapter is a civil case, brought by one or more party plaintiffs against various defendants. Despite the different state jurisdictions involved, the cases generally followed similar rules and procedures. The format for complaints, answers, preliminary motions, and discovery is similar from state to state. In civil litigation, cases are often disposed of in preliminary proceedings based on motions to dismiss or motions for summary judgment or summary disposition, a procedure that allows the court to rule on the principal issues of law, based on facts that are presumptively established. Both *Willis* and *Taylor* were decided on motions for summary disposition. In that type of proceeding, the facts are considered established for purposes of the motion by a legal fiction, one that assumes the facts are true and proven as pleaded. On this basis, the court goes on to decide whether, given those facts, the plaintiffs could prevail as a matter of law. In both cases, the court decided that the cause of action was unsupportable as a matter of law, even if all the facts alleged were proven true. Summary disposition was granted in favor of the defendants and appeals were taken. Since both appeals were unsuccessful, the plaintiffs' causes of action ended.

In the *Turpin* and *Procanik* cases, similar dispositions occurred at the trial level. The complaints in both cases were dismissed based on a form of summary decision, and the plaintiffs appealed successfully, earning the right to return to the trial courts for further proceedings leading to trial on the merits. In all four cases, therefore, decision on the legal issues (embodying the ethical issues that we have identified) was based on procedural devices. The issues, in the first place, were framed into legal language in formal complaints raising strictly legal issues. Only the facts and issues selected by the plaintiff were presented. Only the evidence known to, and ultimately produced by, the parties was known to the court. The court heard the case based on what we might call a cold record, a term usually reserved for the way appellate courts hear cases—on printed records and briefs rather than live witnesses and evidence. What was, at its essence, an intriguing question of bioethics—the status and value of human life and the meaning and scope of personhood—was transformed by legal necessity into a narrow question of law. In that type of process, no room was left for ambiguity, uncertainty, or consensus. In two cases, the plaintiffs were allowed to move on toward eventual trial on the merits; in the others, the legal journey was over. The rules and procedures and the features of the adversarial process controlled.

Closure, Finality, and the Retrospective View: Revisiting the Past

We are concerned here with the fact that the bringing of a lawsuit fixes the matter in time. Usually a court must decide a case based on facts that have occurred before the case is brought. In addition, the rules of law requiring finality of judgment end a case without the opportunity to relitigate based on new developments. Exceptions exist in certain types of cases, such as custody, alimony, and support issues in marriage dissolutions, over which courts have continuing jurisdiction, or in cases in which courts specifically maintain continuing jurisdiction. However, those instances are rare and in most cases judgment is final and binding on the parties by virtue of doctrines called *res judicata* and *collateral estoppel*. At risk of oversimplifying those doctrines, they preclude relitigation of claims and issues that have already been litigated. Decisions may be appealed, of course, but appellate courts (with rare exceptions) decide the issues based on the trial record without an opportunity for parties to submit new facts, even when those facts might affect the outcome. Appellate courts do not hear evidence or make findings of fact, except in rare circumstances. An appeal, therefore, that is heard two years after trial is based on the facts as they were testified to at the time of trial. The combination of the retrospective view of facts fixed in a moment of time plus the closure that comes as a result of a final decision normally leave little room for change, modification, or new developments. New actions can be brought, of course, but they must concern new matters as defined by law. All types of civil actions must be brought within specified time periods or be barred by statutes of limitation. Simply put, statutes of limitations are laws that prescribe when particular types of legal actions must be brought to court or be barred.

In the wrongful life cases under review, even though the cases concerned babies and their parents, whose lives were bound to develop significantly over a period of years, the judgments, whether in favor or against, were final and cannot be revisited. If, in later years, the states in which *Taylor* and *Willis* were decided were to authorize a cause of action for wrongful life, it would be too late for Shelby Taylor and Thomas Willis. Their fates are sealed, so far as the law is concerned, but ethical issues pertaining to their personhood and the quality of their lives will go on.

Courts' Institutional Biases, Assumptions, and Flaws: Unspoken Determinants

The next factor is complicated because it has so many facets. In analyzing decisions with this factor in mind, a number of potential considerations are involved. Not all questions that I listed in Chapter 2 are relevant to each area of law, of course, and I will confine myself to those that pertain to wrongful life actions. The following questions are pertinent. Some are briefly answered; others require more explanation. It is useful to bear in mind that we are looking here at institutional biases and tendencies, those that inhere in or are characteristic of the system, rather than imposed by individual judges.

The following are pertinent questions:

Do courts favor economic interests rather than nonpecuniary interests such as ethical or social interests? Do they disfavor ethical issues unnecessarily?

Do courts naturalize human intervention, explicitly or implicitly, with an uncritical receptiveness to science and technology? Is there a bias in favor of medicine and physicians generally?

Do courts unduly elevate individualism over collective interests, explicitly or implicitly?

Economic interests

The response to this factor is simple. Courts commonly demonstrate an institutional bias in favor of economic interests. While lawsuits may be brought seeking remedies other than monetary damages, the interests represented and the remedies sought are most often formulated in economic terms. Courts do grant specific types of relief such as injunctions and orders to produce documents or restore conditions but, for the most part, economic damages are sought. In virtually all wrongful life actions, courts focus on whether the injury claimed by children and parents can be translated into and measured in economic terms. Unless a formula can be created to enable damages to be awarded, the cause of action itself is not recognized. In *Willis,* for example, the court expressly stated that "the impossibility of measuring damages would in any event preclude recognition of the cause of action.... The primary purpose of tort law is that of compensating plaintiffs for the injuries they have suffered wrongfully at the hands of others...man, who knows nothing of death or nothingness, simply cannot affix a price tag to non-life."[96]

The litigants, of course, framed the action in economic terms because of the institutional requirement that claims be translated into those terms. The effect is that, henceforth, the issues expressly and implicitly involved will be seen and expressed in economic terms. In litigation, we might say that in most cases: *If it is not quantifiable, it is not recoverable.* It is true that seeking relief other than money damages may be difficult to articulate. Likewise, ascertaining and awarding practical, appropriate, and enforceable nonmonetary relief may be virtually impossible at times. On the other hand, asking for money damages is a way of ensuring that some practical relief can be granted, thereby enabling a party to avoid a dismissal on the grounds of mootness (a doctrine that restricts courts from hearing purely academic controversies in which no practical relief is possible). The result may be an example of how legal process forces a party into a certain course of action that fits within the rules.

Naturalizing human intervention: Acceptance of science and technology

Because courts must accept actions the way they are framed and must accept the facts based on the evidence, as presented, the result is to naturalize, that is, to accept new technology and science in an uncritical way. Court, themselves, unless they choose to appoint their own experts (which they rarely do) accept and thereby adopt as authentic and legitimate (unless specifically challenged in the lawsuit itself) whatever the parties allege and present. Once again, the result, institutionally, is to authenticate and naturalize even new and untested technologies.

Individualism and the public good

Since participation in lawsuits is limited to the parties named as plaintiffs or defendants, other interests do not generally participate. Provisions do exist for other parties to seek to join a lawsuit but that is possible only with a demonstrated interest as prescribed by law in the subject of the suit and is not available to generally interested parties. The term interest has a precise meaning, a particular kind of stake in the outcome as defined by case law or statutory law. Occasionally, in matters of public interest, outside individuals are allowed to appear as *amicus curiae* (friend of the court) but, even then, participation is strictly limited to what amounts to an advisory role. Even in a case with grave public policy significance, no party can join for the purpose of representing the public good or collective rights or responsibility (unless specifically authorized), despite the fact that every member of the public may have a stake in the outcome.

Impact of Courts on Future Controversies

Pertinent questions on this subject include the following:
Do courts, by virtue of legal doctrine, have an inordinate and controlling impact on future controversies because a legal determination (and its

characteristic framing of the issues and the decision) colonizes and becomes adopted by implication by other public policy institutions, thereby giving it inordinate effect in terms of governing future controversies and discouraging other types of public policy formulations?

Do courts act consistently and with accountability in establishing boundaries between legal decision and public policy?

By relying on a false or fictitious view that existing legal precedent is adequate to resolve a present controversy, do courts discourage appropriate legislative policymaking?

Judicial decisions constitute precedent—*stare decisis*—for future controversies that meet the appropriate conditions. Some decisions bind only the parties themselves while others, mainly decisions of appellate courts, bind trial courts as well as themselves. Since an identical case rarely arises again, court decisions can be binding when later courts interpret them by way of analogy to a present controversy. The impact of decisions, therefore, extends well beyond the particular facts and ruling. For example, courts still look to case law decided in the nineteenth century if later analogous cases do not exist. There is no end to the impact of a decision unless it is overruled by a later decision.

Beyond that plain and straightforward impact, court decisions often color public discourse in startling ways. When other public policy expressions are absent, court decisions may be discussed widely, with all their own legal characterizations and conceptual limitations, in the media and other forums. In that sense, court decisions can be said to colonize other institutions and affect the way issues are discussed in the future when there is no apparent reason why they should have that extended impact, except that our society is noticeably law-oriented (perhaps law-obsessed) and often other public policy institutions fail to act.

Looking for a moment at the *Willis* and *Taylor* cases, the courts chose to cast the dispositive dilemmas in terms of the impossibility that a trier of fact would compare the impaired life of the victim with nonexistence. Concluding that it is not humanly possible to evaluate, in money terms, that situation, the courts declined to recognize the cause of action at all. That is not, by any stretch of the imagination, the only way to view the problem. The concern here is, of course, that a jury will speculate about damages; the bane of a court system is speculation. No judge or jury is allowed to speculate. Speculation is reaching beyond the bounds of probability into mere possibility. The line between legitimate reasoning and speculation is, of course, not crystal clear. Often it is a matter of semantics. A jury in a wrongful death case is allowed to assess damages for the value of a life. Evaluating such a matter is commonplace in the law. Why is assessing the value of an impaired life so different? For that matter, why is assessing damages for an impaired existence using as a base line no life at all so difficult? At the core of the matter is the courts' choice to cast the dilemma in those terms. Why could the problem not be stated in terms of comparison of an impaired life with a whole, unimpaired life? As courts wrestle with the questions posed by the legal actions discussed in this chapter, commentators view the legal arguments and potential judicial decisions in this field with intense interest. The likelihood that courts will eventually be persuaded to assess the desirability of life with disabilities causes alarm to those who are deeply concerned with the way people with disabilities are perceived by society. The effect on lives that, in some sense, may already be precarious is troublesome to many. How courts decide these cases is predicted to have great impact on how these vital issues will be addressed in ethical and public policy settings.[97]

Establishing Boundaries Between Law and Policy

Sometimes overlooked is the fact that, generally speaking, courts, and not legislatures, establish the boundaries between legal decision and policy matters. What courts decide often is properly viewed as a type of public policy. Courts are, after all, public institutions and their decisions, even when rendered in terms of applying the law, are viewed as public policy. On the other hand, courts are not expected to decide cases based on policy, at least, not alone. Policy declarations are for the other branches of government. Courts of last resort in any jurisdiction are exceptions, however, since they may have no binding precedent to follow and must somehow decide the case. Even in that instance, however, if a court does not ground the decision in some legal expression (case, constitution, or statute) the authority of the decision may be weakened and later challenged. Legislatures may occupy areas of law by passing statutes, thereby relegating courts to interpreting the statutes. However, when legislatures have not spoken, courts are free to move in and, in that case, they set the boundaries between policy and law. They may decline to decide an issue, declaring that the issue is one for the legislature. The intermediate appellate court in *Taylor* did just that, since neither the state's highest court nor the legislature should speak on the issue. What is significant, however, is that the court, not the legislature, decides in most cases whether to move into the area or defer to the legislature. In the case of wrongful life actions, it was probably a responsible move to decline to extend tort law without direction from the legislature or, at least, the Supreme Court.

Discouraging Legislative Policymaking

The institutional practice of courts that permits drawing analogies from existing precedent, no matter how remote in topic or time, in order to decide current issues may contribute to legislative inaction. Given the proclivity of legislatures to avoid controversial subjects, they are often content to let courts assume a visible role. Courts have to decide cases and, of course, they are bound to attempt to apply existing precedents rather than embarking on wholly new courses of action. When no precedent actually fits the situation, however, they can decline to reach out and instead simply decide cases based on failure to meet the burden of proof rather than creating new law. Nothing requires courts to make a practice of couching their pronouncements in language of absolute certainty when that is not warranted. They can defer to legislatures outright or indicate the need for legislative action.

Chapter 5

Body Parts: Allocating Organs

In August of 2004, Todd Krampitz, a 32-year-old man from Texas, was fighting cancer. His liver, which had been plagued by a large tumor, was failing. Because of his liver cancer, he could not survive without a liver transplant. Fortunately for him, an out-of-state family agreed to direct the donation of a liver from a family member who had died. Todd received the organ and underwent transplant surgery. His life was saved—for eight months—before he died in April of the following year. What made this case noteworthy was that Todd managed to move to the front of the line ahead of many people on the national organ waiting list and persuade a family to make a direct donation to him, by means of an extensive media campaign by his family. At the time he received his transplant, more than 17,000 people, some in a worse medical condition than he was, were on the national waiting list for livers. More than a thousand of those people lived in his home state of Texas. Although Krampitz and his family were aware of the national system for distributing organs, they decided to circumvent it.[1]

By conducting a media blitz, consisting of billboards, newspapers, an Internet web site, and appearances on national TV shows, they convinced an unrelated family to direct the donation of a liver to Todd. The goal of the Krampitz family was not to increase the number of organ donors in general but to secure an organ specifically for him, regardless of the needs of other recipients who had been on the list long before his need arose. The success of his media campaign in bypassing the national list depends on one's point of view. It was either a heartwarming triumph by Todd and his family, the example of a go-getter whose actions were rewarded by the compassion and altruism of the donor's family or the deliberate hijacking of an organ from some other deserving recipient who had ethically played by the rules and awaited his or her turn on the national list.

This event with all its implications illustrates the complex questions concerning the organ distribution system. There is no way of knowing whether the donor family would have given the liver at all but for the publicity that attracted its attention. How many potential donors could have used the liver successfully? Could the liver have extended someone's life longer than Todd's was extended? Many similar personal appeals followed Todd Krampitz's successful effort to jump the line and secure a transplant organ ahead of many other needy recipients who had patiently awaited their turn on the national registry (which is grounded in federal law but basically relies on a balance of ethical principles for its authority). The increasing practice of individual media appeals for preferential treatment, along with other developments, is challenging the ethically based system which has been in place since 1984 as well as threatening to undermine its effectiveness. The national list for distribution of deceased donor organs, previously used almost exclusively, depends on strong broad-based support for authority. It could fall by the wayside if bypasses become the rule rather than the exception. Although litigation over one's place in line has not yet occurred, litigation involving various aspects of organ donation is becoming more common. When individual initiative threatens the ethical distribution system and litigation over aspects of the donation and transplant process prevails, the ethical framework will be weakened and the field will be changed. Solicitation of organs in efforts to bypass the present distribution process arouses concern about the potential for financial exploitation, unfair allocation of organs, and the subversion of standards for donation. An additional ethical concern is that the practice of private organ solicitation gives an unfair advantage to people who have the financial resources to conduct an extensive campaign. Whether they use their own money or engage in fund-raising, those with resources will be far more likely to prevail. The principle of distributive justice, which has been especially important in this bioethics field, is undermined by private solicitation.

BACKGROUND

In order to understand and appreciate the changes that are beginning to happen in this field, some background concerning the history of organ donation in this country, plus explanation of differences in the handling of living donations and deceased donations, is necessary. The ethical issues involving both types of donation are immensely complicated. The purpose of this chapter is not to address and resolve all the ethical issues. Unconditional resolution is not possible because the issues involve a balancing and weighing of various ethical principles and, like all issues in bioethics, these are intensely fact-based at the core. My purpose is to identify and describe the cultural shift in thinking about the field of organ transplantation and to attempt to predict changes that will occur as a result of a gradual shift from ethics to law in resolving issues. I will also suggest how a well-thought out public policy could help in stabilizing the field before it becomes a free-for-all in which considerations of ethical principles fall to individual aggression.

First, we turn to a brief history of transplantation itself. On December 23, 2004, the 50th anniversary of what is usually regarded as the first successful human organ transplant, a kidney transplant from one living twin brother to another, performed in Boston, was celebrated.[2] Seven years before that event, however, a kidney was taken from a cadaver and attached to the arm of a patient. Although the kidney was rejected by the patient's immune system a few days later, its brief service enabled the woman's kidneys to resume functioning. In 1953, a somewhat successful kidney transplant, one that lasted six months, occurred in Boston.[3] A year later, however, the landmark transplant occurred and the recipient lived an additional eight years. With the development of improved immunosuppressive drugs, the year 1962 witnessed the first successful transplant from an unrelated donor. The first successful heart transplants occurred in 1967.[4] Since those successes, transplantation efforts are now routinely carried out for a long list of organs and other body parts including the pancreases, hearts and lungs as units, corneas, heart valves, skin, bone, bone marrow, partial livers, intestines, blood vessels, tendons, and ligaments. In addition, on a few occasions organs from animals have been transplanted into humans and various mechanical devices have been used as substitutes for organs.

It is apparent that the past five decades have witnessed remarkable progress in organ transplantation. Surgeons have learned how to transplant nearly every vital organ in the human body as well as a wide variety of non-vital body parts. At the time of the 50th anniversary, transplanting the human hand was the most recent and innovative addition to the list of transplants. Facial transplant surgery was then anticipated but still viewed as controversial. Since that time, the first face transplant has occurred and remains a subject of controversy because of the medical risks and psychological implications, among other reasons. A team of French surgeons accomplished that complex surgery in 2005. It appears to have been successful to date.

During these five decades, more than 415,000 people in the United States have received new kidneys, hearts, livers, lungs, pancreases, and intestines to extend their lives and relieve their suffering.[5] Advances in surgery, medicine, anesthesia, and intensive care have increased chances of successful transplants and extended patients' longevity and quality of life. Furthermore, surgeons routinely give transplants even to patients with serious diseases, such as diabetes, who were considered unqualified in earlier years. Techniques of preserving organs from cadavers have improved. Improvements in antibiotics and antirejection drugs have increased the chances of successful transplants. Transplant science has changed the face of medicine in many ways and has led to developments such as acceptance of the Harvard criteria for brain death and passage of anatomical gift acts.[6]

The story of transplant medicine is, in almost all respects, one of almost unbelievable success given the doubts and objections that existed at the time the first successful transplant was attempted. Success, however, has created a problem that will eventually lead to massive change within the organ transplant scientific community. The problem, a product of success, is a vastly increased demand for organs. Demand far outstrips the supply of donated organs, creating a drastic shortage. Organ transplants are now expected as routine medical procedures. A technique that was considered high risk and optional is now viewed as a medical necessity. Because organs from deceased persons cannot supply nearly enough to meet the demand, donations from live donors have been increasingly sought. Since 2001, in fact, the numbers of kidneys from living donors has continued to surpass those from cadavers. The shortage is aggravated by the fact that many recipients require multiple transplants. In 2004, there were about 27,000 solid organ transplants in the United States, nearly 1600 more than in the previous year.[7] According to figures released by the UNOS (United Network for Organ Sharing), the number of transplants had increased to 28,931 in 2006. The number of organ donors in 2006 was reported to be 14,754.[8] The demand for organs continues to increase. By April of 2007, the waiting list for organ donations had climbed to nearly 96,000 people.[9] The waiting list for kidneys alone has climbed to over 70,000 patients; however, based on the number of transplants that actually occur annually, the expectation is that only a quarter of them will receive a transplant in 2007.

The great success in improving the science of organ donation has made it an expected, if not routine, part of medical planning for individuals with the type of medical problems that can be remedied by obtaining new organs. The resulting demand for organs exceeds available donations, at least under present circumstances. Pressure has resulted on the donation process and on the distribution process as well. The increased demand has created a perception of inadequacy and delay. It is obvious that deceased donors represent a category that can be increased only by persuading more people to promise to donate organs but it cannot be effectuated at will. It is difficult to predict how developments in medical science will affect the demand and supply sides of organ donation. Although demand can be expected to increase, scientists are working on alternative means of providing for that need. Improvements in medicine may work to decrease the demand for organs. For example, vaccines and other prevention measures against hepatitis C and alcoholism would help. Animals are one possible source of organs for transplantation. Extending the useful life of transplanted organs will help to reduce the need for multiple transplants. Increased longevity in general will slow down the supply of organs from deceased donors but, on the other hand, organs of older people may be more useful for transplants, given the medical improvements. Growing people's own cells in the laboratory to fashion new organs is another means of avoiding the need for a stranger's organs, although it may not be practical in the immediate future.

In the meantime, while other means of reducing demand for human organs are developed, the pressure remains to increase and reallocate the supply of organs from living donors. The pressure has manifested itself in several ways. Some people, like Todd Krampitz, have sought to bypass the ethical allocation systems in place by seeking out nonrelated donors who will donate to them directly. Others have engaged in what is called "transplant tourism," that is, going abroad to other countries that do not bar payment for organs and having transplants performed there. Still others seek to change the present system, which prohibits compensating donors. With increased expectations of organ transplants as standard medical measures comes impatience with delays, pressure to manipulate the system to move ahead, and desire to prevent others from bypassing the list. Expectations of success will cause lawsuits when delay or failure results. In other words, increased demand plus increased expectations cause people to turn to legal remedies to further their individual needs or, when failure occurs, to seek compensation for their losses. I will examine each of these consequences of increased demand and corresponding perceived delays and inadequacy in turn. In essence, the stresses on the present organ donation ethically based system, which is basically an altruistic system, are causing change. Reliance on a purely ethical arrangement may be replaced by litigation as people who are seeking organ donations seek to meet their needs. As in other areas of controversy, bioethics is on trial and litigation threatens to alter the ethical resolution of issues. The impact of these controversies will have a long-range effect on all aspects of the system.

As transplantation has become safer with successful outcomes more certain, the ethical rules guiding donation and fair allocation have struggled to keep pace. The bioethics field of organ transplantation has long been dominated by two fundamental questions. First, assuming that human organs will still be needed despite medical advances that may supply other types of replacements, how can we increase the supply of transplantable human organs in a fair and just way? Second, how can we distribute available human (or other) organs in an effective, efficient, and just way? The two questions are interrelated. Increasing the supply of organs can help to address the problematical nature of the second question. The public perception of the fairness of the distribution method may well affect the willingness of people to donate, thereby addressing the first question.

Two basic assumptions are involved, although they are not entirely without controversy.[10] The first assumption is that increasing the supply of organs in order to enhance quality of life or to save lives is important. In this time of high expectations of longevity and life quality, this statement is not seriously questioned. The second assumption is that methods of increasing organ supply should be restrained by ethical considerations. One such consideration would be that organs should not be taken from living people without their consent. That is not in dispute. Another consideration, however, which is increasingly controversial, is that donors should not be compensated and organs should not be purchased on the market. Still another is that, in removing organs from donors who are deceased, the organs should not be removed until the donor is declared dead by some agreed-upon medical standard.

At this point, a brief discussion of the existing methods of allocation and distribution for living and for deceased donors is necessary.[11] The U.S. Congress passed the Uniform Anatomical Gift Act in 1968 in an effort to establish a national organ transplantation policy. By 1980, every state and the District of Columbia had adopted some form of the Act and, in 1984, Congress followed up by passing the NOTA (National Organ Transplant Act) to facilitate the organ distribution process. One of the main purposes of NOTA was to establish the OPTN (Organ Procurement and Transplantation Network), a system that both maintains the names of individuals who need transplants and, when organs become available, matches organs with patient recipients.

In 1986, the Health Resources and Services Administration, a division of the DHHS, contracted with the UNOS, a private nonprofit organization based in Richmond, Virginia to maintain the OPTN. The networks share the same board of directors and are collectively known as OPTN/UNOS. UNOS continues to administer the OPTN to ensure the effectiveness, efficiency, and fairness of organ sharing in the national system, as well as to attempt to increase the supply of donated organs. UNOS has divided the country into eleven geographic regions, which are further subdivided into local organ procurement organization service areas.

The OPTN receives most of its funding from a onetime patient registration fee of $459, which is assessed when a transplantation center accepts a candidate for a transplant from a deceased donor or when a person who had not been on the waiting list receives a transplant from a living donor. Historically, consistent with its federal charge, the OPTN has focused on transplants from deceased donors. At the time it was created, donation by living persons was less frequent and usually occurred between individuals who were relatives or friends. Living donor donations were, and still remain, the responsibility of individual transplantation centers. All centers are subject to OPTN regulation but, until recently, the OPTN took little responsibility for living donor transplants.

The OPTN is becoming more active in dealing with living donor situations. In October 2004, the DHHS directed it to develop voluntary-allocation guidelines for organ donations from living donors that are made to an anonymous pool, not to specific patients, and other voluntary policies and guidelines as "it believes necessary and appropriate to promote the safety and efficacy of living donor transplantation for the donor and the recipient."[12] The responsibilities include developing guidelines for public solicitation of organ donors. In November 2004, OPTN/UNOS announced that it opposed solicitation of organs from deceased donors who had no personal or family tie to the patient because such solicitations could "divert organs from patients with critical need to those who are less ill."[13] The OPTN/UNOS Board stated that "[w]e strongly oppose public or private appeals that effectively put the needs of one candidate above all others and pose concerns of fairness. Transplant candidates rely on the public's trust in the fairness of the allocation system and support of that system through donation. Public appeals may jeopardize that trust."[14] OPTN/UNOS said, however, that it would provide resource information for prospective living donors, including medical criteria for who can donate and protocols for live unrelated donation.[15]

In June of 2005, OPTN/UNOS announced that it would not participate in efforts to solicit living donors for specific transplant candidates. Specifically, it would not set up a Web site similar to MatchingDonors.com, a private Web site, devoted to matching living donors with specific unrelated patients. MatchingDonors.com claims to be a nonprofit corporation dedicated to matching donors, doctors, and patient-recipients. A onetime or monthly fee is charged to be listed. MatchingDonors.com was launched in 2004. As of January 14, 2007, it has paired thirty-six living organ donors and recipients. The first transplant, which took place in

October 2004, received widespread media coverage.[16] The recipient, who had been seeking a kidney for five years, said that he did not pay for the kidney but had reimbursed the donor about $5,000 for expenses. The donor reportedly took and failed a lie detector test during which he was asked if he had profited from the transplantation.[17]

One more development on the federal level is a necessary part of the picture. In 2000, the DHHS issued the final version of the Final Rule to replace local and regional allocation systems with a single national distribution protocol. Originally issued in 1998, the new protocol caused alarm on the part of the states and so was amended after vigorous debate. Before the Final Rule, organs donated within the United States were distributed locally or regionally. With this system, organs sometimes went to recipients within the donor's region who needed them less urgently than patients outside the region. A discrepancy existed between organ availability in states with larger donor banks and those with smaller donor banks. This inconsistency led to growing support for a change in the organ allocation system. After the first version of the Final Rule was issued, a number of states expressed public concern that organs donated in-state could be distributed to residents of other states, thereby lessening the interest of residents in donating. They passed laws that limited the transfer of organs out-of-state to situations, for example, in which a suitable match could not be found. The Rule was changed to accommodate the concerns. The amended Rule contains language that allows states to give preference to local and regional organ recipients but, if a match is not made, directs states to offer the organ to patients nationwide. The Final Rule is viewed as ethically proper because it provides for organs to be distributed over as broad a geographic area as feasible and considers a patient's urgency of need.[18]

CONTEXT POINTS

Before examining and analyzing how litigation is about to transform this area of bioethical regulation, several important points must be made by way of context. The urgency of meeting the demand for organs (at any cost) need not be accepted uncritically. While no one would question the legitimacy of individuals' quest for organs or for donors' generosity of spirit in donating their own or those of their loved ones, the fact is that organ transplantation may not be a particularly wise investment for society in terms of its overall health and public health systems. Critics have pointed out that immense numbers of lives could be more easily saved or improved with the financial resources required for organ

replacement. One commentator, who is a supporter of organ transplantation, conceded that "from a public health perspective, more harm than
good has already been done [by organ transplantation]:" in the United
States, "nearly $6 billion is spent [annually] on a handful of solid organ
transplant recipients."[19]

By way of contrast, in the global effort to immunize against measles,
which kills 900,000 children each year around the world, only $0.26 per
vaccine is needed.[20] In this world of limited resources for health care, it
would be difficult to assert fairly that the expenditures necessary to carry
out organ transplantation are the best possible use of money available to
serve the health needs of the living. This is especially true because transplants along with other high technology medicine are generally unavail-
able to those with "inadequate" financial resources. For example, during
the period 1978–1994, only 163 transplants took place in all of Africa,
while 124,000 took place in the United States during the same period.[21]

Another contextual point is that, for all its successes, organ transplantation is not the medical miracle that some claim it is. Given the kinds of
diseases suffered by those who need organs, many might well have died
within a relatively short time even with a replacement organ. Moreover,
some critics argue that the transplant medical community has consistently
overstated recipients' quality of life and has minimized the undermining
effect of the antirejection medication.[22] There is no doubt that the need
for transplants is intense among those who are personally involved with
patients whose lives can be improved or saved by transplants. But the overall context is crucial when public policy is considered and when the ethical
decision-making is done. The anticipation of more litigation involving the
most troublesome aspects of transplantation is a factor that must be taken
into account as well.

A third contextual point is that as a general rule, our common law
"provides that one human being is under no legal compulsion to give
aid or rescue or to take action to save another....The rule is founded
upon the very essence of our free society."[23] Although the rule has traditionally been applied to living persons, the mandate that organs may not
be removed without consent would suggest that no presumptive obligation to rescue exists after death. To be consistent with this long-standing
rule, compulsion to relinquish organs would not be acceptable.

It is evident that distribution of organs for transplant has been governed by ethical consensus based on a complex system authorized by the
federal government for organs from deceased donors and by voluntary
agreement for organs from living donors. That consensus is in the process
of disintegration and realignment, especially with respect to living donors.
We recall that two major changes have occurred. The demand, and thus

the need, for human organs has escalated with the advancing medical success of the procedure. The need, and thus the demand, for organs from living donors has increased accordingly. The demand, which we could call a market demand, has made interested patients less willing to abide by the national ethical formula and system and more willing to bypass the system when it comes to both deceased and living donors. More individualistic, aggressive, and self-serving actions, in turn, produce a willingness to litigate to enforce rights and interests.

The reasons for the breakdown of the consensus are many and varied, and the breakdown itself is not fully acknowledged. One has to read between the lines to see that individualism, advocacy, and general dissatisfaction with both the supply of organs and the methods of allocation are contributing factors. It has been noted that fewer people now indicate that they are willing to be organ donors upon death than in 1968, around the time of the first heart transplant.[24] It may be that one factor in this lack of willingness to donate is increased skepticism or distrust of the medical community on the part of the public because of changes in the patient and physician relationship over time. More of an adversarial relationship may now exist than in the late 1960s. Increased demand for organs is a major factor. My perception is that the improvements in medical science that have increased capabilities of performing successful transplants have raised people's expectations of living longer lives with the benefit of artificial means leading to an increased demand. Given their own expectations, people may be less inclined to focus their attention on donating their own organs upon death. Whether we call it market demand or expectation of enhanced medical services, the result is that the public, in this case the public with a need for organs, is about to cause a sea change in the system. No longer are people content to sit and wait for their names to appear at the top of the list. They are demanding organs now, and they are prepared to advertise their need, bring lawsuits to accomplish their goals, and go abroad to obtain organs. If there is a general adversarial attitude involving the public and the health care industry and medical professionals, it will manifest itself in more, rather than less litigation over all types of disputes and controversies. Issues that might have been resolved by ethical discourse may now end up in courts for decision.

Although as yet no one has sued to gain priority over the national list of patient recipients, the practice of cutting the line has taken on a far more adversarial and individualistic tone in recent years. Whereas prior to the past four or five years, the practice of attempting to get ahead of the line was essentially unheard of, it has become more common and has become institutionalized in a sense, with several organizations created for the specific purpose of bypassing the national list, which is regulated by ethical principles.

LITIGATION ON THE HORIZON

Litigation has occurred in several areas related to organ transplants. They include (1) lawsuits against health care institutions for improperly classifying patients in order to gain priority on the national organ lists (*transplant priority*); (2) claims of delay and inadequate preparation by health care providers in failing to perform transplants for their patients (*delay and inadequacy*); and (3) claims of negligent or improper transplantation practice, essentially in the nature of medical malpractice claims (*negligence*). In addition, some lawsuits have been brought against foreign providers in which transplants have been done abroad pursuant to transplant tourism. This area of litigation does not promise to be highly profitable because it is fraught with problems including jurisdictional issues and, ultimately, collection issues even when judgments are obtained. Although such lawsuits may increase in number as more patients go abroad to seek riskier transplants rather than waiting on a national list, I do not intend to discuss this category of cases since they are marginal to the U.S. system. It is important to be aware of developments in this area, however, because it represents an inevitable result of the increasing gap between supply and demand of organs within the United States.

One area of legal measures, involving federalism disputes, arose several years ago and appears to have attained its objective. When the federal government issued its first version of the Final Rule, a number of states passed laws to protect state-produced organs from being shipped out of state. That issue appears to be resolved with the issuance of the modified Final Rule, discussed above, which took into account the priorities of individual states and regions.

An additional area of litigation is likely to arise in the near future. Because of the increase in individual solicitation of organs from living donors and the proportionate increase in available organs coming from living rather than deceased donors, we can expect to see more stringent regulation of organ donation by living donors in the near future. OPTN/ UNOS has already indicated that it would pass regulations in this field. With more living donors giving organs, there will be increased risks to living persons from removal of their organs. Serious risks and consequences to living donors in the future caused by past donations are highly predictable. We can expect to see a substantial increase in claims based on lack of notice and improper medical procedure, that is, basically medical malpractice type litigation. Living donor litigation (*involving living donor risks*) may well become a cottage industry of the malpractice bar. There are already numerous claims based on the improper taking of organs from deceased donors. These claims are usually based on lack of permission.

Another potential source of claims, however, may be based on the improper taking of organs before death has occurred pursuant to an agreed definition. Already there is talk about changing standards of death to facilitate the removal of organs before they are rendered useless. In addition, incipient claims of unlawful compensation for solicited donations in the marketplace already exist and it is only a matter of time before government officials investigate and prosecute those who probably are engaging in paying for organs within the United States. There is one more problem that arises when people solicit organ donations from living or deceased donors in order to obtain directed donations rather than abiding by the national list priority system. That is unlawful discrimination on the part of potential donors. While directed donations to non-family members have occurred from time to time in the past, they are increasing as more people use widespread solicitation techniques. While this is primarily an ethical issue, it is a legal issue as well since we have federal and state laws prohibiting discrimination. It has not been a major factor to date since directed donations to groups or individuals have occurred only on a small scale. However, it will become a larger problem perhaps requiring government action once soliciting organs increases in practice. While I do not intend to discuss this problem in detail, it will call for close attention.

It is evident that all four of these areas of litigation have occurred or will arise in the future because of changes in the nature and pattern of organ transplants and distribution. Gradually, the culture of organ transplantation as a field of bioethics is beginning to experience a shift, as other fields have done, from being exclusively based and governed by ethical standards to one that is increasingly dominated by courts and regulated, in a sense, by lawsuits. With this cultural shift in regulation, the public policy issues will change and the practices in organ transplantation will be affected and transformed into predominantly legal issues. The ethical issues will continue to exist, but those issues will be affected by the increasing role of courts in resolving legal issues in the field. The ethical questions ultimately will find legal answers and, in some cases, the preemptive force of law will preclude the private, ethically based, resolution of issues.

I will provide an example of each of these different types of litigation that either has occurred or is likely to occur. I will then analyze each in determining how the overall impact of the legalization of organ transplantation is likely to transform this field of bioethics. The four areas of legal intervention are (1) transplant priority; (2) delay and inadequacy; (3) negligence; and (4) living donor risks. Once the various types of litigation have been described, I will analyze the impact by examining the five factors set out in Chapter 2, that is, the idiom of the law; the adversarial nature of litigation; the elements of closure and finality, and the retrospective view; institutional biases; and the future impact.

Transplant Priority: Illinois Federal Actions

In November 2003, the UIC (University of Illinois) paid the United States and the State of Illinois $2 million to settle a whistle-blower (someone who reports misconduct within an organization) lawsuit filed by a transplant surgeon and professor at the College of Medicine. He alleged that the University's Medical Center in Chicago improperly diagnosed and hospitalized several patients in the late 1990s in order to allow them to jump ahead in eligibility for liver transplants sooner than they would have had they not been the victims of the fraudulent practices. The state and federal governments intervened in the lawsuit. Similar allegations were settled for smaller amounts involving two other medical centers, the University of Chicago and Northwestern Memorial Hospital. The whistle-blower received the allowable portion of the settlement proceeds (25 percent or about $250,000) plus his attorneys' fees and expenses (close to $300,000).[25] According to the settlement agreement, the United States and the State of Illinois had claims against the center for submitting fraudulent claims to Medicare and Medicaid during a three-year period based on the following conduct: admitting liver transplant-eligible patients to the intensive care unit when not medically necessary; admitting liver transplant-eligible patients to the hospital when not medically necessary; billing for these medically unnecessary hospitalizations and services; falsely diagnosing patients to justify their placement on the liver transplant eligibility list; falsely identifying patients with high status for the purpose of making them eligible for liver transplants before other patients also in need of transplants; and transplanting a patient who was medically ineligible to receive a transplant.

Specifically, the action alleged that several federally insured patients were admitted to the Medical Center for lengthy liver transplant hospitalizations in intensive care. Two of the patients received liver transplants despite failing to meet the criteria for priority of the national organ sharing network (OPTN/UNOS). Another patient who received a transplant was not eligible because she had liver cancer. The fraudulent diagnoses allowed UIC to transplant enough patients to meet the minimum needed to be certified under Medicare and Medicaid, thus enabling it to receive federal and state reimbursement.

The settlement agreement provided that UIC denied the allegations and claimed valid defenses to all the claims, including an assertion that no patient ever was harmed by any conduct of its physicians. UIC admitted no liability. Although the governments had claimed damages of triple the actual damages, they settled for double the damages. The whistle-blower had filed his lawsuit in the federal court claiming violations of the federal False Claims Act, the Illinois Whistleblower Reward and Protection Act, and his employment rights. The whistle-blower lawsuits had been filed under seal, that is, protected from public disclosure, to give the government time to investigate the allegations and decide whether to take a role in the litigation.

The settlement agreement imposed certain integrity requirements, including compliance and reporting requirements, on the medical centers but did not exclude them from Medicare, Medicaid, or other federal health care programs. The claims against UIC and the other hospitals were civil only.

Delay and Inadequacy: Claims Against Kaiser Permanente and the University of California at Irvine Medical Center

The DMHC (California Department of Managed Health Care) began an investigation of Kaiser Permanente's kidney transplant program for Northern California in late March of 2006. Kaiser Permanente is a not-for-profit organization that administers managed care programs and hospitals in the State of California and elsewhere. Kaiser has more than eight million enrollees nationwide, more than three-quarters of them in California.[26] The medical group purportedly consists of 6,000 physicians nationwide and exerts powerful control over the corporate decisions.[27] DMHC has jurisdiction over managed care services within the state. Until mid-2004, Kaiser contracted with the UCSF (University of California San Francisco) and the UC-Davis (University of California Davis) to provide kidney transplants for Kaiser members. When it decided during 2004 to handle transplants itself, Kaiser cancelled care contracts with the two hospitals and notified approximately 1,500 members that they were to be transferred to the new Kaiser program in San Francisco. The problems that resulted from this changeover produced a series of individual lawsuits plus an investigation and the largest fine ever imposed by DMHC in its history. Kaiser paid a $2 million fine and agreed to donate $3 million to Donate Life California, an organ donation advocacy program, as a result of a determination by regulators that it failed to properly monitor its two-year-old Northern California kidney transplant program.

The DMHC investigation began after the *Los Angeles Times* reported that Kaiser's poor management of the transfer of some 1,500 patients to its own center resulted in delays for some patients' procedures. The *Times* reported that twice as many Kaiser patients died on the waiting list as received kidneys in 2005 because of delays in transferring medical records to the new program. During the same period, reportedly, in California as a whole, more than twice as many people received transplants as died. During the two years before Kaiser instituted its own program, the two hospitals, UCSF and UC-Davis, performed three times as many transplants on Kaiser kidney patients as Kaiser performed during its first year of operation. Kaiser reportedly failed to provide adequate administrative oversight of the transplant program, failed to provide patients with timely access to specialists, and failed to respond to patients' complaints. During the investigation, Kaiser announced that it would close its own Northern California transplant program and transfer patients back to UCSF and UC-Davis.[28]

Because of the settlement with the DMHC based on its investigation, there is no official record of the incidents that led to the penalties. Press reports indicate, however, that the role of the physicians' group within Kaiser was central to the move to establish its own transplant program rather than continuing to farm out the kidney patients for transplants.[29] Unlike the rest of Kaiser, the Medical Group is a for-profit entity that divides profits among the partners, creating a financial incentive to have in-house services. Kaiser reportedly planned to use the San Francisco program as a template for a series of other transplant centers around the country that would save the HMO (Health Maintenance Organization) money by not sending patients to outside hospitals.[30] The principal whistle-blower, David Merlin, stated "I have every reason to believe they're going to resurrect this...[model].... They want to build a strong template to roll out in the other eight states....They said it would save Kaiser hundreds of millions of dollars" to handle organ transplants in-house.[31] DMHC will continue its investigation concerning Kaiser's staff and patient practices. Kaiser did not admit wrongdoing or failures but publicly indicated that the experience has "caused our organization to reflect on how we can continue to improve moving forward."[32] Kaiser's representative stated that there are no "strict indications" that any patients died because of the problems and that "I don't believe that anyone anticipated the complexity (of what) needed to be accomplished to safely transfer these people."[33]

A number of lawsuits raising individual complaints based on the same underlying transplant situation are pending. The general criticism of

Kaiser's actions involved failing to transfer patients promptly to the new program thereby leaving many without eligibility for a long period of time. Transfer of a patient requires registration with UNOS. Without that, a patient is not eligible to receive a kidney. Eligibility for a transplant depends, in part, on the length of time the patient has been on the waiting list, so a patient transfer must include information about the patient's credit for waiting time. One year into the program more than a fifth of the original patients had not been transferred. Two years into the program, a reported 220 of 1,500 had not had their waiting time transferred properly and six had not been transferred at all. The first of the UC-Davis patients were not transferred until four months after the contract with UC-Davis was cancelled.

Individual patients claimed missed opportunities to receive kidneys. Reportedly, UCSF physicians revealed that they had twenty-five cases of kidneys with antigen matches for Kaiser patients, but Kaiser refused to authorize UCSF to do the transplants, causing the organs to be refused. Kaiser patients were not informed of the lost possible opportunities for transplants. Kaiser allegedly failed to provide adequate transplant services for the patients which it was transferring back to itself. Patients were required to accept the retransfer if they wished Kaiser coverage for the services.[34] One individual cause of action allegedly claims the death of a patient while awaiting a transplant after Kaiser "bungled his paperwork, effectively removing him from consideration for a kidney."[35] Another said she became more ill as the HMO delayed her transplant. A third said his Kaiser doctor told him three times to travel to the Philippines to get a kidney, rather than waiting for Kaiser.

The whistle-blower who helped instigate regulatory and media investigations of Kaiser has filed a wrongful termination lawsuit alleging that Kaiser medical group ignored several warnings about mounting problems in the program. David Merlin, who was administrative head of the kidney unit for a short time during 2005, claimed in his wrongful termination lawsuit that he met with several Kaiser executives to raise concerns about operation of the unit. He believed that the new kidney-transplant unit was so poorly organized and managed that it failed to comply with state and federal requirements and was compromising patient care, leading to possible deaths. He alleged that the executives ignored his concerns and refused to let him schedule a meeting with the medical center's physician-in-chief. His lawsuit claimed $5 million in damages.

After being terminated by Kaiser in early February of 2006, Merlin took his case to the news media as well as to state and federal regulators. The report by the Centers for Medicare and Medicaid Services released in June 2006 appears to support a number of Merlin's allegations about quality and management problems. At least one media source, the *East Bay Business Times,* reported that the move to bring services in-house was done for financial benefit to the medical group. In addition, "Kaiser's emphasis on 'population health'—meaning providing cost-effective care for the greatest number of enrollees—carries with it some risk that the interests of individual patients could be compromised in an attempt to stretch health-care dollars across a broad spectrum of care."[36] Population health is recognized as a legitimate public health goal of a community or society and is often in conflict with private health care goals in the United States health care picture. The sacrifice of individual health for population health would not be considered legitimate if the real purpose were to maximize profits for a health care provider.

Transplant Center Controversies

In a related type of controversy, three people filed a lawsuit against the UCIMC (University of California-Irvine Medical Center) alleging negligence, fraud, and conspiracy following a state investigation that found more than thirty patients had died awaiting liver transplants after the hospital turned down organ donations because of staffing shortages.[37] An August report of the California Medical Society found that the hospital received 122 liver offers between August 2004 and July 2005 but that only 12 were transplanted, including two livers to the same patient after the first failed. The lawsuit alleged that UCIMC officials did not inform patients that the center had not had a full-time liver transplant surgeon since June 2003. The lawsuit also asserted that doctors performed other surgeries that would bring "more prestige, more patients, more profit and more research funding" than transplants.[38] The class action claimed that the UCIMC officials improperly rejected livers and did not tell patients that the "vast majority of UCI transplant patients would never receive a liver transplant at UCI."[39]

In another controversy related to competency of medical centers that claim to perform transplants, the *Los Angeles Times* reported in 2006 on an investigation in which it determined that about one-fifth of federally funded transplant programs fail to meet the government's minimum standards for patient survival or perform too few operations to ensure competency.[40] According to the study, the U.S. Centers for Medicare and Medicaid Services has allowed forty-eight heart, liver, and lung transplant centers to continue operating despite often repeated lapses. There are approximately 235 approved transplant centers nationwide. The centers with reported failings have accounted for numerous deaths of patients beyond those that are expected within a year of transplant.

"The bottom line is that there are too many programs in the United States that need to be shut down," said Dr. Mark L. Barr, a cardiothoracic transplant surgeon at USC and president of the International Society for Heart and Lung Transplantation.[41] Medicare, which funds most of the nation's transplant centers, requires programs to perform a minimum number of transplants to achieve a specific survival rate in order to be certified for funding. The number varies according to organs.

These disturbing reports lead to the next area of litigation that has emerged in this field, that is, negligent or improper transplants. While claims of negligence in performing transplants, within the scope of medical malpractice, do not represent a new area of litigation, we can expect an increase in volume and seriousness as expectations continue to soar while performance fails to meet the standards that are required to meet the extraordinary demands.

Transplant Error: Josh Hightower, Jesica Santillian, and Other Victims

When transplant error occurs, the results are often prime material for the media. Early in 2006, a 17-year-old named Josh Hightower made news when his kidney transplant, expected to liberate him from a life of catheters and blood-cleaning machines, instead caused his death from rabies. As with all these stories of medical tragedy, in which the promise of a treasured gift of life turns into a lethal weapon, the media was intensely interested. The story will be one that is often repeated as the volume of organ transplants goes up and the regulation of the organ transplant enterprise fails to keep pace. Even where the failure is understandable, the high expectations for transplants are likely to produce an interpretation that any failure is unacceptable and egregious harm.

In Josh's case, which was the first reported case of rabies transmission through solid-organ transplant and a statistical aberration, the family was appalled to learn later that rabies was not included in routine organ screening. The family believed that the transplant surgeons failed to heed the symptoms that led to the death of the donor and that they improperly failed to notify the family that the donor had previously spent time in jail and had drugs in his system at the time he died. Surgeons were quick to point out that jail time and drug use do not preclude organ donation and they are not linked to rabies, which caused the death in Josh and three other recipients of the donor's organs. The case raised ethical issues common to the transplant community, the balancing of the donor's right to privacy with the recipient's right to know. Commentators pointed out that these issues become more troublesome as the waiting list for organ transplants has lengthened during the past decade while the number of donors has not kept pace. Physicians are accepting marginal organs that they might have rejected a decade ago when the waiting list was one-third the size. Surgeons say that because a patient in need of a transplant may be in a dire clinical situation, decisions are often made to accept organs that have less than perfect functioning. "Though organ banks used to have the flexibility to refuse a donor for such reasons as old age and chronic health conditions, today they automatically exclude only donors who have certain types of cancer," according to the public affairs director of the Southwest Transplant Alliance.[42]

In this case, the donor, William Beed, Jr., was a young man slightly older than Josh. According to physicians, he was thoroughly screened. They determined that he had died of a brain hemorrhage, which they believe resulted from a drug overdose. They did not know that his apartment complex was infested with bats. Transplant surgeons at Baylor University Medical Center, where Josh was, accepted both of William's kidneys plus his liver and some arteries. The family sued the hospital claiming negligence for failure to give them the chance to turn down the kidney based on the facts which the hospital knew or should have known. Although the hospital stated that its transplant teams follow all disclosure and privacy protocols established by UNOS, the guidelines do leave some matters open for interpretation. What information is pertinent and what risks are identified and what are unforeseen are matters within physicians' discretion. Litigation is pending in this case.

Jesica Santillian was a 17-year-old illegal alien from Mexico who came to the Duke Medical Center in North Carolina to get a new heart as a solution to a heart and lung disorder that had been determined to be untreatable. Although her status as an illegal alien made the case especially controversial, her mother worked at a local college and covered Jesica on her insurance policy. A donor was located in Boston and a member of the Duke transplant team, Dr. Shu Lin, traveled to Boston to procure the organ. Although Dr. Lin was informed about the donor's blood type on three occasions, he had never been informed of the recipient's type and did not know that the heart was a mismatch. When the organ reached Duke, not a single member of the transplant team checked to verify that the organ was a blood-type match. UNOS had in place policies that should have prevented a mismatch before the release to the transplant team. What appeared to be very nearly a medical miracle for Jesica turned into a nightmare when the team was informed in the operating room after the transplant that a mistake had been made. Although her condition rapidly deteriorated in the days following the operation, Duke made no public statements concerning the incident. This was so, despite the fact that surgeons realized that the only hope was a second transplant. By the time she received a second transplant, which in itself was a controversial move, she was near death. After Jesica's death, the family made a claim against Duke, which publicly admitted medical errors, and the case was settled shortly thereafter. Federal regulators investigated the incident and cited Duke University Hospital for multiple deficiencies in its organ transplant procedures.[43] This case of classic failure of proper matching did much to undermine confidence in the already overtaxed organ transplant system.

The Problems of Living Donors

Living donors pose special problems. According to Steven D. Colquhoun, M.D., director of Liver Transplantation in the Center for Liver Disease and Transplantation at Cedars-Sinai: "There are risks involved with any surgery, but usually these are balanced by the potential benefit to the patient. In the case of the living donor, they derive no direct physical benefits, so the risks are much more difficult to justify and their safety is of utmost importance. An enormous amount of energy goes into screening potential donors. We need to feel certain that they are appropriately motivated and educated regarding the risks."[44] Speaking of liver donors, Colquhoun said: "When you're dealing with liver transplantation, you're dealing with people who will die without surgery. The only way to make that worse would be to add a complication in a living donor."[45]

Healthy people who donate organs enter a world of unknowns, according to a recent report published by the *St. Louis Post-Dispatch*. A year long investigation by the newspaper found some startling facts about lack of knowledge of risks on the part of the medical community. The newspaper reported:

There is no systematic tracking of living donors, so no one knows how many have died or suffered serious injuries or complications. There is a lack of comprehensive data, making it impossible for donors to assess risks. Agreement is lacking on evaluating potential donors and who can donate. Children as young as 10 and drug addicts have been among donors. Transplant hospitals make their own rules, as the government does not regulate organ donations from living donors.[46]

Regarding the risks reported by the newspaper, Arthur Caplan, director of the Center for Bioethics at the University of Pennsylvania, was quoted as saying: "There is no system and there is no accountability."[47]

Some 27,000 people received organs in 2004. The organs came from deceased and living donors in nearly equal amounts.[48] Overall, it is reported that more than 71,000 people in the United States have given organs to help relatives, friends, and strangers.[49] Although many have had no serious problems, notable cases of injury, sickness, and death exist. Without donor follow-up, it is not possible to give potential donors sufficient data for decision making. One estimate is that 3 of every 10,000 kidney donors can be expected to die and fewer than 10 percent will develop complications, for reasons related to the donation. A UNOS study in 2001 identified fifty-six donors who later needed kidney transplants, themselves. Estimates of problems for liver donors suggest that as many as 15–67 percent of donors may experience complications. Some transplant centers are "pushing the boundaries of who can give an organ. . . . Some centers are accepting donors who are older, overweight or have health conditions —such as high blood pressure—that would have ruled them out a few years ago."[50] The combination of factors, increasing demand that lowers standards for donors, plus lack of follow-up, and risk information, spells trouble for living donors and increased litigation in the future, which will have a severe impact on the organ transplant prospects. Increased litigation brings liability-consciousness and economic consequences, which contribute to an unfavorable atmosphere for transplants.

The federal government has indicated that it will develop guidelines governing living donor transplants.[51] Late in 2004, the DHHS directed OPTN to begin developing voluntary-allocation guidelines for donations from living donors that are made to an anonymous pool, not to specific patients, and other voluntary policies and guidelines necessary to promote safety and effectiveness of living donor transplantation, including the issue of public solicitation. A month later, OPTN announced its opposition to soliciting organs from deceased donors who had no personal or family bond with the patient. In June of 2005, OPTN/UNOS stated publicly that it "will not participate in efforts to solicit living donors for specific transplant candidates."[52] After a process of soliciting responses from transplant organizations, living donors, and live donor families, the HRSA (DHHS Health Resources and Services Administration) has ordered the OPTN to proceed with developing policies mirroring those that govern deceased donors and deceased organ recipients. They should include policies for the equitable allocation of living donor organs. The same public comment process used for deceased donors will be used, and the same enforcement actions will apply as with other OPTN policies. On the issue of directed donation, HRSA decided that the OPTN should develop living donor allocation policies that include the right to direction of donation.

Recognizing the special risks that a living organ transplant donor takes, transplantation doctors have outlined proposals of financial incentives to encourage donations. At the World Transplant Congress in Boston in 2006, Arthur Matas, a professor of surgery at the University of Minnesota, outlined a proposal including a term life insurance policy; guaranteed access to health care through Medicare or the Veterans Affairs system; and coverage of all transplant-related expenses such as doctors' expenses, travel to transplant sites, and other incidentals. He suggested that incentives for families of deceased donors could be offered as well including funeral expenses and tax incentives or credits. One purpose, he indicated, is to discourage patients from traveling to Third World countries to obtain organs from impoverished people. Hans Sollinger professor of surgery and chair of transplantation at the University of Wisconsin-Madison said, "[the] practice often leaves the donors without decent medical help and also creates problems for the people who get the organs because of less than adequate knowledge of transplant medicine."[53]

It is evident that increasing the numbers of living organ donors will contribute to the supply. It would also appear that the gains will be offset by other costs, including costs to donors in terms of medical expenses and health risks, costs to society in terms of incentives provided, and costs to society in terms of increased litigation for the inevitable losses and injuries that will be sustained by donors. All the litigation problems will be exacerbated by pressing for increases among living donors. In addition, the arguments against incentives, including reimbursements and compensation, must be taken into account. On balance, is it worth going to a system of compensating living donors, however well the compensation is disguised as incentives? Should we adopt (and would our legislators be willing to enact) standards of care for organ transplants that protect those who do the retrieving and transplanting? Would that leave donors unprotected and vulnerable throughout their lives for the potential consequences of donation? If they are protected, how could transplant centers bear the risks of future as well as present liability for problems in the transplant process?

ETHICAL ISSUES

Before undertaking an analysis of the legal impact, it is useful to review the major ethical questions concerning organ transplants.

First, it is important to recognize that it is not accurate to speak of organ transplants as a single ethical or medical subject or issue. There are many varieties of transplants involving a wide range of body parts including kidneys, liver, pancreas, heart, lung, skin, connective tissue, eyes, and now facial components. The ethical issues vary according to what body part we are considering. Kidney transplants are the most common and perhaps raise most of the important questions and issues. Kidney transplants, for example, can come from living or deceased donors, are essential to remove people from the costly and limited resource of dialysis, and are free of some secondary ethical issues such as those raised by liver transplants when the recipient can be held responsible for his or her own condition.

Several basic assumptions produce the first line of questions. The first assumption is that we need to increase the supply of organs in order to save lives and to enhance the quality of lives. The second is that our efforts to increase the supply should respect certain ethical boundaries. Numerous other questions arise concerning the supply side of the equation. Should donation be purely voluntary or should some measure of necessity be involved, such as a presumption of donation unless otherwise specified? With living donors, what information and consent are necessary for a donation to be voluntary? With deceased donors, when can an organ be taken? What definition of death is appropriate? Who owns the body and who is entitled to give or withhold consent?

On the distribution side of the equation, what method of allocation is ethically fair and reasonable? Must we enforce the existing UNOS system of priorities or should patients be entitled to use whatever means they choose to procure the needed part? What reimbursement or compensation should be allowed? Should UNOS run the living donor system as well as the deceased donor system? What about the liability factor? Who should bear the risk (according to what standard) of failures or errors within the process? If living donor organs increase in proportion, who will bear the risk of long-term medical problems that cannot be predicted at the time of donation?

If the need for kidneys, for example, continues to outstrip the supply, should transplant surgeons take more risks, for example, by tapping the supply of organs from a high risk pool? Who should bear the risk of that? Should the donor's reasons be considered? How much privacy should be accorded a donor (or the family of a deceased donor) in balancing that with the need for the recipient to have enough information to make a decision whether to accept the organ? If donor and recipient are allowed to make their own arrangements, should they also bear all the risk of their transaction? Why shouldn't free trade of organs be allowed, with some limits, if it would increase the supply? Isn't that better than having people engage in transplant tourism, which carries potentially greater risks?

ANALYSIS

We have examined four different types of legal action. They include fraudulent manipulation of the allocation system by falsifying patient priorities, failure to be prepared to perform transplants resulting in depriving patients of available organs, failures in the retrieval and transplant process, and the potential problems posed by relying more heavily on living donors. We have noted that lawsuits are likely to increase with respect to transplant tourism as well as concerning the premature or otherwise improper retrieval of organs, such as without consent, from bodies of deceased persons. The bringing of lawsuits represents a challenge to the basic transplantation system in place in the sense that they highlight and reveal flaws in the current practices. The impact of litigation and the court intervention that follows, however, has impact on all levels.

The Idiom of the Law (Language and Concepts)

As we have noted before, legal actions are framed in their own vocabulary and concepts. Important features of ethical decision-making are recast in legal terminology. The first two categories of lawsuits or legal investigations, involving the Chicago medical centers and Kaiser Permanente, were brought as challenges to claimed abuses by health care providers in attempting to circumvent the ethical system or in carrying out their responsibilities to provide for appropriate transplants. The nature of these lawsuits, private and public, validates the existing system but asserts that the institutions were violating the principles of the system. Since the lawsuits do not challenge the system but, instead, the way the institutions were operating within the system, the language and concepts do not alter the ethical system. Rather, they divert attention from the ethical decision-making as they attempt to restore equilibrium by requiring the institutions to comply. The negligence cases mount a challenge to the way transplants are procured and carried out. This category of lawsuit does not seek to alter the system. Its purpose is to seek damages for failure to comply in a reasonable and proper manner. To the extent that the lawsuits have merit, they point to failures of the system that need to be corrected. To the extent that they do not raise legitimate challenges, they may represent the natural consequences of failures that will occur from time to time no matter what the system is. Risk is always a factor and occasional failure is probably inevitable in medical procedures no matter what precautions are taken. In each procedure, whether it be human research trials or organ transplants, a balance must be struck between efficiency and practicality of results, cost, and risk. Regulation and safety precautions should eliminate inappropriate risks and the probability of bad results but not be so restrictive as to reduce the potential benefits. In bioethical terms, autonomy must be respected fully, the potential of harm should be minimized, the potential of benefit should be maximized, and the potential benefit should be distributed as evenly and fairly as possible. Lawsuits citing errors and harms should be evaluated carefully as to whether they reveal inappropriate risks or procedures or whether they fall within proper legal standards.

The Adversarial Process

This factor is significant in assessing the impact of litigation. The organ transplant system is an ethically based network that is formalized and established by regulation, legal regulation established by Congress and carried out by OPTN/UNOS. It does not, in any sense, function in an adversarial manner; rather it is essentially a social or community network charged with carrying out the retrieval and distribution process of organ transplants in a way that takes into account individual need and autonomy as well as the public good. It is more closely related to our public health institutional system than it is part of our individual health care system although it functions in both. In that respect, in attempting to serve more the public health need than the private health need of individuals, it stands apart from the mainstream of U.S. medicine and health care, which is more oriented to individual need. It may be inevitable that, as demand and supply have become unbalanced because of medical advances, pressure would be brought on the system to be more responsive to individual needs however asserted. The concerted action of hospitals in Chicago to seek advantage for their patients is an example of malfunctioning. The earlier legislation and litigation by states to challenge the Clinton administration's further nationalizing of the system arose because of similar factors.

The motives of Kaiser to incorporate transplants within its own bounds, despite inadequate preparation, is another example of economic motives at work within our market economy. The whistle-blower lawsuits, which brought some of these actions to light, represented a type of "private attorney general action" authorized to mobilize societal forces to uncover private abuses. These adversarial actions, however, were all designed to reaffirm the present system by exposing and punishing institutions that were seen to abuse the system. The tort actions, on the other hand, impose the adversarial process on the mechanics of the system itself by making transplant institutions comply with legal standards in a way that supersedes ethical standards. It would be claimed, of course, that the errors represented ethical violations as well but, more accurately, they were reminders that certain authoritative legal standards exist to govern the transactions even beyond the ethical basis. In this instance, legal standards and adversarial procedures are imposed on the ethical system and cause language and concepts to change. The prevailing tests become legal tests rather than ethical tests. Courts, rather than the regulatory bodies or the parties, are the ultimate decision makers. The adversarial nature of the process causes the parties, not to search for the facts—the truth—but to prevail by applying legal standards and procedures legitimately.

Closure, Finality, and the Retrospective View

In bioethical issues, legal standards and concepts are poor substitutes for the values and standards used in ethical decision-making by individuals and communities. The retrospective outlook of judicial decision-making has no place in the ethical decision-making process. Negligence lawsuits bring with them the same kind of retrospective view as lawsuits in the field of human research. The lawsuits exist to enable claimants to seek damages as legal recourse after the fact when all the pertinent conduct has already taken place. They do not facilitate or correct the underlying transactions as they are occurring but cause a legal assessment by courts after all relevant matters are concluded. Lawsuits involve a version of what happened as a snapshot earlier in time. There are exceptions to this general rule, of course, such as injunctions and actions seeking specific performance, but those remedies are not involved here. Court proceedings must have finality and so they result in a specific judgment with relief granted or denied. Courts are strictly limited to legal standards and rules as they undertake to resolve the claims of the parties. Ethical standards are not relevant except when they are integral parts of the prevailing standards of professional conduct.

Institutional Biases, Assumptions, and Deficiencies

This cluster of factors attempts to penetrate the way courts operate when they are called upon to intervene in controversies. We attempt to see how the factors can affect the outcome and whether they produce an outcome that is fair and legitimate in the eyes of the public. Biases and assumptions are at work in determining how courts characterize the dispute at hand and in how they resolve the controversy. Legal rules strictly limit who can sue and for what purposes. Potential claimants must be able to frame their claims in acceptable legal terminology and concepts. Individuals who perceive violations of private or public duties on the part of health care institutions must find appropriate legal vehicles for the issues they wish to raise. We have seen how statutes authorizing whistle-blower complaints allow people to raise issues that do not result in personal harm to themselves but raise public claims. For the purpose of raising their individual claims, they must find an acceptable cause of action, such as a wrongful employment termination action, in the Chicago cases. In the Kaiser case, individuals claiming to be injured by Kaiser's conduct had to frame their actions within the structure of permitted individual or class actions. In order to prevail, plaintiffs are obligated to prove the elements of traditional tort actions including duty, violation, causation, and damages. Individualism prevails and all such actions are meant to vindicate individuals' rights rather than societal wrongs.

What Impact Does Judicial Decision-Making Have on Future Controversies?

As in the case of human research litigation, all tort litigation has an immense impact on ethical decision-making and medical decision-making. The threat of liability causes a self-conscious view of everything that occurs during the process. This can have a salutary effect, of course, in protecting individual and public rights, and promoting effective as well as safe results. If regulation is not strict enough, tort liability serves as a warning signal. It can result in better regulation or, if ignored, can impose a cost on the system that may be detrimental to its operations. In the case of the Chicago medical centers and Kaiser, I would submit that individual lawsuits called attention to inadequacies and improper actions. By alerting the media, corrective measures resulted on the part of public authorities. Whether individuals claiming to suffer loss will be vindicated is another chapter in the story. In our societal health care picture, we emphasize the rights of individuals to secure whatever care they can acquire. Tort litigation serves this purpose. If we were to emphasize the overall health of the public to the same extent, tort litigation in the field of organ transplants could be seen to impede our goals.

If we were to evaluate results based on how well population needs are served, a certain number of individual lapses or failures would be accepted as an inevitable result of prioritizing the public's health needs. Similarly, we could decide that the cost of increasing the organ supply or reducing organ demand did not hold up as an effective expenditure of money, given what could be accomplished for the same amount of money to combat the massive public health epidemics and pandemics that occur regularly around the globe, or even the public health problems that exist in our own society. Whether litigation in the organ transplant setting will help to improve the existing system or contribute to its down-fall remains to be seen. If a strong commitment to the existing ethically based system is supported by the public, medical advances plus stricter regulation may save the day. If the system cannot be maintained in the face of market demand for organs on an individual basis, the present surge of litigation will speed the change. Increasing concerns for liability will accelerate the process of change or, if it does not, the system will become so risk-adverse that transplants will fail to meet the needs of the public and we will have to depend on medical advances to reduce or eventually eliminate the need for organ transplants.

Chapter 6

Stem Cells: Promise and Politics

The campaign for embryonic stem cell research has many faces, and the late Christopher Reeve is a prominent one. Before his death in 2004 from a condition caused by his accidental spinal injury years before, Reeves became perhaps the foremost advocate of stem cell research. Another well-known face belongs to Michael J. Fox, the television and film star, who was diagnosed in 1991 with Parkinson's disease. He did not go public about his affliction until 1998. Since that time, he has been a vocal advocate of Parkinson's disease research as well as embryonic stem cell research, which many believe will someday help those who suffer from Parkinson's. Fox established a foundation bearing his name to advance the research and another bearing the name of Muhammad Ali, who also suffers from the disease. Fox has been politically active in supporting candidates who have committed to support research. For example, in 2004, he appeared in a television commercial for Arlen Specter, who was seeking reelection to the U.S. Senate. In the November 2006 elections, he endorsed numerous candidates who support stem cell research, including New Jersey Senator Robert Menendez.

One of Fox's television commercial appearances in late October 2006 caused a storm of controversy. Appearing in an advertisement for Claire McCaskill, the Democratic candidate for the U.S. Senate in Missouri, Fox appeared to be suffering from highly visible tremors. Rush Limbaugh, a conservative talk show host, criticized Fox for purposely being off his medication or acting in the advertisement. In response, Fox claimed to be suffering the effects of dyskinesia, which is a reaction to the medication.

Limbaugh's remarks and the resulting firestorm of controversy kept the issue of stem cell research on center stage in American politics throughout the election.

BACKGROUND

Research on ES (embryonic stem) cells has generated vigorous political and ethical controversy since 1998, when researchers at the University of Wisconsin reported in *Science* that they had isolated human embryonic cells from leftover embryos and created self-perpetuating colonies in culture.[1] The news of the breakthrough caused a public stir in light of the potential of the ES cells to differentiate into a wide variety of human tissues. Hopes ran high that ES cells had the potential to revolutionize medicine and ultimately cure many diseases and conditions, including Parkinson's, heart disease, diabetes, and spinal-cord injury along with a host of others. The scientific triumph was immediately tempered, however, by the recognition that human embryos had to be destroyed in the process. The Wisconsin research involved human embryos that had been obtained by the consent of donors from several IVF clinics.[2] To some people, ES cell research represented the hope of near-miraculous cures; to others, it amounted to the killing of human beings in an early stage of life.

The Wisconsin report triggered a polarizing three-year public debate, which culminated in a decision announced by President George W. Bush on August 9, 2001, that the National Institutes of Health could issue federal research grants only for ES cell lines that were existing on that date. Since that time, in the view of many scientists and bioethicists, ES cell research has been held hostage (on the federal level at least) by the Bush policy. The quality and quantity of existing lines are not considered to be adequate for continuing research. As a result, scientists have turned to the states and privately funded research organizations. Beyond that, many leading scientists have been lured abroad by the promise of foreign funding.

Presidential Veto

Proponents of ES cell research were hopeful when the Republican-controlled Congress passed a bill in the 2006 session that would have permitted a modest extension of research. The bill called for federal funding that would enable the creation of ES cell lines from fertilized eggs stored in freezers and already designated for destruction. President Bush, however, chose this occasion to exercise his veto power for the first time in his six years in office. In vetoing the bill, Bush said that "stem cells . . . can be drawn from children, adults, and the blood in umbilical cords with no harm to the donor, and these stem cells are currently being used in medical treatments." [3] Despite the exaggerated claims of benefits from adult cells, most scientists believe that the President missed an opportunity to support research on the types of cells that have the potential to differentiate into many different kinds of tissue. As a result, tens of thousands of fertilized eggs that resulted from IVF will be destroyed without any being used in research.

In June of 2007, Congress passed another bill that was designed to "allow researchers to obtain stem cells from embryos created for in vitro fertilization that would otherwise be discarded by fertility clinics." [4] Specifically, the bill, entitled the Stem Cell Research Enhancement Act of 2007, would authorize HHS (the Department of Health and Human Services) to support research involving embryonic stem cells that met certain criteria, without regard to when the stem cells were derived from embryos. The bill authorized funding only for stem cell lines that would otherwise be discarded by fertility clinics. The bill also authorized alternative stem cell research, that is, obtaining stem cells without destroying embryos. The margin in both chambers fell short of the two-thirds needed to override a veto. On June 20, 2007, President Bush vetoed the Act. At the same time he issued an executive order encouraging federal agencies to support research that did not require the destruction of human embryos. Two senators who support stem cell research promptly included a provision in the 2008 Labor-Health and Human Services-Education appropriations bill to make more embryonic stem cell lines available for federally funded research.

State Research Grants

While ES cell research has been stalled on the federal level, a number of states have filled the void with laws authorizing state-financed research. California led the way with a major research authorization, which will be explained later. Progress, however, has been impeded by a series of lawsuits challenging the legislation on a variety of grounds. Several other states have also authorized significant research grants. Although the states cannot fund research grants in amounts that could compete with funding that the federal government could offer, it is possible that the obstacles created by lack of federal funding may stimulate the creative process in a way that may be beneficial in the long run.

Although research will continue in private and state-financed laboratories, the lack of federal support hinders research in the United States.

Many scientists will choose to work abroad in such places as China, Sweden, Singapore, and the United Kingdom. Scientists are quick to point out that it is not possible to predict what will come out of ES cell research and that patients should not be misled with false promises that the research will result in cures for a long list of chronic diseases. Considerably more research is necessary to explore the full potential of ES cells and to establish whether adequate stem cells exist in adults. Some recent studies, however, have given reason for optimism about the clinical benefits. For example, in two studies reported at the March 2007 American College of Cardiology Conference, scientists used adult stem cells to treat patients and observed marked improvement in their health. In one study, the researchers extracted stem cells from the thigh muscles of patients who had poor heart function or heart failure. They grew the cells in a laboratory and introduced them into the subjects' hearts through a catheter. The subjects, after six months, showed improvements in health and life quality, while the health of those who had standard therapies became worse. In a second study, conducted at ten medical institutions, researchers took bone marrow cells from unrelated donors and infused them directly into heart patients within ten days of heart attacks. After six months, the patients showed improved heart and lung function. More studies need to be done to confirm the results. Experts point out that stem cell therapy could be significantly less expensive than heart transplants, if later studies bear out these early findings.[5]

Stem Cells: Science

The question has arisen as to whether adult stem cell research is sufficient to make ES cell research unnecessary. While adult cells can be used for some purposes and research in this area is continuing, the present consensus is that they are not a substitute for embryonic cells because they lack the capability of embryonic stem cells to be totipotent (able to form any and all human tissues and to become an entire organism) or pluripotent (able to develop into many types of human tissue). ES cells are derived from the inner cell mass of embryos at the blastocyst stage, about five to nine days after fertilization. This occurs after the zygote (union of sperm and egg) has divided enough times to produce about 200 cells but before it has undergone a process called gastrulation and differentiation into the three primary germ layers. Each of the layers, ectoderm (outer), mesoderm (middle), and endoderm (inner), develop into different organs and tissues of the embryo. They are called "primary" because all organs and tissues of the body will be developed from them. The inner cell mass is the part of the blastocyst-stage embryo whose cells normally go on to become the body of the new individual. To date, the process of removal of stem cells results in the destruction of the embryo. At this point, the embryo has not undergone implantation in the lining of the uterus so some describe the embryos as pre-implantation embryos or preembryos. In fact, the only embryos available so far to derive stem cells are ones that have been created by IVF, that is, conceived by egg and sperm combined outside the body.[6]

Stem Cells: Ethical and Policy Questions

According to the report of the President's Council on Bioethics,[7] ethical questions arise because the most useful stem cells are derived from early-stage human embryos and the embryos are destroyed in the process of obtaining the cells.[8] The basic controversy concerns the ethics of using a form of human life for research purposes. This question first arose in the 1970s after IVF was first accomplished. When the practice of IVF had become more common and an excess of unused embryos accumulated, issues arose concerning the fate of the so-called "spare embryos."[9] The current controversy began in 1998 when reports were published about methods of deriving cells from the inner cell mass of very early embryos (ES cells) and from the gonadal ridges of aborted fetuses (embryonic germ cells or EG cells).[10] Two main public policy ethical questions have dominated the discussion. Is it permissible to support or sponsor research that depends on the exploitation and destruction of nascent human life? Is it permissible to withhold support from research that holds the promise of significant medical benefits?

The President's Report points out that:

ES and EG cells are not, themselves, embryos; they are not whole organisms, nor can they be made (directly) to become whole organisms. Moreover, once a given line of ES or EG cells has been derived and grown in laboratory culture, no further embryos (or fetuses) need be used or destroyed in order to work with cells from that line. But it is not clear whether these lines can persist indefinitely, and only very few lines, representing only a few genetic backgrounds, have been made.[11]

The debate encompasses discussion of adult stem cells, which can be derived from tissues in the bodies of adults or children. Because obtaining these cells does not require destruction of human life, they are considered to be "exempt" from problems of embryonic cells.[12]

Beyond the core issues, which remain in a state of tension, many other policy questions of an ethical nature have arisen in the public debate. Should moral or religious considerations play a role in deciding what sort of research may or may not be funded? What public policy should be promulgated as to issues on which significant numbers of Americans hold strong and conflicting moral beliefs? How can the present situation be allowed to continue in which private research is unregulated, except for that sponsored by a few states? Is it acceptable to use for the potential benefit of humans the scores of frozen embryos that will otherwise be discarded? What are the proper limits of embryo research, if it is funded to some extent? How can it be regulated? Who will have access to any benefits derived? Will they be available on some fair basis to those who lack the ability to pay? How will the allocation of scarce resources be affected if public policy supports fully backed research? What are the implications for other forms of human life (including fully developed humans) of experimenting on one form of nascent human life? What significance should be given to the fact that embryos are incapable of consent, even though someone else gives consent? What are the social implications of the lack of consent for others whose capacity to consent may be limited? How can claims of potential medical benefit be evaluated and controlled so that the promise of benefits is not overstated and misrepresented in the process of urging that research be funded? Should public policy on this issue hinge, as so many argue that it does, on how embryonic stem cells are defined, that is, whether they are entitled to full personhood or, at the other end of the spectrum, property, or as some form of life with less status than full personhood?

The last question is especially compelling to me. In the literature on this controversy, most commentators begin by stating that policy decisions concerning how to treat stem cells hinge on how we define the human embryo. It may be pertinent to question what is in the petri dish—person or property or something else. The question does not seem useful because the answer depends more on beliefs than analysis. These and many other issues remain unresolved as far as a national consensus on public policy is concerned. Some states have resolved the issue and gotten underway with funding research. The development of a federal policy that can encourage a consensus or, at least, an accommodation of the various points of view, has not occurred. The President's Council studied the issue and produced a report that, as in the other areas of bioethics, explained the various points of view but failed to suggest any meaningful way to accommodate the conflicting positions.

Religious and Moral Objections

The fact that this crucial scientific enterprise, perhaps more than any other scientific field, remains mired in controversy after so many years is evidence of the powerful impact of political activity that is grounded on theological premises. The fact that recent polling data show that two-thirds of the American public supports ES cell research even when it destroys embryos does not deter the opponents. Commentators have noted that the survey "reveals a public opinion landscape that bears little resemblance to the polarized, deep moral divide expressed on the floor of the Congress and in the op-ed pages of American newspapers."[13]

Litigation and the law are important components of this controversy. Although the main impetus for opposition to ES cell research comes from religious institutions and constituencies that believe it violates fundamental moral principles, much of the argument relies on traditional definitions and concepts supplied by existing law, namely, involving personhood and property. While the ethical issues involving ES cell research can be addressed on a variety of levels, the current controversy mixes the religious with the legal and the scientific. As a result, the ES cell research debate raises First Amendment-related issues about the role of religion in public life. The role of law and, specifically of litigation, in this field is different from the ones previously discussed. Three areas of litigation are involved. First is the litigation involving the state-authorized ES cell research grants. The lawsuits here do not confront the religious and moral issues, but, rather, challenge the legislation on technical grounds. Second is the area of traditional case law concerning personhood and property, which is an integral part of the religious and moral issues. Much of the discourse is framed, whether intentionally or not, in recognizable legal terms. Pervading the discourse is the third area, the body of First Amendment case law which, although not specifically raised in the public controversy over ES cell research, is part of the context of the debates. What is, or should be, the role of religious institutions and principles in the shaping of social and scientific public policy?

The issue of stem cells goes to the very core of human life so it is bound to touch the religious conscience and invoke fundamental moral beliefs. In terms of secular public policy, however, it is a medical science issue with social and ethical significance, not to mention economic and political implications as well. Due to these concerns, religion and morality invade the debate. Although one group of religious and moral belief systems is pitted against another group, the religious points of view tend to be reframed in legal terms, such as personhood or property, when discussed in the public policy debate. The legal classifications are not the real concerns though. What is at stake for many of the interested participants is whether the research does or does not violate religious and moral beliefs.

There is nothing wrong with religious groups addressing political issues or advocating political points of view. Those activities constitute protected speech and do not violate the First Amendment. The tension between religion and government clearly has deep roots in American history. In the late eighteenth century, many prominent figures supported the idea of state establishment of religion. While the issue of religious involvement in government has always been a concern, one that led to the drafting of the First Amendment, it became a heightened concern in the latter part of the last century when more church–state entanglement began to be promoted in the political arena.[14] Religion and the state are not separated by a wall, despite the popularity of that common metaphor. The boundaries between them are specified with particularity in the language of the First Amendment. There are two ways in which religion can be improperly entangled with the state. They are well known and defined although some cases have contributed to blurring the issues. The first way is that the state is prohibited from establishing a state religion, that is, from officially preferring one religion over another. The second way religion is improperly entangled is when the state impedes the free exercise of religion by individual citizens.

Although the meaning of that language seems remarkably clear, it has led to equally remarkable confusion, perhaps due to the high emotions that accompany First Amendment debate. Although the "wall of separation" is a metaphor probably coined first by Roger Williams,[15] Thomas Jefferson used the phrase "a wall of separation between church and state" in a letter written in 1802.[16] The U.S. Supreme Court later used language of "separation of Church and State"[17] although that expression is not constitutional language and suggests a more distinct gap than the Constitution requires. The First Amendment was designed most likely to protect individual religions from the state.[18] The state was prohibited from restricting the free exercise of religion and from establishing one religion as the state religion thereby undermining and silencing others. The political climate seems to have changed in recent years. Some religious groups have secured political support for obtaining special grants from the government when they provide social services. These so-called *faith-based initiatives* are seen either as favorable developments or as threats to the separation of church and state, depending on the viewpoint.

In view of the blurring and obscuring of religious, moral, social, and legal ideas and distinctions, it is important to define carefully the legal questions in this field. A religious or moral claim masquerading as a legal argument or a political argument does nothing to resolve the issue or even to further the public debate. When arguments and scientific facts are misstated trouble erupts because the conversation becomes confusing and misleading. Public policy must be based on factual and legal accuracy in order for it to make sense.

The stem cell issue is being discussed in religious, political, and scientific terms as well as legal terms. Although there is disagreement in the science field, these issues will be resolved in time by research and scientific consensus. In politics, the debate is driven mostly by religious argument, which relies on legal terminology, that is, classifying stem cells as either persons or property. The correct answer seems to be found in neither category, or perhaps in both. As long as some participants in the debate hold inflexibly to the position that the earliest embryos are complete persons entitled to precisely the same status and respect as adult human beings, the real issues in science and medicine cannot be addressed openly. Absolutism in such matters stifles the discussion.

Political Solutions

There are no legal solutions for political questions, but there can be political solutions for religious and moral questions. Compromise is unlikely, but accommodation can be used if the parties are willing, even though they hold opposing positions on principle. By this method, circumventing the issues on which absolute positions are taken can allow for solutions. In a democracy, that is essential since opposing views on crucial issues are commonplace, especially in a pluralistic nation like the United States. To be full members of a democratic society requires thinking in terms of universal rather than religious-specific values.[19] Some form of accommodation of conflicting positions must take place in order to move forward on issues without resulting in a harsh conflict that can destroy the fabric of society.

The debate on ES cells can be confusing because it often occurs in legal and scientific language when it is really not about law or science but, about religion. When religious views pose as legal and scientific views, the resulting discussion becomes unproductive.

Legal Classifications

The reliance on concepts of person and property, traditional legal categories developed centuries ago, to resolve issues involving life forms recently discovered and never imagined at the time, is basically unsound. Recent cases have attempted to apply these traditional concepts to life forms or products. Issues involving ownership of human tissues and ownership of frozen embryos in divorce cases are examples of recent applications. Law can be a resource for public policy arguments but it restricts discussion of broader issues of social concern. Litigation can be used to distract public policy discussion and action as the California stem cell lawsuits demonstrate.

Stages of Human Life

Manipulating existing legal categories to fit new biological developments does not work well. A newly recognized stage of life that is a form or derivative of developing life does not necessarily fit existing legal categories. End-of-life issues give rise to similar problems concerning autonomy. In end-of-life situations, there is recognition that, at some point, the autonomy of the individual has diminished and surrogate decision-making is legitimate. One suggestion that has been made with respect to classifying prenatal forms of human life in addition to people who, for any reason, are not fully competent is to say that they are not entitled to identical autonomy or rights as fully capable adult humans. In other words, it may not make sense to attempt to create new categories of life but, instead, to assign different levels of autonomy according to a person's particular status. It appears realistic to say that there is not a single immutable human life form; rather, there are many different forms. Although no human life form should simply be deemed property, it can be argued that some forms may be accorded less autonomy and fewer rights when weighed against interests of other human entities. All may be persons but some have potential (increasing) capacity, some full capacity, and some are in stages of waning (diminishing) capacity. It is impossible, of course, to draw clear boundaries between life stages, since they are dynamic and changing, but distinctions are possible based on agreed factors.

The stem cell controversy is usually discussed in a variety of contexts, including political, legal, religious and moral, scientific and social. Each context has its own embedded values, which are often reflected in the language used. A major problem with the dialogue, as it is presently conducted, is the use of terms, categories, and assumptions that are not explicitly acknowledged. Before discussion can be meaningful, the values need to be sorted out to avoid confusion. Different types of facts, claims, and arguments need to be accurately identified if any kind of intelligent dialogue and understanding is to take place and if consensus or accommodation is to occur. Of course, if the purpose is to resist or undermine reaching consensus or accommodation, then blurring the lines and mixing arguments is an effective strategy.

In the field of reproductive research and technology, which covers issues such as cloning and stem cell research, as well as abortion, categorical arguments are commonly found. The opponents of stem cell research argue that destruction of embryonic stem cells is equivalent to murder of human beings. Classifying the arguments in categorical terms such as life versus death makes compromise, consensus, or accommodation impossible.

PUBLIC POLICY CONSIDERATIONS

No sensible reason exists to use categorical terms for selected issues and to ignore the implications of others. All critical choices, in bioethics and elsewhere, involve trade-offs of values and results. All bioethical choices produce benefits to some and detriment to others. It is not uncommon for these choices to involve life and death. In many political choices outside the field of bioethics, life and death can be at stake. Decisions to wage war, to use force in law enforcement, to make vehicles less or more safe, to extend or restrict health care services, and to enforce or ignore housing code violations are examples of situations in which life and death choices can be involved.

In the field of bioethics, the implications of critical issues are often patently obvious. Beginning and end-of-life issues as well as triaging, allocating medical resources, allocating health care services, allowing public health infrastructure to deteriorate or to flourish, and distributing organs involve life and death choices. All these choices involve life and death with respect to autonomous human beings. Decisions to destroy stem cells, on the other hand, concern embryos. No rational basis exists on which to classify one choice as "life and death" and ignore that aspect with regard to others. Decisions to restrict or to permit ES cell research will have potentially far-reaching consequences.

Whether public funds should be used for ES cell research is a political choice to be made by taking into account the scientific and medical benefit, the cost, and the benefits and harm to society. Issues of morality and ethics are relevant but should not be determinative. The issues should be dealt with on all appropriate levels by addressing political arguments, legal issues, moral and ethical concerns, and scientific data. Each area of concern is open to discussion and debate, but none should be approached so categorically that meaningful public discussion is precluded.

In public policy, a gap always exists between the public discussion and the political and economic realities that underlie the issues. Concerns of political power are involved in all political controversies. Democracy depends on open discussion of pertinent facts and concerns and decisions based on policies that do not disguise improper interests.

Public policy, which constitutes law in one form or another, relies on various methods of resolution and accommodation including so-called bright line rules and balancing tests. Both can be useful depending on circumstances and both are used by legislature and courts. A purpose of both is to resolve controversies and disputes and bring about practical solutions to ongoing problems. Categorical thinking interferes with this process. That is not to say that principles are not relevant. Although principles guide the process, they are sometimes in conflict and their application is challenged by new fact situations.

LAW AND LITIGATION

Law and litigation are often used as tools in the political process. Litigation can be time-consuming, expensive, and inconclusive in resolving political issues. Litigation is also extremely costly in terms of doing permanent damage to relationships. Litigation, once undertaken as a method of political pressure, can become a problem in itself as it drains resources and further polarizes political adversaries. If the process of political accommodation is used openly and honestly, it can produce positive results. Once litigation produces a specific result in terms of the legal framework of a lawsuit, larger questions often remain. At that point, the parties may have suffered irretrievable losses, making the ultimate political solution less satisfactory than it would have been had it been negotiated sooner.

With that background and having identified the major ethical issues in connection with ES cell research, we proceed to examine how law and, in particular, litigation has been used to address the issues. How exactly has litigation affected the struggle over ethical, moral, and political issues concerning stem cell research? The answer is threefold.

First, the legal status of embryos has been resolved on the federal level, at least for the time being, by the U.S. Supreme Court in *Roe v. Wade*[20] and later reproductive cases and also on the state level by cases on a variety of related topics. With few exceptions, courts have ruled that embryos are not persons, even though various legal protections may be extended. The U.S. Supreme Court ruled in *Roe* that "the word 'person' as used in the Fourteenth Amendment does not include the unborn."[21] Second, several major cases in the states have decided issues concerning property rights in and to parts of the human body, including tissues, cells, and cadavers.[22] Although these cases have not ruled directly on ownership of embryos, they have some bearing on the issue because courts have ruled on who is authorized to use or dispose of frozen embryos. Third, specific state laws authorizing funding for research, notably in California, have been challenged on many grounds aside from the core ethical or moral issues. The California funding controversy illustrates the problems and pitfalls that can happen when a hotly contested issue emerges in the political process.

As we noted earlier, religious groups have played major roles in the political and legal controversies over stem cells. Religious groups have been as prominent in the public discussion of stem cell research as they have in other beginning and end-of-life issues. Although there has been no outright First Amendment litigation concerning the role of religious groups in this process, the case law dealing with the interaction between church and state is part of the context.

I have pointed out that much of the public discourse has been carried on with legal terminology and concepts. For example, much of the discussion of the status of embryos revolves around whether they are person or property. It is clear that the participants have borrowed from legal and popular legal culture. The problem with adopting a polarized way of looking at this subject is that it discourages accommodation, negotiation, and mediated solutions.

After explaining what has happened in these three areas of litigation, I will address the question of whether litigation has helped to resolve the ethical questions that lie at the heart of the stem cell controversy or whether it obstructs and impedes resolution. If litigation serves to distract attention from the main issues, how does it operate to prevent ethical resolution? I will apply the factors outlined in Chapter 2 to evaluate law's impact on this critical area. We will find that, in some respects, law has been used as one method affecting the outcome of the controversy but it has not generally been used to address the main ethical issues that must be resolved if our society is to move forward with a practical resolution.

In the case law interpreting the First Amendment, courts, notably the U.S. Supreme Court, have attempted to define the role of religion in secular society to create a framework for religious intervention in political affairs of society. That is not to say that the pertinent Supreme Court cases have necessarily been consistent or clear, but at this point we have some idea of the place of religion and religious beliefs in the public life of our society. Can ethical discourse lead the way to social and political solutions that respect all points of view or are we destined to remain at an impasse, leaving the crucial research to states, to the private sector and to other countries?

State Action

Statutes concerning embryonic and fetal research vary from state to state.[23] Some states have passed legislation to forbid embryonic stem cell research while others have acted to permit or even encourage research.

Among those permitting research are California, Connecticut, Illinois, Maryland, Massachusetts, New Jersey, and Ohio, all of which have authorized funding on some basis in order to initiate stem cell research. Virginia and Washington have taken the first steps toward the project but have not provided funding yet. On the other hand, South Dakota prohibits all research on embryos while other states, such as Arkansas, Indiana, Louisiana, Iowa, Michigan, and North Dakota, prohibit research on cloned embryos. Many other variations exist among the states.[24] I will begin with a brief survey of the political process and the lawsuits that have been brought to challenge state-funded research.

California

The events and lawsuits in California present a unique opportunity to study the political and legal systems in action. Funding for stem cell research was authorized, not by legislative action, but by virtue of a state constitutional amendment embodied in Proposition 71, an initiative that was approved by 59 percent of the voters. Proposition 71 created the CIRM (California Institute for Regenerative Medicine) and authorized bonds that would provide $3 billion in funding for stem cell research. The opponents of the measure, having failed to defeat it at the polls, brought lawsuits challenging it on various grounds, including state constitutional grounds. The legal actions included claims that the stem cell research institute was not a legitimate state agency and that its managers had conflicts of interest. One action challenged the plan on policy grounds, asserting that Proposition 71 did not provide enough oversight of disbursing the research money. The California constitution requires the state to exercise "exclusive management and control" over state agencies, and the initiative did create an unusual state agency in CIRM. The courts, however, have ruled in the past that the state constitution does not forbid unusual structures so long as they maintain the requisite control.[25] The groups challenging the program in court also claimed that because Proposition 71 authorized financing for both stem cell work and other kinds of medical research, it violated state laws against proposing two subjects on a single ballot measure. In early 2006, the state prevailed in the California state trial court in two of the actions, which had been consolidated for trial and the matters were appealed.[26]

In February, 2007, the First District Court of Appeal in San Francisco affirmed the trial court, ruling that Proposition 71, the stem cell initiative approved by voters on November 2, 2004, does not violate the California constitution.[27] The Court of Appeal noted that "our review of the various constitutional and other objections appellants have addressed to the stem cell initiative involves no normative evaluation of the merit of the measure. Nonetheless, the objective of the proposition is to find, 'as speedily as possible,' therapies for the treatment and cure of major diseases and injuries, an aim the legitimacy of which no one disputes. The very pendency of this litigation, however, has interfered with implementation for more than two years. After careful consideration of all of appellants' legal objections, we have no hesitation in concluding, in the exercise of 'our solemn duty to jealously guard the precious initiative power' that Proposition 71 suffers from no constitutional or other legal infirmity. Accordingly, we shall affirm the well-reasoned decision of the trial court upholding the validity of the initiative."[28] The California Supreme Court announced in May, 2007 that it declined to review the decision of the Court of Appeal.

In another California lawsuit, this one brought in the federal court, the plaintiffs sought a ruling that embryos outside the body are full citizens of the United States with all the rights that children have.[29] If that lawsuit were to be successful, IVF and other reproductive technologies could be rendered unlawful as a result. The implications for the thousands of frozen embryos would be enormous. What responsibilities would exist to protect and nurture those embryos? A federal judge in Los Angeles dismissed the action in late 2005, but the action may be filed in other federal courts in the state.[30]

Because of the lawsuit regarding CIRM, the institute was unable to sell securities on the bond market to raise the $3 billion it was authorized to borrow. The agency, however, financed its first set of research grants when six philanthropic organizations lent it $14 million to be repaid from bond issues, once they are allowed. Although Governor Arnold Schwarzenegger ordered the state Department of Finance to lend the program $150 million, taxpayer and religious groups sued to prevent the loan from being made. The state Supreme Court refused to take jurisdiction over the bond challenges, leaving the matter for the trial court. The CIRM later received, in November 2006, a $181 million loan from the state general fund. The stem cell finance committee also approved the sale of $31 million in bond anticipation notes to philanthropic organizations. Although the combined loan and sale allowed the funding of research to go forward, the bridge funding had risk for the lenders and buyers. Neither the state nor the private groups would be repaid if the California appellate courts were to rule against the CIRM.[31]

The California proposal and ensuing controversies provided insight into the workings of direct democracy (the initiative), the legislative process (the legislative process was bypassed by the ballot initiative), executive action (the governor obtaining initial temporary funding from public and private sources by various methods), as well as various state and federal court rulings on a wide variety of legal challenges. Interestingly, the initiative succeeded through an exercise of direct democracy but was delayed because of the legal challenges posed by various interest groups.

Ethical and Political Questions in California and Other States

For the most part, the lawsuits attacked the California initiative on procedural or structural issues rather than substantive issues involving the ethical legitimacy of stem cell research. The federal action, of course, did go to the core of the issue in its legal challenge.

The central issue, however, remains to be addressed along with many questions concerning how states should go about implementing ES cell research. How much transparency and oversight is appropriate for state-funded research? What intellectual property and commercialization policies should be in place? How should women who donate oocytes for research be protected? The bioethics community has been so focused on debating the moral status of embryos that issues pertaining to the actual carrying out of stem cell research have not been directly resolved.[32] It is clear from existing standards, such as the *National Academies of Science Guidelines for Human Embryonic Stem Cell Research*,[33] that donor consent is a necessity and that clinical trials must be supervised and controlled by institutional review boards. The Academies' guidelines prohibit paying for either embryos or oocytes.

Two safeguards appear to be in place with the California initiative. The CIRM funds are overseen by the IOCC (Independent Citizens Oversight Committee), which is composed of people appointed by elected officials and by state university representatives. This structure would appear to allow control of conflicts of interest and commitment by virtue of its composition, which balances the roles of the different stakeholders.[34] In addition, the public and the legislature have roles in the process of setting priorities.

The development of policies to protect intellectual property and to ensure a financial return on the investment by California taxpayers is another crucial issue. Private and public interests will have to be taken into account. Proposition 71 calls for the committee to balance the state's need for a return on investment with the public's interest in developing medical treatments as efficiently as possible. The issue concerning how to protect potential donors of oocytes for research remains a controversial one especially in view of prominent cases where ethical abuses have occurred.[35] Donation by people directly involved in the research process must be prohibited and adequate screening must be provided for.

The political and economic aspects of implementing state-funded stem cell research have been the subject of scholarly attention.[36] While the federal government has long been in the business of managing grants for scientific and medical research, states are new to this area. Major issues come into play. There are difficulties associated with using government grants, loans, and contracts to promote development research. Organizational challenges in creating a merit-based method of providing financial support within the constraints of a government agency pose another problem. As noted, the assignment of intellectual property rights presents another challenge. Lurking in the background are the uncertainties of federal policy and politics. Much of the planning has been done with Proposition 71, but these additional ethical, economic, and political problems remain to be addressed if and when all legal challenges are resolved in favor of the CIRM.

We will return to analyze the impact of the California litigation on the ethical and political processes after examining the impact of traditional legal discourse in the public policy discussion and debate about stem cell research.

Traditional Lawsuits Involving the Status of Embryos and Human Tissues

Public policy decision-making is a process. No decision should be fixed for all time as though the factual and situational context does not change. Even legal and constitutional decision-making must be viewed in that way. Principles should be consistent but the application should be different, recognizing change. This is essential in a democratic society where technological, economic, and social changes can happen rapidly.

Although ethical decision-making can adapt to change most efficiently because it is not bound by formal limitations, legislative action has the potential to adapt effectively as well. Legal and constitutional changes are far more cumbersome because they cannot be self-initiated and because they are bound by strict procedural limitations.

Ethical decision-making does not involve preemption of positions but, instead, a process of reasoned and pragmatic negotiation or mediation based on articulated principles until a particular result is reached. The result is usually a temporary decision, and the matter must remain open for future developments. Ethical decision-making is a continuing process. As the situation evolves, the decisions must change. For example, in an end-of-life situation, decisions are made based on current status and subject to medical changes in the patient. Medical intervention may be based on one assessment and then withdrawn, based on changes.

Legislative public policymaking should be based upon public opinion as well as current information. It should involve drawing broad guidelines that enable local action and individual decision-making. Public hearings and legislative fact-finding should accompany and provide context for decisions. Statements of legislative purpose should ordinarily explain the objectives. Legislative decisions should be based on common ethical standards.

Legal decision-making is the most formalistic and least flexible. Courts decide only what must be decided for the case at hand and properly restrain from reaching out to other issues by calling on a variety of procedural devices. Judges should not initiate their own agendas. Courts should avoid trumping issues by constitutional pronouncements unless necessary. Constitutional decision-making, although necessary at times to protect rights, is inflexible, categorical, and infringes on public policy decision-making by legislatures.

Public Policy Debate

The subject of public policy debate leads me to a central question in the stem cell controversy—the unnatural focus on defining the embryo as a way of excluding policy positions and trumping the debate. The public policy discussion of stem cells has become legalistic rather than ethical. The true issue is how to weigh and accommodate two legitimate interests in the least offensive way. On one side is the public interest in encouraging scientific and medical development to alleviate suffering and extend or save lives. That involves respecting and improving quality of life. On the other side is the public interest in respecting all life, especially human life, with reference to very early stages of human life in this situation. This conflict is not limited to the stem cell controversy but is involved in many decisions about vital factors in human life such as availability of education, shelter, food, health care, liberty of all sorts, discrimination, etc. In all cases, people strive to accommodate competing values with limited resources.

As we noted earlier, the current public policy debate focuses on the identity and nature of the human embryo. This definitional question has become a central, perhaps *the* central, question in the stem cell controversy as it has been discussed in the public square (in academic literature as well as the popular media, print, and visual). While it is important to keep up with scientific information that explains the unfolding story of the biology of each stage of human development, precise definitions are evolving, elusive, and not conclusive.

The legal decisions do not apply directly to the ethical discussions for a variety of reasons. They arise in very different contexts, involve a limited number of participants, and were litigated for the purpose of resolving specific controversies. Beyond that, the legal approach is not appropriate for the public policy discussions. In the ethical context, participants should be focusing on an entirely different issue—how to balance and weigh the competing legitimate interests in preserving and respecting life as it exists at early stages of human development and prolonging and improving the quality of life of children and adult persons. The debate, however, is stuck at a preliminary point of contention, one that, even if answered, will not resolve the core ethical question. The point is that legalistic thinking too often dominates the public discourse. Although jurisprudence has addressed the question of embryo status, the definitional question has reemerged in the political and social debate as an open question. Court decisions have not accomplished a resolution of the crucial issues for public policy purposes.

Language is very important in legal matters and, in fact, the choice of language often determines the outcome of a case. Courts spend much of their time interpreting and applying the language of constitutions, statutes, and precedent as they decide cases before them. Courts generally do not create new language to describe issues in cases to be decided; instead, they decide how new issues can be resolved with reference to already existing language. Existing language has the advantage of prior court definition and interpretation. New language would involve writing on a clean slate and creating or finding meaning for the new language. Public policy debate and discussion are not so inhibited. No valid reason exists for confining public policy discussion to existing legal language. Nowhere is this more important than in areas of law directly affected by the revolutionary change in technology, such as in the reproductive field. Changes in technology have had a great impact on family law issues as well as privacy issues. Most cases that have dealt with defining embryo status have arisen in the family law or privacy areas. For example, technology has changed the very meaning of motherhood and fatherhood. The science in this field has also proven capable of identifying the complex process of prenatal human development, thereby distinguishing between the changing stages of preembryo, embryo, and fetal development, to mention a few, even while recognizing that the stages are not actually separable but rather part of an ongoing process.[37]

From a legal viewpoint, the current stem cell controversy (in public policy forums) seems to focus on the question of whether sperm–fertilized eggs, either left over from IVF or created for research by sperm and egg donors, should be available legally for approved privately or publicly funded research.[38] In the policy debate, the answer to this question is said to turn on how the embryo (or preembryo) is defined or characterized, that is, basically whether it is a *person* or not for purposes of the law.[39] No court has ruled directly on this question, but many courts have ruled on the personhood status of unborn humans. As discussed earlier, the 1973 decision of the U.S. Supreme Court in *Roe v. Wade* held that fetuses were not considered persons for purposes of the Fourteenth Amendment.[40] More than thirty years after *Roe v. Wade*, the debate continues and American society is no closer to a state of equilibrium on the subject of that case.

Preembryo Status

A series of court decisions, starting in the 1980s, have addressed the status of preembryos. The lawsuits in question fell into two main categories. The first involved disputes between medical professionals and couples whose preembryos they controlled.[41] Those cases did not give personhood status to preembryos. The second and larger group of cases arose when divorcing couples contested the control of unused frozen preembryos they had created for reproductive purposes. The issues revolved around whether and under what circumstances the preembryos could be used, donated, or destroyed. The first case involving a divorced couple, *Davis v. Davis*, was decided in 1992 by the Tennessee Supreme Court.[42] The *Davis* court ruled that "preembryos" were neither persons nor property but were entitled to "special respect" because they had the potential to become persons. The court also decided that preembryos implicated constitutional rights of procreation and nonprocreation for the couple and that, absent a prior agreement between the couple, the constitutional right of the one who sought to avoid procreation had priority over the one who wished to use the preembryos.[43]

After *Davis,* appellate courts in Alabama, Florida, Iowa, Massachusetts, New Jersey, New York, and Washington have ruled on similar issues involving frozen preembryos.[44] Although those courts have used a variety of terms to describe preembryos and have not mentioned the same level of "special respect" as potential persons, they have acknowledged that preembryos are special and distinctive entities. The courts have generally enforced prior agreements that did not involve procreation but have refused to order "forced procreation."[45] That is, even when spouses initially agreed to allow one spouse to use the preembryos after a divorce, a later decision not to permit use has been given priority.[46] In the decisions since *Davis,* the courts have tended to treat preembryos more like property of the disputing spouses than as potential persons, which has encouraged supporters of stem cell research.[47] The decisions have clearly not had much impact on the issue in a public policy context. Public policy discussion remains stuck on the definitional level. A great deal of scholarship in the field is devoted to discussing scientific terminology[48] as well as the pejorative use of language in the public policy debate. Beyond argument over the choice of language to describe the unborn human, knowledge of which is continually increasing, argument exists over whether the language chosen elevates or devalues the moral status of the preembryos.[49]

It is difficult to understand how language chosen to distinguish between recognized biological states of development can be considered to devalue the preembryo. While the language used to describe an unborn human at various points in the developmental process is important, it does not go to the crucial ethical issue. Regardless of what terminology is used, it is unmistakable that the preembryo is a living entity with the potential to be born but it has not joined the ranks of born human beings. On the other hand, the world is full of born human beings who face suffering and premature death from diseases for which there is no effective treatment or cure.

Although I will not go into detail about the related issue of the property interest in human tissue, I should note that several prominent cases have addressed the issue of the status of the living human body or its parts. *Moore v. Regents*[50] is the classic foundational case that appears in all bioethics textbooks. Moore was the seminal case determining what interest a patient had in profits from patents on a cell line that was produced by his own tissue. The Supreme Court of California declined to find an interest and denied his cause of action for conversion, a civil action asserting the wrongful taking of the property of another.[51] Twenty years after that leading California case, U.S. jurisprudence has reached no coherent consensus on the deceptively simple question: Do we own our own bodies?[52] This area of legal inquiry has increasing importance as genetic information acquired from human tissue is used in research and is shared more and more widely. It clearly has a bearing on issues involving research on preembryos. In addition, although end-of-life cases also address aspects of the nature of human autonomy and personhood status, I will exclude these for the moment, since they will be the subject of the next chapter.

Religious Involvement in Political Issues

The stem cell political debate serves to emphasize the powerful influence of religious institutions and doctrines on critical public policy issues. They appear, almost uniformly, as voices of caution about experimenting with the human body or limiting the autonomy of human life in any form, including embryos, fetuses, and adult humans in every stage of life. Although the voice of religion was commonly heard in political discourse and debate throughout American history, the tension between religion and politics has recently become a source of heightened controversy.[53] As we noted previously, critics of religious participation in public life often raise First Amendment objections, asserting the importance of a "wall of separation" between religion and the state.

Religious views, as we have noted, are not barred from public expression on matters awaiting decision by political institutions. It is well established that the First Amendment was adopted to protect religion and religious expression from state control rather than to protect the state from religion. In recent years, however, a concern has been that the establishment clause may have been violated by promoting religious roles in all kinds of social services. It is noteworthy that religious groups, whether knowingly or not, have adopted legalistic tactics in the debates. By using definitional arguments, they seek to control the ethical issues by claiming that views opposing theirs on ethical questions are not legitimate. The legislative approach seeks to circumvent the ethical arguments that relate to efforts to balance embryo preservation with pursuit of disease treatments for children and adult human beings.

ANALYZING LAW'S IMPACT

The Idiom of the Law (Language and Concepts)

In this case, some of the legal decisions that bear on the central ethical controversy predate the inception of the controversy. I refer to *Roe* and its progeny and the array of cases involving family conflicts over disposition of frozen preembryos. The California cases were brought on a variety of legal grounds to challenge Proposition 71. Those cases did not attempt to reframe the ethical debate but merely to defeat the result of the initiative. Proposition 71 acted on a public consensus in favor of proceeding with stem cell research. The legal actions sought to stop that popular democratic action based on legal flaws in the process. Although the initiative and the actions arise from the ethical controversy, they did not address it head-on. Obviously, the lawsuits were framed exclusively in legal language and concepts. If successful, they would block the result of the initiative but would not preclude other similar efforts. At least with popular democratic and legislative action, no interest group is precluded from participating in the ongoing process. As public opinion changes, new action is possible.

That is not so easily the case with court decisions. In litigation, the specific controversy is settled by a final judgment although legislative or popular action can take place in the future. In the meantime, the actions remove the decision making from the democratic process (the initiative trumped the legislative process at the outset) to the judicial process.

In the case of the controversy on personhood or property status of preembryos, legal decisions, methods, and culture have been imported into the public policy debate, but they have not served it well. The translation of ethical issues into legal concepts and language has taken place in order to affect the outcome of the controversy. The pertinent cases have resolved particular controversies over cryopreserved (or frozen) preembryos among divorcing spouses and, in the abortion cases, among individuals and public authorities concerning privacy rights of the individuals. Court decisions involving frozen preembryos have no effect, other than persuasive, beyond the particular controversies they resolve. The U.S. Supreme Court's decisions in the abortion cases obviously set public policy throughout the country at least until further state or federal legislative action, which has already occurred.[54]

Court decisions address specific controversies and resolve those controversies based on existing law. Typically, there is no room for creation of new law, new legal standards, or new ethical standards for the underlying issues. The U.S. Supreme Court, of course, has more freedom in this regard than other courts since its decisions are not subject to judicial review. Congress may, however, effectively overrule the Court's decisions by legislative action circumventing the rulings.

In the case of ES cell research, new definitions, categories, and ethical standards are clearly needed. As progress is made in developing therapies from stem cells[55] and new discoveries are made about the process of human development, old categories are no longer adequate. New ways of approaching the issues cannot be created in the course of judicial decision-making but must come from ethical or policy decision-making carried out through legislative (or popular democratic) action, such as initiatives. The previous judicial decisions on reproductive freedom have generated rules and principles that apply to unborn children. This is contextually very different from the situation of preembryos created in laboratories through IVF or for research purposes. The frozen embryo cases determined preembryo status for the purposes of particular lawsuits. It was logical for courts to determine that one spouse or the other had priority of choice regardless of the status of the preembryo. None of the courts determined that all the frozen embryos were persons, requiring the appointment of guardians, and entitled to full autonomy. Legislative action by states is possible along those lines in the future.[56]

It seems desirable in the long run to develop public policy to balance the relevant considerations, which should include the medical benefits of stem cell research, the sanctity of potential human life of whatever stage in the process, and the need to respect female reproductive autonomy.[57] Since life is a continuum that exists from conception to death, it seems unrealistic to take either extreme view on the subject of embryos, that is, designating them as either an entity of biological property or, on the other hand, a complete person of equal status with a fully adult human. Rather, according special respect to embryos while allowing them to be considered in some interim category that includes the vital factors described above could be workable. There is precedent for interim conceptual categories of quasi-property status for in vitro preembryos such as those used to classify a stillborn fetus. Special categories need not remain static through the early stages of development but could shift according to defined developmental criteria. There are alternatives but they cannot be easily created within the context of specific lawsuits.

The Adversarial Process

The previous discussion applies here. Courts are ill-equipped to initiate new concepts or standards because the cases before them are framed by the parties. Courts are limited for the most part by what the parties have pleaded and produced in evidence. With some seldom used exceptions, courts cannot reach out to generate new issues or summon witnesses or produce evidence. The function of courts is to adjudicate the disputes brought before them on the terms in which the parties have presented them. Courts have an obligation not to decide issues that are unnecessary to the litigation before them. The public has a right to expect the courts to practice self-restraint in taking on issues and in exercising coercive powers over the parties.

Closure, Finality, and the Retrospective View

Virtually all court cases involve controversies that have already occurred with a result that at least one party disputes. The evidence serves the purpose of establishing what happened and what relief should be given to whom. Courts must reach a decision based on applicable burdens of proof and evidence rules. Judicial restraint does not lend itself to establish a comprehensive public policy since there is little chance that the parties seek anything other than a favorable decision in their particular case. Only parties who have legally defined stakes in the outcome will be joined in the lawsuit, thus precluding relevant information that would be vital for purposes of establishing a broad public policy. While the decision itself will become public policy in a sense, it will be factually limited to the dispute at hand and limited by the evidence. Courts speak retrospectively—not prospectively. Evidence does not relate to all the economic, social, and political implications of the decision as would be needed for establishment of legitimate public policy. Results do not center on ethical principles, but rather on legal principles. Courts do not necessarily attempt to guide other parties with similar disputes. Decisions may do that by their very nature as precedent but that will be incidental to the process except in the case of appellate courts, whose duty it is to take future applications into account so far as possible within the confines of the case at hand.

Institutional Biases, Assumptions, and Deficiencies

Some traditional institutional biases of courts will impact the litigation in this area. The California CIRM cases mainly focused on practical and economic aspects of the project authorized by Proposition 71. Economic implications flow from the conflict of interest claims and from the supervisory authority claims. The claims are well suited for courts, although they do not raise the underlying ethical and moral issues that presumably drive the litigation that impeded the move toward ES cell research. Economic, political, and constitutional claims fit well with what courts do best. These cases do not raise any wide-ranging ethical issues that would give difficulty to courts.

Roe v. Wade and the continuing line of cases that it engendered focus on weighing conflicting rights of privacy and self-determination. The cases reach as broadly into social and political issues as any line of cases has done. The Supreme Court was strongly inclined to give deference to the reproductive rights of women but, increasingly, the states' authority to regulate has been expanded. The court has probably been influenced by awareness of the practical economic and social realities that would result from compelling young women to bear children, and raise them or pay the consequences, against their wishes.

A similar inclination can be seen in the cases of divorcing couples. Compelling people to be parents against their will has been seen as a greater evil than disposing of unused preembryos. Whether courts will continue to endorse this practical point of view remains to be seen as the political challenges to preembryo use and destruction grow at the same time as an increasing percentage of the population supports ES cell research.

Impact on Future Controversies

Court decisions in this and related fields will continue to have impact as they are marshaled on one side or another in the political and social debates. Hopefully, at some point the issues will be directly engaged allowing for a full consideration of the legitimate concerns of medical research to save lives, respect for reproductive rights of parties, and respect for entities that have full life potential. Only when our society grapples with the difficult questions that are inevitably at stake can a credible public policy be developed. In the meantime, private and foreign researchers, along with those who secure state funding, will carry the day. When the legally based categorical arguments subside in favor of debate over the central ethical issues, our society can move forward to discuss all the other pertinent ethical questions that need resolution. They include questions involving donors, research standards, funding guidelines and restrictions, development of cell lines, development and approval of new drugs and therapies, assignment of intellectual property interests in the results and, equally important, fair allocation of the medical benefits derived from the research to all those who need them.

This ethical issue is subject to drastic change as new developments come along. It is not beyond question that many of the ethical problems can be answered by new procedures by which stem cells can be derived without destroying the preembryos or discoveries that stem cells can be obtained from other materials, such as amniotic fluid.[58] New developments may not answer all the objections, since there will be some who still object to research on human life forms, but it may answer the major concerns of the majority of those who object. It remains to be seen whether courts ultimately will be brought into controversies that raise constitutional issues arising from the central ethical issues. When that happens, courts will be faced with establishing boundaries for public policy decision-making as well as resolving the substantive questions presented by the litigation.

Chapter 7

Boundaries at the End of Life— The Strange Case of Terri Schiavo

Terri (Schindler) Schiavo grew up in a suburb of Philadelphia and was an overweight and shy teenager throughout her high school years. At one point Terri weighed as much as 250 pounds, but she eventually lost 100 pounds by strict dieting. A few months later, in 1983, while attending community college, she had her first date with Michael Schiavo. After five months, they became engaged. They married in 1984 and spent their honeymoon in Florida at Disney World. After living with Terri's parents for several months in the Schindlers' condo in Florida, they took over the condo and eventually moved to their own apartment. In 1988, Terri and Michael tried to have a baby, but Terri had trouble becoming pregnant. She saw an obstetrician for fertility treatments. Friends and family observed that Terri was very thin, about 110 pounds. In retrospect, they speculated that she may have suffered from anorexia nervosa. Michael's brother noticed that her skin seemed "to hang off her like sheets."[1] Friends also noted that Michael was very controlling, that Terri and Michael fought, and that Terri had thought about seeking a divorce.[2] On February 25, 1990, at the age of twenty-six, Terri had a heart attack and fell unconscious in her apartment. Her husband called the paramedics, but she was without oxygen until help arrived and never regained consciousness.[3]

Observers who have sought meaning in the litigation involving Terri Schiavo have described it as a "private tragedy, public danger,"[4] "an important medical, legal, and ethical controversy,"[5] a dispute about when personhood ends,[6] and a political conflict between privacy and the right to life.[7] One critic suggested that it resembled *The Truman Show,* a movie in which a man's daily life was watched, unknown to him, by millions of viewers, except that the Schiavo saga was complicated by clinical and legal misinformation, as well as being fueled by a voyeuristic media, political opportunism, and vitriol.[8] Many saw it as a classic *end of life case,* a successor to the foundational cases such as *Quinlan* and *Cruzan.*[9] Others saw it as a typical legal hard case involving the "politics of righteousness"[10] or a paradigm case in the ongoing constitutional controversy over separation of powers.[11] Others, who could not resist using apocalyptic language, saw it as the end of autonomy, the failure of litigation, or as the ultimate struggle between personal dignity and decision-making authority and the unwarranted taking of a person's life.

Many commentators have sought to determine the meaning of the case. For some, the case arose because of the failure of ethical decision-making by the family and the medical profession. For others, it illustrated the failure of the courts in end-of-life decision-making. Still others saw it as a failed experiment of our political and public policy system, in which rational decision-making was overwhelmed by vitriolic special interest groups. Hardly anyone saw it as any kind of success. While many sought to strip away the layers of controversy to find hidden meanings, few were able to articulate the core meanings of the long controversy. The fact is that all the above characterizations are partially true and all the lessons drawn are partially valid. The Schiavo controversy does speak about end of life, litigation, separation of powers, politics, public policy, religion, and culture as well as the results of medical technology. None of those concepts, however, capture the essence of the case nor do they explain why Terri Schiavo became the unwitting proxy for so many special interests.

The long-standing Schiavo controversy had elements of a classic morality play, American-style, involving the traditional clash between good and evil. Whether Michael Schiavo was hero, vindicating his tragically-ill wife's privacy, or villain, seeking to end her life prematurely to secure his own freedom with her money, depended on one's point of view. Whether the Schindlers, on the other hand, were the forces of good, seeking to protect their daughter from her husband's manipulations, or selfishly trying to keep alive for their own purposes a daughter who had no desire to remain on life support, depended on one's belief system. As one commentator, Bruce Jennings, pointed out, facts were of little significance to those who sought to use the Schiavo events for their own purposes.[12] The Schiavo drama had all the elements necessary to capture the imagination of special interests and had implications for a wide range of topics, especially for those already engaged in the abortion controversy. It involved literally a life-and-death confrontation between two opposing forces. As it gathered momentum in the courts and became a featured media story, it attracted the attention of groups and individuals who sought to exploit it for their own agendas. As politicians and interest groups joined forces on one side or the other, Terri became a symbol for a wide range of political and social agendas.

THE LEGAL BACKGROUND: QUINLAN AND CRUZAN

We must set the stage by reviewing the prior case law that forms the context for the *Schiavo* litigation, that is in particular, the *Quinlan* and *Cruzan* cases. Following that, I will outline a history of the relevant facts of the *Schiavo* case. We will then explore the forces at work in the *Schiavo* matter that combined to enable it to hold center stage in American culture for so many months.

A discussion of the *Quinlan* and *Cruzan* cases requires a word about the brain death standard that began to be used in 1968 as an operational standard in determining death. Prior to that time, physicians determined death only by noting cessation of breathing and heartbeat. With development of ventilators and other technology that could maintain and prolong those functions, a new standard was needed for cases in which a patient had a healthy heart but had suffered serious brain injury. The brain death criterion[13] was developed at Harvard Medical School in 1968 and has supplemented, but not replaced, earlier standards. Although variations of the brain death standard exist, they are not necessary for our purposes.

Karen Ann Quinlan

The New Jersey Supreme Court began to lay the foundation for end-of-life cases in 1975 and 1976 in the case of Karen Ann Quinlan.[14] Even though the *Quinlan* decision has been discussed extensively since its publication in 1976, it remains one of the foundational cases in the health care field and has continuing applicability to contemporary issues. It is a striking example of the intersection of medicine and law in a courtroom setting, and an illustration of why judicial resolutions of such tragic cases are unsatisfactory on a cultural basis.[15]

A brief synopsis of the facts of the *Quinlan* case may be useful. Karen Ann Quinlan was hospitalized in New Jersey in April 1975, at the age of twenty-one, when she was found in a coma of unknown origins. Her parents began legal proceedings five months later, after Karen's physicians refused their request to remove her from the ventilator that assisted her breathing. Her parents later appealed to the New Jersey Supreme Court after receiving an unfavorable decision from the trial court. The New Jersey Supreme Court granted relief to the plaintiff, Joseph Quinlan, Karen's father, who served as her guardian. The court determined that, with the concurrence of the guardian and family of Karen, if the guardian-selected physicians, in consultation with the hospital "Ethics Committee," should determine that "there is no reasonable possibility of Karen's ever emerging from her present comatose condition to a cognitive sapient state and that the life-support apparatus now being administered to Karen should be discontinued, then the present life-support system may be withdrawn without any civil or criminal liability" on the part of anyone.[16] The decision was widely interpreted to vindicate the patient's right of privacy, which now included the right to be withdrawn from the life-support machine.

It should be noted that, in addition to all pertinent medical personnel and institutions, (specifically Doctors Arshad Javed and Robert J. Morse, and St. Clare's Hospital, being parties to the case) the Roman Catholic Church, specifically the New Jersey Catholic Conference, was allowed to file an *amicus curiae* brief to present its views on the matter.[17] The opinion, in fact, is one of the rare cases in which the court actually discussed a religious view on the issue.

In addition to being a landmark case on the right-to-die issue, the *Quinlan* case has had an important historical role in a social sense. The controversy spurred the "right-to-die" movement, focused public attention and anxiety on the role of technology in human life, gave rise to legislative redefinitions of "death" throughout the country, and fostered the legal development of widespread use of "living wills" across the nation.[18]

An important feature of the case, however, is what it reveals about the restrictive judicial and legal treatment of this difficult issue. This is so despite the fact that the decision written by Chief Justice Hughes was remarkably broad and encompassing in terms of discussing the religious and social aspects of the problem. The decision is noteworthy for what it says about the issue of liability, which did not appear to be the central issue. The central issue, in fact, appears to rest on a misunderstanding of the medical practices germane to the case. This illustrates how tragic issues are distorted and misapprehended by courts, based on the peculiar legal practices that shape the controversies into issues that the court system is able to decide.

Although the decision purports to focus on the right of privacy of a patient (and her family representing her interest) to refuse to be maintained indefinitely in a comatose state, the case is really about the issue of legal responsibility of those who bear the duty of shutting down the life-supporting machinery. The role of this issue is referred to in the opinion as a "brooding presence."[19]

As to the issue of liability, the court stated,

[t]he modem proliferation of substantial malpractice litigation and the less frequent but even more unnerving possibility of criminal sanctions would seem, for it is beyond human nature to suppose otherwise, to have bearing on the practice and standards as they exist. The brooding presence of such possible liability, it was testified here, had no part in the decision of the treating physicians. As did [the trial judge], we afford this testimony full credence. But we cannot believe that the stated factor has not had a strong influence on the standards. . . .[20]

The court went on to specify that "[t]he termination of treatment pursuant to the right of privacy is, within the limitations of this case, *ipso facto* lawful. . . . [T]he exercise of a constitutional right such as we have here found is protected from criminal prosecution."[21]

Critics have pointed out that several circumstances made the potential liability in the *Quinlan* situation particularly acute. There was awareness on the part of the medical profession and the insurance industry of a growing "medical malpractice crisis."[22] An increasing number of lawsuits had driven up insurance costs, and the matter had been deemed a crisis.[23] Moreover, the *Quinlan* decision also involved potential criminal liability on the part of physicians. The exposure to criminal liability was heightened by the adoption, in 1968, of certain criteria for brain death. The standards were adopted in connection with the issues surrounding organs that could be transplanted and were, therefore, very narrow and strict. Karen Quinlan's situation did not fall within the brain death criteria, thus increasing the physicians' exposure to criminal liability.[24] In addition, a Boston physician, Kenneth Edelin, had been convicted of manslaughter in 1975 in connection with the death of an infant resulting from a late-term abortion.[25] Despite all this controversy, the issue of liability was understated in the case. The court, however, clearly understood the significance of the concern.

In retrospect, the *Quinlan* case has been cited as an example of the incapacity of courts to apprehend correctly the prevailing standards of medical practice. In the view of many commentators, the *Quinlan* decision was at least outwardly premised on a misconception of the realities of medical practice. The misconception, if there was one, was foisted on the courts by the profession itself out of fear of potential exposure of those practices under oath, "under the white light of litigation."[26] According to medical sources, it was common for physicians to remove respirators from patients in situations like that of Karen Quinlan's. Although that standard medical practice was well known within the profession, and even admitted to in remote journals or interviews, no physician was willing to testify to the practice in a court of law.[27] Thus, the courts were not capable of assessing the "realities of medical behavior"[28] and the "white light of litigation" created a false portrait of medical practice that was conveyed to the public by the press.[29]

The New Jersey Supreme Court rendered a comprehensive opinion, covering all bases, including commenting on religious views of the case.[30] The case was "considered by the Court only in the aspect of its impact upon the conscience, motivation, and purpose of the intending guardian, Joseph Quinlan, and not as a precedent in terms of the civil law."[31] The legal foundation on the right of privacy issue was established by *Eisenstadt v. Baird*,[32] *Stanley v. Georgia*,[33] and *Griswold v. Connecticut*.[34] The real impact of the New Jersey Supreme Court's decision, however, was to give control of the situation to the medical profession, which could withdraw the life-support system without civil or criminal liability.[35] As one commentator has noted:

> The great irony of the...litigation is that the lower court, although it explicitly stressed the importance of preserving a physician's autonomy, actually raised the possibility of narrowing that autonomy by confirming the potential for criminal liability; the higher court, although it explicitly stressed the importance of expanding a patient's right, actually expanded medical autonomy by freeing physicians from criminal liability.[36]

The practical result of the litigation bears witness to the empowering of the medical profession in the matter. The respirator was not removed until additional medical technology was employed to control Karen's maintenance. Eventually "weaned" from the respirator, she continued her existence for another nine years.[37]

The case exemplifies the hazards of court determination of complex bioethical issues involving the necessity of knowing the practices and policies of other professions. The restrictive nature of judicial decision-making not only encourages the conversion of issues into legal concepts and language, which is restrictive and distorting, but actually allows egregious and misleading representations as to facts and opinions, as occurred in *Quinlan*. Moreover, the *Quinlan* court either misunderstood the significance of the liability issue, which is unlikely, or having understood, purposely cast the decision in terms of privacy while knowing the real impact of the holding. Either way, the public is not served by discussion and resolution of vital issues based on incomplete or erroneous facts and opinions, and apparent holdings that vary from the actual import of the decision. Decisions so reasoned and decided, when principles and practice are not in accord, speak of excessive resort to politics, rather than reliance on principle. Although there is no bright line that creates an absolute distinction between political and principled decision-making, it is fair to say that the legislature is the proper place for political decision-making. Decisions involving the application of principles that are not relevant to the practical realities of the case run the risk of being viewed as politically motivated, arbitrary, or biased and, thus, lacking in legitimacy. The sins of judicial decision-making, bias, partisanship, and arbitrariness deprive the court of moral authority.

We can see that a public policy decision was made by the court to leave the choice ostensibly to the patient but, in reality, to the physicians. The issue was identified as a right of privacy issue, which was a misleading characterization. All legitimate interests participated, including the Church. Because the result appeared to be sensible public policy, perhaps that supports the view that the court was politically sophisticated. Whether it was sound legal decision-making is a different question. The weighing of the common good versus individual rights was carefully explained. In the whole scheme of things, however, that seemed to be part of the fictional camouflage. The analysis was sound and comprehensive as to the privacy issue, but in some respects, was also a diversion from the real issue of significance. The decision brought closure to the issue and, in that sense, it was a considerable political accomplishment. The case was decided in the governmental sphere, but the ultimate decisions were left to be made privately.

Nancy Cruzan

Fifteen years later, in 1990, the U.S. Supreme Court heard the case of Nancy Cruzan, a young Missouri woman who had been in a PVS condition for seven years. The case involved her parents' request for removal of her feeding tube. Prior to this decision, twenty states had recognized the right of competent patients to refuse medical life support, and all of those states except New York and Missouri had recognized the right of surrogates to make decisions for incompetent patients. The *Cruzan* decision was the first to recognize explicitly the rights of dying patients.

Nancy Cruzan, at age twenty-four, lost control of her car on the night of January 11, 1983, and was thrown thirty-five feet. The paramedics who arrived at the scene discovered that her heart had stopped. They successfully restarted her heart with a stimulant and a shock but, because her brain had been without oxygen for fifteen minutes, she was in a PVS.

While the *Quinlan* case revolved around the withdrawal of a ventilator, this case focused on withdrawal of a feeding tube. With a feeding tube, the natural deterioration of the body can be put on hold for decades. Whereas Karen Quinlan's parents did not seek to withdraw nutrition, Nancy Cruzan's parents sought court permission to disconnect the feeding tube. Nancy's care was paid by the state of Missouri. Hospital employees refused to honor their request without court approval. The probate court ruled in favor of the Cruzans, but the Missouri Supreme Court reversed the decision because the evidence did not meet the clear and convincing standard required by Missouri law. The court refused to read into the Missouri constitution a broad right to privacy. The state had an interest in preserving life regardless of the *quality of life.* The U.S. Supreme Court, which upheld the Missouri Supreme Court, specifically recognized the right of a competent patient to decline medical treatment even if doing so would lead directly to death. The court also determined that with drawing a feeding tube did not differ from withdrawing any other form of life-sustaining medical equipment.

Finally, the Court decided that a state could, but did not have to, pass a statute requiring clear and convincing evidence about what a formerly competent patient would have wanted done. Missouri's law was constitutional and the feeding tube could not be removed since the Missouri courts had determined that the standard had not been met. In Nancy's case, the parents and a sister testified as to what her wishes would have been. As a result of further proceedings based on new evidence that met the clear and convincing standard, the feeding tube was legally removed five months after the Supreme Court's decision. Nancy died upon removal of the tube. Although most legal scholars agreed with the decision, there was no agreement on what the result would have been under a *best interests of the patient* standard. Medical professionals, however, thought the decision produced an impractical and burdensome result.

During the span of years from *Quinlan* to *Cruzan,* many state statutes were passed and many appellate cases were decided, developing a body of law to govern end-of-life cases in the age of developing medical technology. Following the Quinlan case, medical professionals and hospital ethics committees contributed to the decisional reservoir as well. The basic elements of the ethical and legal framework, starting with *Quinlan* and encompassing all the work done during the fifteen-year period, have been said to include the following standards. Competent patients have constitutional and common law rights to refuse medical treatment, even if refusing it will result in death. Incompetent patients have the same rights although their rights are obviously exercised in different ways. The clinical setting is preferred for resolving issues. Surrogate decision makers should apply the following standards: subjective (patient's own living will or health care power of attorney); substituted judgment (doing what the patient would have wanted, if that can be established); and best interest (doing what is in the patient's best interest). No ethical difference exists between withdrawing and withholding life-sustaining medical treatment. Artificial hydration and nutrition are medical treatments for this purpose. The right to refuse does not depend on a patient's life expectancy or terminal illness. Pain medication is acceptable as palliative care even if it will hasten a patient's death. Active euthanasia and assisted suicide are legally and ethically different from withholding LST (life-sustaining treatment). The determination is patient-centered, thereby focusing on a patient's autonomy and self-determination, even if that is a fiction in the context of surrogate decision-making.[38]

TERRI SCHIAVO

To their credit, the judges in the lengthy Schiavo case refused to take the bait and be drawn off course by the battling parties. Other institutions of government did not act so admirably. Both state and federal executive branch officials, as well as state and federal legislators reached beyond their constitutional and legal authority in carrying out their political agendas. The clear consensus of medical experts was not sufficient to prevent the opponents and their allies from relying on medical absurdities to serve their political purposes. In the end, the battle of attrition ended, not through reason and common sense, but by exhaustion of resources and legal options.

After outlining the key facts and the time line of events, we will examine the issues that were litigated in light of the real context of the controversy. Indeed, the political ramifications gave rise to a traditional legal and ethical controversy over personhood as well as serious concerns about separation of powers and correct interpretations of federalism. We will ask whether the level of integrity and civility in American politics reached its nadir in the Schiavo case or whether it will continue to deteriorate. The legal analysis will illustrate the role of the state and federal litigation and the deficiencies in the judicial system for handling this type of cultural battle. The most difficult task is determining whether the controversy could have been resolved in a way that did not involve litigation.

History of Relevant Facts

The relevant facts of the Schiavo case are well known and available from a wide variety of sources, including Web sites, newspaper accounts, periodicals, and court documents. A team from the Mayo Clinic, for example, produced an impartial factual account of the history.[39] Additionally, O. Carter Snead, a professor and general counsel to the President's Council on Bioethics, offered his own recounting of the critical events that led to the passage of Terri's Law by the Florida legislature.[40] The saga began on February 25, 1990, when Terri, age twenty-six, suffered a cardiac arrest and fell unconscious in her apartment in St. Petersburg, Florida. Her husband, Michael, called for paramedics, but Terri was anoxic (lacking in oxygen) until they arrived. The paramedics resuscitated her, but she never regained consciousness. Doctors inserted a PEG (percutaneous endoscopic gastrostomy) tube to provide her nourishment and hydration. Her heart attack is believed to have resulted from an imbalance in her potassium level, but the cause of the drop has not been identified; however, it has been suspected that this drop was caused by anorexia coupled with assisted reproduction attempts.

When the police investigated, they found no evidence of abuse or a physical struggle either in the apartment or on Terri, herself. An inquiry after her death was closed without finding any wrongdoing by her husband. After hospitalization for about two and a half months, Terri was moved to a skilled care facility and on June 18, 1990, her husband, Michael, was appointed her guardian. Terri had not signed any advance directive, such as a living will,[41] durable power of attorney,[42] or appointment of a health care representative. There was, therefore, no written expression of her wishes regarding future medical treatment in the event that she became incapacitated. Terri's parents, Robert and Mary Schindler, did not object to Michael's appointment as guardian. After a brief attempt by Michael to provide home care in September 1990, and an effort to get experimental treatment, Terri was placed in a rehabilitation facility in Brandon, Florida in January of 1991. Neurological evaluations revealed only reflexive behaviors consistent with a PVS. A PVS is, in brief, "a vegetative state present one month after acute traumatic or nontraumatic brain injury or lasting for at least one month in patients with degenerative or metabolic disorders or developmental malfunctions."[43] A PVS has also been defined by Florida law as "a permanent and irreversible condition of unconsciousness in which there is: (a) the absence of voluntary action or cognitive behavior of any kind, and (b) an inability to communicate or interact purposefully with the environment."[44] Terri, nonetheless, was given intensive physical, speech, and occupational therapy.

After Terri's collapse, Michael lived with the Schindlers until May 1992. By all accounts, he was devoted to Terri's care for the first four years of her illness. The Schindlers encouraged him to see other women and even met the women he was dating. The relationship between Michael and the

Schindlers began to collapse in 1993, however, after damage awards in two malpractice suits regarding Terri's infertility treatments and the possible connection with her cardiac arrest. The first action produced $250,000 and the second, $1,050,000, of which Michael received $300,000 and the balance was put in a trust for Terri. The trust fund was controlled by South Trust Bank, not Michael, although there is disagreement over whether he had access to some of the funds. The damage awards were calculated based on Michael's testimony that his wife would live out her normal life span and that he would provide care for her. The balance of Terri's award would pass to Michael by virtue of Florida's intestacy law (the law that directs who inherits property of someone who dies without a will) but would go to her parents if he divorced her in the meantime. The Schindlers attempted to remove Michael as Terri's guardian in July 1993. Their effort to remove Michael failed and the first guardian ad litem[45] reported favorably about Michael's attention to Terri's needs. Regardless, the relationship between Michael and the Schindlers continued to deteriorate thereafter.

Little changed from that time until May 1998, when Michael petitioned the Florida court to authorize the removal of Terri's PEG tube. When the Schindlers objected, claiming that Terri would have wanted to be kept alive, the court appointed a second guardian ad litem. This guardian's report fueled the controversy. He noted that Terri was in a PVS state and that her treating physicians thought she had no chance of improvement. The guardian also stated, however, that the only evidence of Terri's wishes concerning LST was from Michael and that he did not believe it met the clear and convincing standard in Florida established in 1990 in *In re Guardianship of Browning.*[46]

The guardian also called to the court's attention Michael's potential conflict of interest. He noted that Michael's hearsay testimony about his wife's intent was "necessarily adversely affected by the obvious financial benefit to him of being the sole heir at law."[47] The guardian recommended removal of the tube if the court disagreed with his evaluation of the evidence as to Terri's wishes. The court did not appoint a new guardian when the second guardian completed his assignment.

Trial of First Florida Action

A trial to determine Terri's wishes and intentions began in January of 2000. Judge George Greer of the Pinellas-Pasco County Circuit Court was assigned to the case and remained involved for the next five years. The evidence as to Terri's wishes was hotly contested. One of the witnesses was Father Gerard Murphy, chaplain of the Catholic Medical Association. Father Murphy testified that removal of the feeding tube would be authorized under Roman Catholic teachings provided that Terri had stated her wishes not to be kept alive artificially under these circumstances. He was asked for his view about the Schindlers' assertions that they would want to be kept alive by any and all measures, including amputations for gangrene, even if it meant impoverishing their family. He indicated that the Roman Catholic Church had no such vitalistic requirement.[48] He was also asked about their claims that they wished Terri to be kept alive because it gave them pleasure, regardless of the extent of life support or disfigurement by amputation. He indicated that this was contrary to the Gospel and to the teachings of the Church.[49]

Judge Greer ordered the removal of the PEG tube on February 11, 2000. According to the court's ruling, Judge Greer found credible and reliable statements that Terri had made to several individuals on different occasions, including her husband, to the effect that she would not want to be kept alive by life support. Judge Greer found that the testimony satisfied the clear and convincing standard. After Judge Greer stayed his decision to allow the Schindlers to exhaust their appeals, the Second District Court of Appeal upheld Judge Greer's original ruling permitting removal of the PEG tube. In so doing, however, the appeals court reaffirmed the applicability of the *Browning* decision in cases in which a patient's wishes are unknown, by adding: "We confirm today that a court's default position must favor life."[50] Legal proceedings followed resulting in a refusal by U.S. Supreme Court Justice Anthony Kennedy to stay the case pending a formal review by that court. The PEG tube was removed on April 24, 2000.

Second Stage in State Court

More legal proceedings followed and Terri's feeding tube was reinserted two days later. The Schindlers claimed that Michael had perjured himself. That claim failing, they started a civil action against him. More legal moves followed and, on August 7, 2001, Judge Greer once again ordered that the tube could be removed. The Schindlers' appeal of that order resulted in an indefinite stay of the removal order.

Third Stage of State Court Proceedings

For nearly four years after this second ruling authorizing removal of the tube, the parties engaged in virtually continuous litigation, culminating in the ultimate removal of the tube in early 2005. To begin with, on October 17, 2001, the Second District Court of Appeal ordered that five physicians examine Terri to determine the possibility of recovery with medical treatment. Michael chose two physicians, the Schindlers, two, and the trial court, the fifth. Mediation concerning which tests should be performed failed and, ultimately, the physician witnesses testified a year later. The physicians chosen by the Schindlers testified that Terri was not in a PVS and could benefit from treatment. The other three agreed that she was in a PVS with no chance of improvement. One physician was controversial because of previous statements favoring withdrawal of AFN (artificial fluid and nutrition). His testimony was thought to arouse members of the public who thought that amounted to euthanasia.[51] The Schindlers again petitioned to remove Michael as guardian claiming that he was neglecting Terri and that he may have abused her initially. The court rejected this claim again and Michael was not removed as guardian. Judge Greer once again authorized removal but stayed his order pending an appeal. Once the reviewing court affirmed the order, the date for removal of the PEG tube was set as October 15, 2003. Despite many additional proceedings including an appeal to the Florida Supreme Court (which declined to hear the case), the PEG tube was sealed with a cap, thus ending its function, on October 15.

The appeals court expressed its view that the case was about Terri Schiavo's right to make her own decision, independent of her parents and independent of her husband. In circumstances such as these, when families cannot agree, the law has opened the doors of the circuit courts to permit trial judges to serve as surrogates or proxies to make decisions about life-prolonging procedures.... [T]he trial judge must make a decision that the clear and convincing evidence shows the ward would have made for herself....[52]

This might be viewed as typical legal fiction. The case was about everything but Terri Schiavo's personal decision. Her views, ambiguous and uncertain at best, were an obscure part of the controversy.

Fourth Stage of the Proceedings: The Court, the Legislature, and the Governor

The situation heated up at this point and a wider range of participants joined in. On October 19, 2003, the Advocacy Center for Persons with Disabilities filed a federal lawsuit challenging the withdrawal of AFN. Interest groups representing disabled people got involved and argued that the devaluing of people with disabilities was a threat to all disabled people. On October 20, 2003, the Florida House of Representatives passed *Terri's Law* (HB 35-E).[53] This bill contained a statement authorizing a onetime stay to prevent withholding or withdrawing nutrition and hydration in a patient who met the unique description of Terri Schiavo. On the same day, Michael, assisted by the ACLU (American Civil Liberties Union), filed a lawsuit in the state court claiming that *Terri's Law* was unconstitutional. A few days later, the third guardian ad litem, Dr. Jay Wolfson, a professor of medicine, law, and public health,[54] was appointed by the trial court. Wolfson spent a great deal of time with Terri and not only issued a report but also wrote independently about the situation.[55] He reported that his observations and assessment of the medical information led him to conclude that Terri was in a PVS with no likelihood of improvement. He expressed his view that the courts had followed Florida law and constitutional principles. Florida's governor, Jeb Bush, rejected his conclusions and recommendation that AFN be terminated.

The challenge to *Terri's Law* was upheld by Florida Circuit Judge W. Douglas Baird who, in May 2004, declared the law to be unconstitutional as a violation of separation of powers, due process, and right to privacy doctrines in the state constitution and similar provisions of the U.S. Constitution.[56] Governor Bush appealed the decision. The Florida Supreme Court, which took jurisdiction directly, unanimously affirmed the trial court and declared Terri's Law unconstitutional on September 23, 2004. In making that decision, the Supreme Court relied on two of the main grounds argued. The first was that the act was an unconstitutional delegation of lawmaking powers to the executive branch. The act violated the separation of powers doctrine because it did not include specific guidelines for the governor to use in exercising his discretion. The second was that the law represented an encroachment on judicial authority. Governor Bush's motions for rehearing were denied, but the order to remove the tube was stayed to allow for an appeal to the U.S. Supreme Court. The U.S. Supreme Court refused to review the decision and Judge Greer gave permission for removal of the tube on March 18, 2005. The tube was removed and various last-minute petitions to state and federal courts by the Schindlers were denied.

Action on the Federal Government Level

More political intervention was still to come. Earlier in March 2005, a Florida Congressman, David Weldon, had introduced in the U.S. House of Representatives H.R. 1151, named the Incapacitated Persons Legal Protection Act.[57] The bill called for judicial review of state court orders by the federal courts when withdrawal or withholding of AFN is involved. A bill calling for the same kind of "reverse federalism" was introduced in the Senate. The Senate bill passed by a voice vote, a method in which individual votes are not recorded, by only three Senators on March 20. Early in the morning hours of the next day, the House bill passed by a vote of 203 to 58. Culminating this extraordinary action, President Bush returned early from a vacation to sign the bill at shortly after 1 A.M. on March 21, 2005.

Federal Court Proceedings

When the case was brought before a federal judge, the judge denied a request to overturn Judge Greer's order. A three-judge panel of the Court of Appeals for the Eleventh Circuit denied a similar request on the next day and the court voted en banc, that is, by vote of all the judges on the court, to reject the appeal. Governor Bush, refusing to capitulate, announced that he would seek to have the Florida Department of Children and Families take custody of Terri. Judge Greer issued an order preventing this action. The U.S. Supreme Court again declined a request to hear the case and overrule the Eleventh Circuit's decision. After more appeals to both federal and state courts failed because the courts refused to hear the case further, the legal proceedings came to an end. Terri Schiavo died on March 31, 2005, after years of legal and political intervention in this unusual case.

As a footnote to the legal proceedings, an autopsy was performed after Terri's death.[58] The autopsy revealed no evidence of trauma or abuse by anyone, putting to rest the Schindlers' accusations against Michael Schiavo. It also revealed that her heart was clinically unremarkable, that is, it showed no signs that a heart attack had occurred. No clinical evidence of an eating disorder existed, ending the speculation that such a disorder had caused her initial collapse. Perhaps most significant in terms of the controversy about her mental condition, the autopsy revealed that she was *not* merely in a minimally conscious state, a condition less grave than a PVS. She had massive brain damage. Her brain was half the expected weight. The most logical conclusion is that the autopsy basically supported Michael Schiavo's position as to her condition, rather than that of her parents.

With that overview of the history of the litigation, we will consider whether the issues litigated in the major court proceedings parallel the issues that would have been confronted if ethical resolution had gone forward. The issues line up closely. The issues that the courts decided, so repetitively, were essentially the same as those that would have been important in an ethical resolution involving the patient, family members and medical providers. The exception is the issue regarding separation of powers, which would not have arisen had the case been resolved privately. The issues were as follows:

1. When can an individual be allowed to die by withdrawal or withholding of LSTs?

2. When is an individual not a person for decision-making purposes (capacity)?

3. Who is entitled to speak for a patient (surrogate) who lacks capacity to speak for himself or herself? What standards govern the surrogate? When can a surrogate be replaced?

4. What would Terri Schiavo have wanted in this case?

5. What is the proper constitutional role of each branch of government in the resolution of end-of-life cases and what standards apply?

The first four questions, crucial to ethical decision-making, were decided over and over by the trial and appellate courts, with a number of variations, of course.

In an ethical setting, the concepts of autonomy, non-maleficence, and beneficence would have controlled the decision making once the appropriate decision maker had been identified. The concept of distributive justice is rarely introduced in the case of individual end-of-life situations but clearly, had it been considered, it would have weighed in on the side of allowing life to end. The questions were answered in different terms in the legal proceedings than they would have been in ethical discussions or negotiations. Strict legal standards dictate the language and concepts to be used. The pivotal points of both legal and ethical proceedings in this case, however, are remarkably similar.

In *Schiavo,* the courts made sensible decisions consistent with what the ethical result likely would have been. Lawyers can readily understand and appreciate why so many court proceedings occurred in this case. Each new installment came about because of a legitimate legal claim. Requests for rehearings, stays for new appeals, offers of new evidence, appeals, emergency motions, motions in the federal court as well as the state court, and other special proceedings caused postponements after rulings by the trial court. From the point of view of a nonlawyer, it would be difficult to explain how, because of subtle points, each major issue could be challenged and decided again and again. The financial cost and emotional toll of so many years of intense litigation in state and federal trial and appellate courts is difficult to justify by any exercise of common wisdom. Surely that is no way to decide a case of such personal sensitivity and pain to the litigants.

This situation involving Terri Schiavo is not vastly different from many cases that are resolved weekly, if not daily, by consensus of patients, families, and medical providers. It is easily conceivable that this case could have been resolved amicably and without adversarial strife. The husband and parents are neither heroes nor villains but, rather, decent people caught in a tragic situation. They were trying to reconcile conflicting views and interests in an effort to resolve a critical dilemma and move on with their own lives. Had they retained confidence in each other's good faith and intentions, they might eventually have agreed on terminating LST for Terri. Once the trusting relationship broke down because of money and self-interest, mistrust and suspicion took over. The Schindlers were driven to extreme positions which they might not otherwise have taken. They did not seek to serve their self-interest although they made extreme statements in the heat of passionate battle. They fell easy prey to the exploitative social and political special interests who sought to appropriate their tragic dilemma for their own agendas. Both sides were pushed to extreme positions and became more adversarial as the litigation heated up, fueled by extremists on both sides. The idea of compromise or accommodation disappeared as they fought to vindicate their positions.

There were no heroes in this situation. If there were villains, they were the special interests and political figures who exploited a tragic situation for their own gain. Perhaps the politicians were the most culpable of all, since they appeared to act not out of principle but of self-interest. In the end, they retreated from the battlefield and tried to distance themselves from the result. A tragic personal dilemma, not brought on by either Michael or the Schindlers, that could have been resolved within a reasonable period exacted a high price over the ten years of litigation. Although the courts kept to the issues, despite the external pressures, the executive and legislative branches disgraced themselves by pushing the boundaries of law and decency in their self-aggrandizing efforts.

In the end, the litigants probably remain hostile and unreconciled. They cannot recover the cost or repair the emotional damage suffered during years of litigation. The religious and moral gulf between the various interests cannot be bridged. All the temporary supporters have moved on to other causes, no doubt, leaving the survivors to suffer alone. The Schindlers probably suffered the most. The husband is not likely to be viewed as a hero or champion of Terri's rights. The case was not so much about Terri and her human right to determine her destiny. She was the unwilling and unwitting proxy for all who sought to exploit the situation. Whether this case rightfully belongs in the bioethics texts alongside cases like *Quinlan*, *Cruzan*, *Bouvia*,[59] *Martin*,[60] and others remains to be seen. The Schiavo case is more than a case about bioethical issues of medical futility. It is a case that reveals the serious deficiencies in the political process by which our public policy is made.

Before proceeding to an analysis of law's impact on this bioethics problem, I will review some of the main factors that contributed to the difficulty in resolving the Schiavo case. The first is the conflict and breakdown of the relationship between the Schindlers and Michael Schiavo. This developed over a span of twelve years from 1993, when the Schindlers first tried to have him removed as guardian, to 2005, when their last legal move failed. The conflict originated with disagreements concerning how Michael's malpractice damage recoveries should be spent. It was accompanied, at least in the Schindlers' opinion, by a change in his attitude toward Terri. Whereas before that time, he had been devoted to her care and committed to her recovery, he appeared to change his mind. The Schindlers thought he now wished her to die so he could move along with his own life. Character issues, therefore, became important and the dispute became as much about opposing Michael's new agenda as about Terri's well-being. The fact that Terri's initial collapse was shrouded in mystery and that previous relationship problems between the Schiavos were reported contributed to the dynamic.

The second factor contributing to the difficulty in resolving the case is the cessation of personhood and autonomy. This is a multifaceted topic, involving the patient's medical condition, the legal context for determining personhood, and the role of a surrogate. The dispute involving Terri concerned not only whether life support should be ended but also whether her medical condition warranted even considering such a move. Although various courts, relying on experts, decided consistently that she was in a PVS and was incapable of recovering, the Schindlers were unpersuaded. Their experts even promoted a new concept of unconsciousness—the minimally conscious state. Although several New York neurologists hypothesized about such a state, lying somewhere between comatose and vegetative, that new category had not been clearly established. The courts were unpersuaded by the theory, and the autopsy seemed to put an end to the matter. The legal context, which consisted of the *Quinlan* and *Cruzan* cases and the body of legal scholarship concerning end-of-life was well developed by the time the *Schiavo* litigation began. Despite that, however, it seemed as though the parties to the dispute were determined to continue the controversy regardless of the issues at hand.

Whether autonomy ought to govern decision making at the end of life is seriously in dispute.[61] The fiction of a surrogate and a court attempting to carry out the presumed intent or ascertain the best interests of a PVS patient seems ludicrous to some observers. Whether autonomy should direct courts to appoint a single decision maker is questionable (and perhaps designed simply for the convenience and benefit of medical providers) in view of the legitimate and often competing interests of numerous family members. Some commentators advocated the need for a more workable objective standard. The fact that the first court order to remove the tube was made on the basis of rather flimsy evidence of Terri's wishes, as compared with the *Cruzan* or *Quinlan* evidence probably fueled the determination of the Schindlers to fight on.

Media impact is the third. Once the media was attracted to the story, the daily developments became one of the featured news stories. When there were no developments to report, the media created them with interviews and commentaries. The widely viewed 2002 video clip of Terri and her mother, in which Terri's eyes seem to respond, may have played a major role in fueling the controversy. When it was first shown, no one pointed out that it was already three years old and did not reflect her current condition. Nor did anyone convincingly explain that although the eye movements made her look alert and responsive, they were not uncommon in PVS patients and did not prove her mental alertness. The story, aided by the tape, took on a life of its own. At the same time, the constant reporting attracted various personalities, political and otherwise, and special interests.

Third parties played a major role. After the case became headline news, many third parties joined in, most of them on the side of the Schindlers. Christian religious groups, both Roman Catholic and Protestant Evangelical, joined in to support the Schindlers with vocal support. One commentator noted the difficulties with "hard cases and the politics of righteousness."[62] The case became a new right to life cause for groups opposing abortion. Advocates for people with disabilities joined in the crusade as well, raising fears about the prospects of allowing disabled people to die prematurely. The next step was for the case to be highly politicized. Politicians, recognizing the political capital to be made by joining forces with one side or the other, most with the Schindlers but some who advocated Michael's protection of Terri's privacy and autonomy, were not to be left behind. Some political figures, trained in the medical profession, even ventured their professional opinions on Terri's condition, without taking the trouble to examine her. They did not fare well, ultimately, in the media or on the political scene. Politicians, it seemed, were not ready to leave any stone unturned and, rather than merely offering vocal support, they passed legislation and signed bills regardless of constitutional doctrines. The political reaction was, to say the least, extraordinary and unprecedented. After the political moves had proven futile and were criticized from the bench, the politicians retreated, leaving the family members to bear their grief alone.

ANALYZING LAW'S IMPACT ON BIOETHICS

The Idiom of the Law

I noted earlier that the issues addressed by the courts are, for the most part, the same issues that would be addressed in an ethical setting. Had the case been decided in a hospital setting with husband and parents present, the inquiry would have focused on Terri's medical condition, her level of mental functioning, the likelihood of her recovery, if any, the likely result of withdrawing life-support systems, the cost and other factors involving continuation of support, what she would have wanted, and who should make the decision with or without consensus of other family members. A decision could have been reached over a period of days, weeks, or months after repeated conversations. The trial courts made these decisions, instead. Rather than being deciding by consensus over a period of time, by obtaining input from all family members, the courts had to decide the issues within the legal framework and based on adversarial pleadings and evidence. Terri's condition was testified to by numerous physicians in terms similar to those that would have been used in a clinical or ethical setting. The positions of the parties were presented in court similarly but in a more adversarial and extreme way given the controversy.

The courts were compelled to make decisions concerning her medical condition, prognosis, and the implications of withdrawal of life support based on precise legal standards. Although those standards were similar to the factors that would be relevant in the clinical setting, the court proceedings had far less flexibility. Rather than achieving consensual decisions, which could be reached by parties in noncourt settings, the court decisions came about through adversarial conflict. Consensus and reconciliation became more and more unlikely, as the parties invested money and emotional energy in the struggle to prevail, and were supported by outsiders with uncompromising positions on related issues. It is not always possible to reach consensus, of course, in the clinical setting and perhaps this controversy was destined to proceed to the bitter end. In this case, although the parties were supported by outside parties whose interests were broader than those of Michael and the Schindlers, the people who had the most at stake were represented in court. Although the result has legal implications for other end-of-life cases, the impact will be limited by factual distinctions.

The Adversarial Process

The missing ingredients for an amicable resolution of what was basically a personal and family problem of tragic proportions were consensus and accommodation. The adversarial process is ill-suited for this type of case although it surely can produce a decision—ultimately. In this situation, it took more than a decade. With due respect to the rights of parties to every available remedy, it is fruitless to litigate virtually the same issues again and again. Winning is the primary goal of litigation and that is what the parties wanted in this case. Evidence rules and procedural rules slowed the process down and prolonged it while increasing expense but they were essential in the thorough exploration of issues. The physician witnesses had to be heard. The burdens of proof seem appropriately placed on those attempting to bring life to a close. Given what we know about the Schiavo controversy and the legal context in which it arose, the courts probably reached the correct result albeit after an extraordinary number of years of litigation.

Closure, Finality, and the Retrospective View

This requirement is reasonably well suited for the Schiavo type of litigation. The main flaw in a court decision of such a personal matter is that it rules out consensus and amicable resolution. The process does so much damage that the level of harm escalates as the litigation goes on. Public combat over an intensely personal subject leaves permanent battle scars on relationships. The types of court decisions in this case enabled action by Michael Schiavo rather than ordering it. Whether the rulings were final or not is fair game for assessment. The fact that it took a dozen years of litigation and, even then, the result was merely to enable him to act, attests to a startling lack of finality. The retrospective view is basically suitable for a situation that does not keep changing. The constant court activity, in fact, enabled witnesses to keep the court informed of continuing developments. If all end-of-life controversies required court resolution, little else would get done. Fortunately, most controversies are resolved in the private clinical setting by use of ethical conversations and counseling over a period of time until family members are able to accept the inevitable results.

Institutional Biases

It does not seem to me that institutional biases played a role in the Schiavo litigation. Economic considerations were absent from consideration although the use of scarce medical resources for Terri Schiavo over a long period of time should be a major public policy concern. Money did not determine the outcome of this litigation nor did political considerations. The outside interests, in fact, seemed to receive little acknowledgment, and minimal deference, from the courts, federal and state. To the credit of the state court system and the federal courts, which played less of a role, the judges kept to the issues and were not influenced by highly visible interventions by a state legislature, Congress, a Governor, and a President. Neither were they influenced by tremendous media pressure and lobbying, and even threats, by special interest groups.[63] The courts were faced with conflicting opinions of expert witnesses and they seemed to be able to sort them out and reach an appropriate result.

Future Controversies

My prediction is that the Schiavo case will have less impact on the development of end-of-life law and ethics than its notable predecessors, *Quinlan* and *Cruzan*.[64] Although those cases were not nearly as protracted as *Schiavo*, they broke new legal ground. The courts in *Schiavo* did a remarkable job of withstanding public pressure and of maintaining boundaries between law and policy. They did not hesitate to declare unconstitutional the outrageous efforts by politicians, state and federal, to influence the outcome of the case by using and encouraging the public lawmaking authority to shape the outcome of a single case, in my view, for patently obvious political motives rather than for principled reasons. If the litigation has any lasting effect, it may be to define the boundaries between the branches of government and to demonstrate the capacity of courts to maintain their independence from the influence of special interests, political and religious pressure, and prolonged and repetitive efforts to determine the outcome. Schiavo provides an illustration of successful judicial independence. The Florida Constitution, as well as the U.S. Constitution, provides for government in which the three branches are separate and distinct. The Florida Constitution specifically states: "The powers of the state government shall be divided into legislative, executive and judicial branches. No person belonging to one branch shall exercise any powers appertaining to either of the other branches unless expressly provided herein."[65] The separation of powers principle was based on a concern "that the fusion of the powers of any two branches into the same department would ultimately result in the destruction of liberty." [66] The Schiavo litigation took place in a highly charged political atmosphere in which both the state legislative and executive branches attempted to influence the outcome of the cases, especially with the passage of "Terri's Law." These two branches of the federal government attempted to interfere in the controversy as well. The state and federal courts stood firm against the attempted interventions. The Florida state courts, in particular, acted properly on the behalf of the independent and coequal judicial branch of government rather than yielding to the enormous political pressures imposed by the other two branches. If ever courts carried out the responsibility of the judicial branch to withstand political pressure against the boundaries of judicial independence, Schiavo exemplifies that ideal.

Once the litigation ended and Terri died, the case dropped from the public spotlight and, after the usual run of commentaries and retrospectives in medical and legal periodicals and in the media, it has all but disappeared from sight. Although it will be a staple in bioethics textbooks, how much the controversy will contribute to medical and legal literature remains to be seen. Schiavo was, first and foremost, an acrimonious intra-family dispute over authority and money involving a PVS patient. Had the family agreed on a course of action, the public would not have learned about the case despite the difficult question as to how long Terri should have been kept alive. Had interest groups and politicians not joined in the fray for their own purposes, the dispute would have been resolved without fanfare, even if litigated. A change in the facts of the scenario might have produced a different outcome. What if settlement proceeds had not been at stake? What if Michael had not developed a relationship with another woman? Would Terri's medical condition have been enough, without those aggravating factors, to attract media attention and political interlopers? The case surely would not have been the same compelling drama.

As the case did develop, it revealed much about current American culture, in particular, how Americans deal with end-of-life issues. In addition, *Schiavo* illustrated American thinking about the polarized abortion controversy, media and political exploitation of issues and controversies, and the trivialization of American politics. It also revealed the competence and courage of judges within the state and federal court systems. At the same time it showed how flawed our system of justice is to allow for years of repetitive trials and appeals. While the case has been cited as an example of how poorly suited litigation is to resolve such a case, it also shows how capable the judicial branch can be. It revealed much about what happens in a classic cultural clash of politics, medicine, law, and religion in American society. It reveals the best and the worst of American culture.

The *Schiavo* case was significant as a media mega-event because it had the elements of a classic drama. The media became even more interested as the controversy developed. Special interests were attracted once they realized that they could attract public attention as they used the dispute for their own purposes. Having reshaped the controversy to suit their political and social agendas, they fueled the lawsuits. Once political figures realized the potential political advantage of joining forces with the special interests, they supported the oversimplified life or choice sides. Terri became a poster child for one side or the other, and the husband and parents were portrayed as heroes or villains. Judges in both court systems performed their individual jobs admirably, but the inadequacy of the court system as a way of resolving efficiently and amicably was exposed in the process. *Schiavo* revealed both strengths and weaknesses in the American system of conflict resolution but, most of all, it revealed how shallow and unprincipled American politics can be and how powerful the American media can be. The *Schiavo* case was about winning—winning a personal dispute, winning a social conflict, winning a legal dispute, and winning elections. While it teaches much about tactics and strategy, as well as about American culture, it does not teach much about how end-of-life controversies should be resolved. Rather, it teaches how they should not be resolved. Perhaps that is the greatest lesson of all.

The case of Terri Schiavo speaks to all of us but for different reasons. While it evolved from a private ethical dilemma about a young woman's sad decline into a PVS state, into a media event that pitted, not only a husband against his wife's family, but also religious interest groups and political personalities against each other, it raised a virtual cascade of questions that concern the state of American society and culture. What is the nature of personhood and when does it end? What level of respect and, with it, autonomy accompanies an individual into old age or incapacity? Is there a limit to the medical resources that should be used to keep alive an individual who is in a PVS state or, at least, fundamentally unresponsive and unable to function normally? Who should act on behalf of an incapable individual? To what extent is such a situation a private matter for a family and to what extent is it a public concern? What individual liberties does an individual in a PVS state have? If the public, through its government, has a role, what branches and what agencies should intervene? Who should intervene, by what means, and for how long? Are physicians who speak in their political capacity bound by professional ethics? What role should religious beliefs and moral beliefs play in political and public policy decision-making? What does the episode say about the priorities and objectives of American society?

Another crucial question concerns the role of litigation. Is litigation an effective means of resolving disputes and differences concerning the care to be given to an individual who lacks full capacity? The *Schiavo* court saga provides significant insight into the effectiveness (or lack of effectiveness) of litigation as a means to resolve this type of controversy. The exhaustion of legal avenues eventually may have forced one of the contending parties to accept the inevitability of the result, but it did nothing to restore peace and harmony. Once again, we see that litigation is a limited resource. It produces decisions about legal issues but has no way to bring about a solution of the underlying problems. In some ways, litigation exacerbates the underlying problems.

The personhood question that we addressed in Chapter 6 carries over full force into end-of-life situations. The concept of personhood (respect for personhood and autonomy) is, in fact, at the heart of all bioethical issues including the legal aspects. One might think that the question would be even more difficult to resolve in end-of-life situations because the persons involved are, or were, fully capable adults rather than prenatal forms of human life. However, that is not necessarily the case. The threat of lessoned respect for the personhood of human life with potential often seems to generate more alarm than depriving an aged or ill person with limited life expectancy of a few months or even a few years of life. This so especially when the individual appears to be less than fully mentally alert and capable. Although that reaction may be understandable, the basic question appears to be the same. If the presence of a human soul is brought into the controversy, it is not likely that anyone would contend that an embryo has a soul but that a dying person, with or without full capacity, does not have one.

End-of-life cases that produce serious conflict or litigation sometimes turn out to hinge on an agenda of secondary factors that lie at the heart of the controversy. Those factors often include conflicting interests in property or money, relationship conflicts, or struggles for power or control. Beginning-of-life controversies usually involve conflict between individuals or groups with opposing moral or religious views plus opposing views and priorities about what constitutes choice and what constitutes life. The terms pro-life and pro-choice, commonly adopted by one side and the other in the abortion controversy, tell us nothing about the positions since both terms could be used interchangeably by either side. A few end-of-life cases do generate as much turmoil and controversy as beginning-of-life issues. The strange case of Terri Schiavo is the most recent of these, and perhaps the most notorious of those that ended up in court. Why the Schiavo case became the focal point of battles that consumed tremendous media attention and involved all branches of government, state and federal, is explained by the peculiar constellation of factors involved.

The seemingly endless conflict generated by the Schiavo situation has been analyzed from many perspectives. They include separation of powers, federalism, religious intervention, medical and psychiatric opinion, and the breakdown of the relationship of Terri's husband and the Schindlers. Other perspectives include the economic factors, the struggle for political power, the intervention of anti-abortion interest groups, media exploitation for economic gain, political exploitation by public figures seeking attention, and misuse of the legal system for religious and political goals. Although all of these elements and interests were involved, it was, in the end, the peculiar alchemy of all that produced the explosive mix. In some ways, the result was emblematic of the forces in American society before the case arose to take center stage. Litigation served as the vehicle by which all these forces could interact. If hostility between Terri's husband and the Schindlers was one catalyst, the political exploitation, shameless media overexposure and hyperbole and the intervention by various interest groups also served as accelerants.

Without the stage provided by litigation in both state and federal courts, it would have been difficult for the drama to capture public attention as long as it did. Litigation was chosen, less to resolve the conflict than to activate and develop it. In the end, court decisions did bring an end to the dispute. All that happened serves to reinforce my belief that litigation is a poor choice to resolve ethical, social, and religious issues. Despite our strong attraction to litigation as a means of resolving disputes, it is important to recognize that it often fails to bring timely resolution to problems. Even when it does, the cost, human as well as economic, may be a terrible burden.

Chapter 8

New Frontiers

We have been examining five major fields of bioethics for the purpose of identifying how the ethical questions that arise in these areas are affected by the intervention of litigation. We started with human research, the foundational field of bioethics, then moved to beginning-of-life issues, organ allocation, embryonic stem cell research and, finally, end-of-life concerns. Although each field produces a different set of ethical issues, and each has witnessed different types of litigation, the impact of litigation has similar elements. In this concluding chapter, we will consider three separate inquiries. First, what can we conclude about the impact of litigation on bioethical decision-making? Second, what new developments in bioethics may give rise to additional—and perhaps less traditional—litigation? Third, how can courts and judges overcome the deficiencies of litigation in bioethics and better preserve ethical decision-making for individuals?

WHAT IS THE IMPACT OF LITIGATION ON BIOETHICAL DECISION-MAKING?

Legal regulation in the field of bioethics should be expected. As new developments occur, it is appropriate that regulation should be done in terms of broad principles, leaving room for individual action, breathing room, so to speak. Regulation should not be so hasty or so far-reaching that it suffocates the action of democratic people and institutions and the growth of ideas and innovation. But in order to direct the growth and development and to protect people, legislatures must be willing to take action. Judicial decisions also serve to regulate on a case-by-case basis. Both institutions, the judiciary and the legislature, draw on the constitutional framework. The executive branch does a substantial amount of regulating through agency rule-making and orders, subject to legislative and judicial oversight.

The field of bioethics involves voluntary decision-making by individuals and institutions. Although ethical decision-making should be permitted to take place without excessive regulation, some direction is needed. Law provides normative standards. Excessive legal regulation and litigation, however, can be harmful to the health of democracy. There are some newly developing areas of bioethics in which it may not yet be clear what regulation is needed. It is possible that judicial decision-making may occur first. I will try to predict where litigation may arise and what its impact is likely to be.

I will proceed to summarize the analysis as it applies to the five major fields of bioethics and examine the potential impact of new developments in biotechnology.

The Idiom of the Law

We focus here on determining whether translating ethical issues into legal language and concepts (the legal idiom) in the course of litigation changes the nature of issues in the process. A secondary inquiry is whether the impact of legal language continues thereafter when the issues are addressed in ethical settings. It seems clear from the analysis of all five fields that law and litigation have such a transforming impact.

In the field of human research, litigation is a relatively new development, having begun at the turn of the century. Claims arising in this field have to conform to existing legal frameworks, mainly, of tort claims or constitutional claims. Distinctions and categories that are important in the field of ethical regulation often become blurred when translated into legal terms. Human research issues do not necessarily fit easily into a traditional malpractice framework but, for purposes of litigation, they must conform. Causes of action are stated in traditional legal language rather than ethical terms. Courts typically do not address ethical issues even when they are apparent. Whether consent has been obtained, for example, is an issue that arises in both ethical and legal contexts but the standards used to address it differ depending on the context.

In a legal context, the fact that benefit to subjects is *not* an element of human research is often overlooked. The belief or assumption that physicians and other medical professionals have a universal duty to provide care to patients in all circumstances may be be an institutional bias of courts. The idea that benefit to patients is not part of the equation is a difficult one for legal decision makers. We have noted that the threat of litigation against researchers and IRBs has had a major impact on human research activities. The effect may be beneficial, in some respects, because it may cause regulations to be strictly enforced and review standards, to be tightened. Some research studies that should not go forward may be modified or abandoned. Conflicts of interest may be more closely examined and avoided. On the other hand, some innovations may be lost or delayed in the process of conforming to standards that are designed to minimize the possibility of litigation. Some studies may be too expensive, given new regulations, and will be abandoned. The human research field is acutely aware of the threat of potential litigation.

In the reproductive field of bioethics, a similar impact occurs. Whereas the ethical issues involve philosophical questions of the nature and intrinsic value of life or encumbered life, lawsuits deal with evaluating the conduct of professionals and the economic value of life under various circumstances. In the legal context, unanswerable questions of philosophy or ethics are occasionally encountered. The way they are addressed is to translate them into economic questions. Far-reaching ethical claims, such as whether no life at all is preferable to an encumbered life, may fall too far outside the boundaries of law to be recognized in court. In effect, ethical questions must be subordinated to the necessities of practical decision-making in traditional terms. Sweeping ethical issues are often translated into narrow issues of duty, damage, and liability so that decisions can be made within normal legal limits.

Litigation in the field of organ transplants and allocation is just beginning. While organ allocation has been handled almost exclusively on an ethical basis to this point, as the gap between supply and demand for organs continues to grow, litigation is beginning to intervene. That situation could change; however, if alternate sources of organs become available through developing biotechnology. The present types of lawsuits challenge claimed abuses of the existing ethically based transplant allocation system and improper or defective transplants. They do not undermine the present system, but, rather enforce it by providing legal oversight for abuses. Since people who need organs are more frequently attempting to bypass the ethical system, however, this may eventually lead to claims of priority made in legal actions. That kind of litigation would challenge directly the ethically based system. Although the present types of lawsuits do not transform the ethical issues into legal ones, that may be on the horizon.

The current litigation in the stem cell field does not fit the typical pattern. Since this is a developing field of biotechnology, still in the research stage for the most part, the lawsuits generated to date do not impact the ethical issues directly. The entire ethical field is affected by the abortion controversy and the decisions of the U.S. Supreme Court. The California litigation is directed at attempting to prevent the use of state funds for stem cell research. Those cases do not deal with the core ethical issues but, rather, with political decisions pertaining to state funding. Once the biotechnology of stem cell research has more widespread applications in clinical practice, litigation may become more common. It may encompass ethical issues regarding the use of stem cell research both for medical conditions and for enhancement purposes.

Litigation was directly involved with the basic issues in the end-of-life controversy generated by Terri Schiavo's medical condition. The underlying ethical issues, ordinarily resolved through discussion and mediation at the personal or clinical level, were removed to court. Although ethical and legal issues overlapped, they were translated into legal terms and decisions were made according to legal standards. Despite the use of legal language, the issues that the courts decided closely resembled the ethical issues that would have been decided otherwise. What was missing in the legal forum was the opportunity for nonadversarial resolution.

What we see overall is that moving issues to the legal forum impacts the issues in different ways depending on the type of litigation.

Adversarial Process

The effect on bioethics of the adversarial process, which sets the tone for litigation, is easy to appreciate. Bioethical issues are best resolved in ethical settings where the participants can find ways to resolve differences through mutual understanding, compromise, and accommodation of conflicting points of view. The ethical setting also allows parties to take into account changing situations without the formality of structured procedures and rules for obtaining information. Mediation is the favored process. Resolution of ethical issues calls for flexibility and the capacity to take change into account. Winning, the goal of adversarial process, is foreign to mediation. The adversarial process pits participants against each other by forcing them to take sides on issues. That process tends to polarize the parties even more. The adversarial process cannot take into account ambiguities and complexities that do not fit into neat legal categories. Stating claims that arise out of bioethical situations in legal terms obscures the ambiguities and subtleties of the underlying ethical issues.

Some controversies are well suited to the adversarial system. Determining responsibility according to legal standards, for example, is well served by the adversary system. We have looked at traditional litigation forms in the human research field and the beginning-of-life field. Once the underlying ethical issues were translated into the terminology of negligence claims, the adversarial system could decide them. A situation such as the Gelsinger case, for example, was addressed as a legal claim even though it involved many claimed ethical violations. Once characterized in terms of legal issues, the controversy extends beyond the realm of bioethics, in a sense.

In the beginning-of-life field, claims of professional misconduct or negligence are well served by our system of adjudication. One problem is that when ethical issues are recast as legal issues, a court decision does not necessarily resolve all the underlying problems. Only the legal issues are decided. When the real issues encompass essentially ethical questions, courts cannot decide them. My point is that there are legitimate legal disputes arising in these bioethical fields that are well suited for litigation but there are ethical queries that cannot sensibly be resolved in court. In the organ allocation field, the lawsuits so far address claims of improper conduct. Other types of litigation may be on the horizon to challenge the weaknesses in the regulatory system that presently governs the field. In the stem cell field, to date, the litigation has involved challenges to stem cell funding authorization, which involves purely legal issues. As the field develops and more research is translated into practical uses, more litigation is likely.

The *Schiavo* case is a prime example of excessive litigation and overreaching political intervention. As it evolved, the case did address many legal issues but, at the heart of the matter were two main sources of controversy. The first was a family dispute about money and control over Terri's future and, the second, a moral conflict concerning when a life may be terminated by withdrawal of life support. Litigation was used as a method of contesting the basic personal and ethical issues. Once the basic dispute was reframed in legal terms, there was no dearth of legal issues in this ongoing conflict. Although the courts did exemplary work in deciding the issues, the case was over-litigated with repetitious proceedings and endless reprises of the basic claims. The struggle to prevail on the personal, as well as the ethical or moral level, was relentless and in the end, the decision seemed appropriate given all the available information. The underlying bitter family dispute, bolstered by the intervention of third parties, knew no bounds except the eventual exhaustion of legal and political possibilities.

All in all, we can say that, while the adversary system is appropriate (at least, given American predisposition to resolving disputes in this manner) for purely legal controversies, it is ill-suited to solving problems that demand adaptation to changing circumstances and accommodation or compromise of conflicting points of view.

Finality, Closure, and the Retrospective View

There are various aspects to these features of litigation. The requirements of finality and closure, in this context, mean that a court decision freezes the parties at a fixed point in their relationship. Although they can litigate further, new causes of action must be invoked to assert new claims. They cannot litigate the same dispute again, and they cannot return to court claiming changed circumstances, except in special situations such as family matters or enforcement of court orders. In most cases, once judgment has been rendered, and the appeal process has run its course, the case is over regardless of what may happen thereafter.

The retrospective view is implicated by the fact that the court often decides a controversy based on the situation that existed when the lawsuit was brought. The controversy, which may have been ongoing, and which may continue in some respects afterward, is fixed in time and, in many instances, changes that happen during the course of litigation are considered irrelevant. These features of the court system do not match the reality of human life, which is anything but static.

This feature of litigation, in which the court looks back at events that have already happened, has a bearing on the ultimate resolution. The system is adequate for controversies that involve a single event or a series of occurrences that can be isolated in time. It is not well suited for situations that are not time-limited. Most bioethical issues are not so discrete and specific. They generally involve changing situations and relationships. When they are limited to specific claims of improper conduct, they can be litigated. Litigation, however, rarely accommodates the real controversy that has generated the alleged misconduct. Inflexible categories and rules of law were not designed to address realistically the ongoing controversies of life. Generally, court resolution may end the particular dispute but the underlying problems and issues continue. Other related, but different, controversies will arise in the future. The precedent that has been settled will impact the future cases and controversies in various ways. While legal precedents can be useful guides for resolving future controversies, they can also restrict participants in future controversies in ways that may not be beneficial. Parties in future lawsuits will be bound by precedents unless they can persuade courts to distinguish them, that is, to show how they do not apply.

Once ethical issues are litigated as negligence claims, they lend themselves to judicial decision-making, restricted by law and subject to the legal effects of precedent. We have seen this in the case of human research and beginning-of-life lawsuits. The particular kinds of claims litigated in the organ allocation field and stem cell field were better suited for court decision. The broader kinds of issues that may in the future arise in these fields may not be. In *Schiavo*, the parties to the multifaceted litigation surmounted the retrospective problem by bringing multiple lawsuits and by attempting to relitigate issues. The cost to the parties and to the courts was substantial. The cost to other litigants, awaiting their turn in court, was considerable, although difficult to measure. The patience of the public was severely tested by this all-consuming process. Few would contend that the use of the court system in that case was effective or productive. It is surely not wise to encourage the use of court resources for excessive litigation as a way of resolving a family dispute.

Courts' Institutional Biases, Assumptions, and Flaws

We have observed that courts tend to favor economic interests, when decisions are made determining what potential litigants should have access to courts. Most litigation must be framed in terms of quantifiable injury and relief. That is not surprising and not necessarily unreasonable, although it represents a weakness in the capacity of courts to resolve disputes. Courts have difficulty dealing with ambiguous or intangible claims. They do not fit the fixed categories of litigation. The fault in this, if any, lies not just with courts for being unable to decide ambiguous or unclear ethical issues, many of which have no discernable solution, but with litigants who try to convert such issues into recognizable legal claims. Courts are designed to decide a relatively narrow category of disputes—those that fit within recognized categories of law. The decision-making process is geared to that process.

The types of litigation that we have seen in the human research and beginning-of-life fields, as with the organ allocation lawsuits and the California stem cell lawsuits, are readily handled by courts. All of them deal with discrete legal issues. Although the Schiavo litigation did not involve economic interests, the legal claims were reduced to those that could be litigated according to precedent in this type of case. Broad ethical questions were not presented. Rather, the questions were narrowed to conform to existing legal categories and interests.

The institutional bias in favor of a public policy that supports preserving life is evident in the beginning-of-life cases, where courts have difficulty even considering whether nonexistence could be preferable to existence that is impaired. This bias probably contributes to the idea that physician/researchers should treat patients rather than subjecting them to research and experimentation. In the stem cell controversy, we noted that the California litigation was brought to challenge state funding of research that involved the destruction of any form of human life or, in fact, the tampering with life forms. In *Schiavo*, the strong resistance to allowing Michael Schiavo to authorize withdrawal of basic nutritional life support evidences the extent to which people are allowed to litigate to prevent the ending of life. It took more than a decade for Michael Schiavo to prevail and remove the feeding tube, thereby bringing about the termination of Terri Schiavo's life.

The strong bias against court-ordered termination of life is by no means a negative feature. We see this same predisposition in death penalty cases and in the resistance to allowing physician-assisted suicide. Courts, which are considered to be essentially nondemocratic institutions, with no public constituency and no way of directly gauging public opinion, naturally are reluctant to rule in a way that brings about death. A qualifying comment is appropriate here. Although all federal judges and some state judges are appointed rather than elected, most state judges either are directly elected or face a combination of appointment and retention review by vote of the electorate. How to categorize these judges, as democratic or nondemocratic, is difficult. While some judges must participate in the election process, involving fund-raising and limited campaigning, all judges are chosen for an office that requires fair and impartial decision-making rather than carrying out the will of the people, such as by legislative and executive officials.

Courts elevate individualism as opposed to broad-based community interests, except where specifically allowed by statute. Aside from allowing *amicus curiae* briefs (advisory *friend of the court* briefs by nonparties) in appellate cases and occasionally in trials, nonparties are rarely allowed access to participate in litigation. This is so even where common sense dictates that legitimate public concerns and interests may well be affected by the litigation. Since courts are geared to make decisions in particular controversies, it is easy to see why the interests allowed in are narrowly circumscribed. All the cases that we have examined involve specific individual interests except for the plaintiffs who instituted the California lawsuits challenging the stem cell funding. The interests of the litigants had to meet specific standards. Our examination has reinforced the concept that courts operate with specific institutional biases. However understandable this may be, it does not change the fact that this feature limits access to courts and limits the type and extent of relief that can be obtained.

Impact on Future Controversies

The impact of lawsuits in each of these five areas of bioethical decision-making is significant, although as varied as the types of lawsuits are different. In the field of research using human subjects, the introduction of malpractice litigation has had a substantial impact notwithstanding the fact that, to date, few lawsuits have been successful for plaintiffs. We noted that this field of bioethics, once basically left to the ethics of researchers, began to be monitored by the adoption of federal regulatory standards around 1980. Until the advent of adversarial litigation, researchers and local IRBs functioned without regard to negligence claims and the regulatory effect they produce. Since that time, the consciousness of potential legal liability in court has been a constant presence. In view of the earlier notorious abuses in this field, such as those associated with Tuskegee, Willowbrook, and the Jewish Hospital case, serious oversight of research is a necessity. Recent criticism by DHHS of FDA oversight of clinical trials, as reported in the New York Times on September 28, 2007, has given emphasis to this point. The matters involved in the major legal claims, such as *Gelsinger* and Roche, demonstrate that litigation may be an appropriate supplement to federal regulation.

There is no doubt that heightened scrutiny on the part of IRBs has occurred in the aftermath of the legal claims. More attention is paid to conflict of interest problems involving researchers and IRB members, although the regulations already mandated such attention. The threat of litigation is perhaps the most effective means to create a heightened liability-consciousness. That result can be destructive of legitimate activities, however. Numerous factors already exist to impede or discourage productive medical research that can benefit the population. The expense and delay inherent in clinical trials often discourages potential sponsors from pursuing research that does not promise to bring large profits. It is not to society's advantage to discourage researchers from investigating treatments and medications when risk and expense are involved if the results may benefit people who suffer from devastating illnesses. Additional obstacles in the path of legitimate research projects may have a disproportionately adverse impact on research.

The negligence lawsuits in this field, because they are directed at and challenge the very essence of the ethical decision-making at issue, tend to have the transforming effect that we have discussed. Once litigation occurs, all the controversies tend to be viewed in legal terms. Legal language and concepts are substituted for their ethical counterparts. The legal implications of every decision and every action can no longer be overlooked. The culture of the ethical field is changed without the investigation and representation of interests that should occur in the case of legislative change. New standards may be set, and new duties and rights may be created based on a single court decision, which involves only the immediate parties. The intervention of courts (invoked by parties) has a powerful normative effect simply because it has the potential in the future to bring oversight and offer economic relief to parties who claim injury.

The changes brought about by judicial decision-making (or brought about by settlement induced by the threat of judicial decision-making) in this field do not necessarily encourage legislatures to step in. Because negligence litigation is a traditional legal action, the implications of a particular court decision may not be seen as so innovative or significant as to warrant legislative intervention. Although it is, in some ways, a stretch to apply tort law to research relationships, it is not so extreme as to generate an immediate legislative response. Courts have a powerful boundary-defining role in this type of intervention.

In the reproductive field, legal doctrine has a similar transforming effect. Again, negligence lawsuits are the primary mode of legal regulation. The ethical dilemmas that are produced by the beginning-of-life situations become transformed by legal language. The same normative effect occurs as future controversies are seen in terms of legal duties and rights rather than primarily as ethical ones. Ethical decision-making continues, of course, and resolves many situations but once legal intervention has occurred, its potential cannot be disregarded. Failure to reach decisions based on ethical discussion and mediation may result in lawsuits. If an ethical resolution does not produce satisfactory results for everyone involved, a negligence lawsuit against medical professionals is a likely occurrence. Again, judicial decision-making requires reframing issues and concepts in legal terms. Courts cannot decide based on ethical analysis. There is good reason why courts openly decide cases based on legal precedents that are publicly available to all parties. Judicial decision-making may not discourage legislatures from becoming involved in legislative measures concerning reproductive issues since the core issues in this field implicate controversial public policy issues. Legislatures have become involved in some states to determine which type of beginning-of-life lawsuits would be recognized and which would not.

The impact of litigation on the fair allocation of organ transplant resources has not been as far-reaching as in other areas of bioethics. The lawsuits have been directed at isolated instances of misconduct and negligence in the implementation of organ allocation rules and in performing transplants. Rather than challenge and potentially undermine the system of ethical regulation, these instances of litigation have tended to reinforce the present ethically based system by insuring that it works as it was designed to do. The actions of some individuals in seeking to bypass the system have so far not been the subject of litigation. If that happens, the system may be undermined. It may well be that the present system should be modified or perhaps drastically changed. Once litigation begins to occur in a way that challenges the basis for the system by a direct attack on the allocation scheme, change will be inevitable. One obstacle that would have to be surmounted is that people who need vital organs, such as kidneys, do not have the time to bear with the long delays inherent in litigation. The potential of using lawsuits to secure priority is less likely than using the media, especially the Internet.

The history of judicial intervention in this country has been, in part, the story of stimulating social, economic, and political change. While this has not always been for the best, it has often caused highly beneficial change. It is not likely that the present allocation system will continue indefinitely. This area of medical science is witnessing dramatic change. Cultural change has produced increased demand for organ transplants and other longevity-producing treatments and procedures. New methods of meeting the demand are in process, but it is too early to tell whether they will be sufficient. It is evident that individuals are no longer willing to wait patiently for their turn to secure organs but are taking the initiative to obtain priority. The new developments in communication and information dissemination make these individual efforts possible on a broad scale. Ethical objections to payment for some organs may be diminishing, especially since payment for reproductive materials is allowed. There is good reason for legislatures to address these issues.

Recent lawsuits in the field of embryonic stem cell research have not had great impact on the ethical controversy. That is not to say that the California litigation has not directly affected the development of research opportunities, given the withholding of funding. The lawsuits, however, have not attacked directly the core ethical issues. They have instead sought to impede progress by attacking issues on the margins. On the other hand, the vast reservoir of judicial decision-making that has given context to the stem cell debates, the abortion litigation, and the family law disputes, have already cast the controversy in legal terms rather than ethical terms. The litigation over the course of many years, much of which preceded the stem cell controversy, has had impact. The power of legal culture in America, which has translated many social and cultural issues into legal terms, has literally transformed many aspects of American society. Courts will doubtlessly continue to play a significant role, especially if legislatures decline to become involved. Courts will not only decide many important issues but also will define the boundaries between legislative and judicial decision-making. The stem cell research issue, a part of the constellation of the ongoing abortion controversy, will remain a dynamic, changing, and evolving social issue for the indefinite future. This will be so at least until serious medical advances are made or until biotechnology makes the disputes academic by developing alternative sources of suitable stem cells.

The Terri Schiavo case was a unique conflict, following its forerunners, the *Quinlan* and *Cruzan* cases. Each controversy was submerged in the judicial system once the parties sought court intervention. After the problems became legal issues, the judicial system took over. There is no question about the impact of the *Quinlan* and *Cruzan* lawsuits. Those cases not only established the jurisprudence for end-of-life decision-making by courts but also contributed to laying out the framework for ethical decision-making. They affected the standards for medical professionals in these situations and established the framework for hospital ethics committee decision-making.

It is likely, for several reasons, that the Schiavo litigation will have less dramatic consequences for future bioethical decision-making. While the case will serve as an illustration of what happens when end-of-life issues are contested relentlessly, the decisions did not establish new legal ground in end-of-life issues to the extent that *Quinlan* and *Cruzan* did. The litigation was the result of a bitter family dispute and was fueled, almost beyond recognition, by the political and social agendas that led to third-party involvement. While a certain amount of political boundary-defining resulted, the overstepping of proper boundaries by both the legislative and executive branches of state and federal governments was so egregious that it trivialized the American political process. This case will stand as an example of how the political system should not function as well as an example of how courts should function. In that respect, *Schiavo* may be an important separation of powers case. It was a spectacle (neither the first nor the last in our history) of the malfunctioning of the American political system. It was also an example of a phenomenon that exists occasionally in American courts—the misuse of the court system by people who act as virtual *engines* of litigation. The case, in all its excruciating detail, speaks to us as the strongest possible argument in favor of ethical resolution of end-of-life issues.

We have looked at problem areas in which a wide range of litigation was used for a variety of purposes. Some lawsuits challenged directly the ethical decision-making methodology, some worked to reinforce the existing mechanism, and some operated at the margins. While we can say that, in some respects, litigation serves a public policy regulatory function, that is secondary to its main purpose of securing decisions in specific controversies. Public policy regulation is not the purpose of the kind of litigation we have addressed.

WHAT NEW DEVELOPMENTS IN BIOTECHNOLOGY WILL GIVE RISE TO LITIGATION?

Court intervention, whatever its purpose, has a significant impact on bioethical decision-making. What are the implications for the future? What new developments in biotechnology will produce problems that will encourage more litigation? Will future litigation produce similar impacts on the underlying ethical issues and on our culture, itself?

At the outset, it seems clear that many of the existing issues will continue to evolve. Ethical and legal issues that arise out the abortion controversy and issues that touch on defining when life begins and when life ends will not be permanently resolved. They will continue to change and develop. Although there may be periods of apparent equilibrium, they will be destabilized by new developments or new decisions. They will be affected by, and will affect, the political and social environment of the nation. The ethical and legal controversies will ebb and flow in the tides of technological and social change. All issues that arise out of deeply held moral beliefs, which will always fall short of achieving consensus in our diverse society, will remain controversial. Some aspects may be resolved by biotechnological change but others, previously unforeseen, will rise to take their places. This is because beginning and end-of-life issues are likely to elude attempts to resolve them in final terms based on objective information. Most issues will be complex and involve more than one subject area. Some major themes in biotechnology are identifiable although the areas of inquiry that they affect are complicated.

Research

In research involving human subjects, we can predict that more issues will arise concerning ownership of human tissues and cells and that more efforts will be made to protect the rights of research subjects. Issues concerning the safeguarding of genetic privacy and the patentability of life forms will arise, as will those involving protection of intellectual property rights of patient groups. The moral status of stem cells, cloning, and embryos will dominate a substantial portion of the legal discourse. The legal forum will be used for many of these questions since ethical study groups and committees tend not to produce consensus, and legislative forums often produce much controversy but little positive action. The dramatic developments in genetics have played a role in the research field and dominate the life enhancement fields. Genetic discoveries and applications have been the foundation of dramatic developments in biotechnology. We are in the beginning stages of genetic research, which has the potential to impact the social structure of families, communities, and society, itself. Genetics may even change, in some ways, traditional concepts of what it is to be human. I believe that fears about changing the fundamental nature of human life are overstated, however. Consider the changes in technology and social structure that have brought us to the present time. Even if biotechnological change is accelerating, still, change tends to be incremental. The immense potential of genetic research is bound to generate controversy and conflict that we cannot now imagine.

Enhancement of Capacity

A second general topic is the enhancement of human life both in terms of increasing longevity and in terms of increasing capacity and performance. This field encompasses organ transplants and other types of transplants that are designed for performance rather than saving or lengthening life. In the latter category are traditional life-saving transplants such as kidney, heart, and lung transplants. In the former are not only joint replacements but also facial transplants. While some transplants relate to essential functions of the body, others address less critical life quality problems. All transplant cases raise issues of fair allocation of resources as well as whether the medical procedures themselves are properly performed. Those issues will result in more litigation especially as increasing expectations of quantity and quality are generated.

Reproductive Enhancement

A variation on the second theme deals with enhancement of the characteristics of babies. The reproductive field has already been deeply affected by genetics, and litigation has occurred in the wrongful life, wrongful birth, and wrongful conception areas. As biotechnology develops new and better techniques of genetic enhancement and selection, we can expect heightened demand, heightened expectations, and increased litigation as a result of improper or perceived improper performance. This field will be a blessing and a curse in terms of what people anticipate and what they receive. This area of biotechnology and bioethics, like other areas of enhancement, is at an early stage of its potential impact.

Life's End

A related theme arises as a result of the continuing development of end-of-life technology. While perhaps somewhat less far-reaching than the beginning of life field, the problems are just as controversial and subject to change. As end-of-life technology gives people the promise of longer life, that potential benefit will not be free of consequences. Paradoxically (or perhaps inevitably) individuals wish to be free to control their own lives to the end. With longevity comes an increasing pressure to have the freedom to terminate life or at least to allow natural death to occur when the quality is no longer acceptable. This accounts for the demand for increased autonomy in terminating life support and for physician-assisted suicide. These issues will intensify as technology makes longer lives possible.

Privacy

With the prospect of increased and enhanced life comes the need for individual liberties throughout life. The desire for privacy, in general, has been consistent in American society, but the concept of privacy has been subject to change. Privacy has, in fact, no uniform or standard meaning. It has meant many different things in American history. At various times, it has meant the need to be alone, to be free of intrusion by others, to protect vital relationships from public scrutiny, to enjoy free expression and unconstrained action, and to protect personal information or opinions, among others. The present age of information and biotechnology has brought with it new, different, and seemingly contradictory meanings. While Americans have voluntarily surrendered many aspects of their privacy in commercial transactions and by way of the Internet, they demand freedom from government surveillance of personal and telephone conversations and freedom from searches and monitoring of activities. They willingly relinquish some information but demand protection for other types. Individuals can be allowed their idiosyncrasies and inconsistencies. If they part with personal information to obtain medical treatment, insurance reimbursement, for credit card purchases, or even to seek out new social relationships, they are entitled not to have that trust abused, by private enterprise or by the government.

While businesses may seek to exploit personal information for marketing purposes, the government may have darker motivations. The Constitutional protections apply regardless of those apparent inconsistencies. Statutory protections in the case of commercial exploitation or misuse of information exist as well. The prospects of brain scanning, memory retrieval, lie detecting, brain fingerprinting, or DNA identifications in government files, are alarming in any social or cultural context. As technology enlarges the range of possibilities for intrusion, so litigation will remain a vital tool for protection against the government and against private enterprises that misuse them.

Public Health

Another area in which litigation has obviously gotten a foothold and will continue to increase concerns the pharmaceutical industry. This is a new development, related to the direct-to-consumer marketing of pharmaceuticals. Increased expectations have brought more attention to the visible failures. Recent litigation involving Vioxx, a widely used anti-inflammatory medication may be a precursor of what lies ahead in court actions. The public health field is another area ripe for more litigation. The swine flu epidemic scare in the 1960s produced a mass of lawsuits, as did the eventual public outcries against use of asbestos and promotion of smoking. What is it about these areas that led to lawsuits? Was it failure of regulation? Did companies push one step too far? Did changes within legal culture force lawyers to launch into new areas? Did overregulation factor in? In the areas previously addressed, what caused regulation by lawsuit to begin? If we can identify what changes produced litigation, we can predict what will happen in untouched areas and can take steps to encourage litigation or ward it off?

Litigation will determine who is entitled to make decisions for people who have decreased capacity. Litigation will remain a vital tool in enforcing ethically based systems as well as in raising appropriate challenges to deficiencies in those systems. As possibilities increase, expectations rise, and disappointments and dissatisfactions also increase. As people expect new drugs to be provided, for example, new medical research will be needed, and mistakes will be made. When new drugs are developed, patients will demand them and, if professionals withhold them for reasons of conscience, frustrations will be vented in lawsuits unless legislatures intervene with protections. People will expect genetically tailored drugs for themselves but, at the same time, will insist on maintaining the privacy of their personal genetic information. Others will seek to invade their genetic information for legitimate and illegitimate purposes. Litigation will be used to restore the balance but, in the process, it will disturb the equilibrium in some instances.

We can see that lawsuits and court decisions will be major forces in protecting individual rights and establishing public policy in the future. We are in the initial stages of the genetic and information revolution. If legislatures fail to develop broad standards (or even if they do) courts will fine tune the standards and, in a legislative vacuum, will create substantive law as well as define the boundaries that separate the political branches.

HOW CAN COURTS AND JUDGES MINIMIZE THE PROBLEMS THAT LITIGATION PRODUCES FOR BIOETHICS DECISION-MAKING?

We can safely say that in each field of bioethics decision-making, a methodology ought to exist that will enable participants (medical professionals and interested participants) to resolve most of their problems without turning to courts. Lawsuits, after all, are time-consuming, expensive and, as we have seen, usually resolve only the legal issues. A bioethical decision-making process ought to be self-contained with professionals properly trained and responsive to patients' needs and with participants equipped to solve problems through negotiation or mediation. This should be true whether the topics are beginning-of-life problems, end-of-life problems, transplants, or others, such as research issues. Litigation should be used only as a last resort in especially difficult dilemmas or in cases where the system has not worked properly because of negligence or other misconduct.

As noted earlier, private lawsuits of the type we are discussing are not ordinarily brought to regulate a field of bioethics or any other field, for that matter. They are brought principally to secure relief claimed for certain violations of duty. The relief may be public, as in the California cases, or private, as in the various malpractice lawsuits. Lawsuits can also be seen as a warning signal that a system of ethical decision-making is not working properly. Some mistakes will occur in any enterprise, of course. The mere allegation that someone, such as a medical professional, has breached a duty or committed negligence or acted on a conflict of interest does not signal a systemic malfunction. Does the action strike at the core functioning of a system or does it operate at the margin, calling attention to isolated mistakes? The Kaiser and the Illinois claims in the organ transplant field called attention to major problems. The infrequent human research issues or the wrongful life claims tend to highlight occasional malpractice that is probably bound to occur from time to time. The need for fundamental corrections in a field of bioethical inquiry, however, must be detected. Action should be taken before serious malfunctioning or serious harm occurs. Ethical systems should be largely self-regulating, with appropriate oversight, of course.

How can court systems operate more effectively? Radical change in the way courts operate is not necessary. The roles of the three branches of government are well established in constitutional law. That does not mean, of course, that boundary issues will cease to arise or that answers to future questions will be obvious. The branches of government will continue to coexist in a state of uneasy equilibrium. Developments in science, medicine, and technology will continue to present difficult challenges to the judicial branch. There are many ways in which court systems can prepare judges for proper handling of lawsuits arising in the diverse fields of bioethics and biotechnology.

Training in Bioethics

One important measure is to ensure that the judges who will handle cases arising out of fields of bioethics are properly educated and trained, not only to preside over the lawsuits themselves but also to understand the implications and impact on the field of bioethical decision-making. They should understand how the ethical decision process generally takes place and what the ethical considerations are. The goal should be to guide the judges to decide cases in ways that will avoid undermining ethical decision-making. Decisions should be narrowly made, without sweeping pronouncements that may inadvertently (or purposely) disturb or change ethical decision-making.

Consequences

Judges must also be aware of the consequences, clinical and personal, of the decisions people make. While this is true with respect to any area of judicial decision-making, it is perhaps most important in family, juvenile, and bioethical decision-making. Without an informed understanding of the significance of the case in its clinical and personal context, serious mistakes in judgment may do harm.

Restraint

Judges, whether in trial or appellate courts, should avoid moving dramatically ahead of the leading edge of social change in society. This implies that judges have an obligation to be aware of developments in society generally. I believe strongly in that proposition. Judges must be well informed in every respect, even though they do not directly apply or engage their knowledge in judicial decisions. Although legislatures should be similarly self-restrained, they have more freedom to be at the forefront of social change and even, in proper situations, to lead social change. They stand for election regularly and should be in a position to conduct a thorough investigation and study of the impact of proposed legislation. Judges have before them only the specific parties in interest to the lawsuit and have little means by which to initiate research or investigation. I do advocate, however, that when judges are deciding cases that will create significant public policy, either in the absence of legislative policy or for the purpose of further defining and applying it, they should take advantage of their authority to call court-appointed experts far more often than they do.

Broaden Participation

Judges should also interpret liberally their authority to allow potential interveners (nonparties who wish to participate in the lawsuit) to participate when rules allow it. In cases with strong public policy overtones, it is desirable to have many points of view represented. This does not convert courts into mini-legislatures, of course, but simply ensures broader perspectives on the issues.

Encourage Legislation

Judges should specifically alert and encourage legislatures to act when they see problems that are appropriate for legislative action. This is much wiser than constructing opinions that imply or assert that existing law is perfectly adequate to resolve the issues. Courts should indicate frankly and with candor the state of the law as it applies to cases at hand. While courts must make decisions, in close cases they can give accurate messages that the statutory or case law they are applying (especially if it is a case of first impression) has limited applicability to the issues but is the only existing authority and must, therefore, be applied by analogy. Courts should acknowledge ambiguity or uncertainty in the law as they work to produce the best application, under the circumstances. This is essential to judicial authority and transparency. Judges must explain their reasoning in detail with candor and thoroughness. While legal fictions are a complicated matter and not easy to generalize about, they should be minimized and explained.

Lack of Expertise

Since judges cannot be experts in all matters that they undertake to decide, they must acknowledge their sources of information in detail. This is one purpose of findings, to provide the factual basis of the decision, attributing it to the evidence submitted in court. Without an accurate accounting, the factual predicate of the decision will not be known. Findings of fact should never be constructed to insulate the decision from effective review on appeal.

Judicial Notice

Judges and legislators have done an admirable job keeping evidence codes up to date with modern society but continuing vigilance is needed. A court may take judicial notice of a fact, that is, consider it without evidence being introduced as long as it is based on common knowledge and not subject to reasonable dispute. In this information age, judicial notice should be used more liberally, adhering to proper notice and hearing requirements, of course, in an effort to make litigation more effective and to focus on the real disputes.

Continuing Jurisdiction and Future Developments

Although some areas of law allow for courts to have continuing jurisdiction over cases, most do not. Where possible, judges should exercise this prerogative in order to avoid the need for more litigation. If parties can return to the same court for further action, judicial economy and the interests of the parties will be served.

Appellate Review

Although appellate courts cannot find facts, they can take into account recent developments under certain circumstances, such as mootness or other jurisdiction issues. They should lean toward liberal interpretation of this opportunity to avoid the cost and delay of new appeals. Final judgment rules should be liberalized to allow for quicker resolution of disputed issues. The problem of trial interruption while interlocutory (during the course of trial, before final judgment) appeals are resolved must be solved by expeditious appellate process for interlocutory appeals in appropriate cases.

Access to Court and the Problem of the Excessive Litigator

It is crucial that all people who have a legitimate right to present their matters to courts must have reasonable access for that purpose. "Access" is often taken to mean the opportunity to see and hear what is going on in courts through media coverage. "Access" in the sense of enabling people to overcome burdens of expense, delay, and proper representation is often given less attention than it deserves. The cost of litigation must be reduced for people who cannot afford court fees and attorneys' fees. The greatest danger to the legal system in this country may be the lack of access of ordinary citizens because of the rising levels of attorney's fees. Recently, a top official of the American Bar Association stated "No one in our nation should have to go to court unassisted when facing a problem that could result in loss of shelter, family dissolution or serious health consequences. Americans should not be subject to grievous harm at the hands of a legal system that they cannot navigate or even understand on their own."[1]

The right to court-appointed counsel should be expanded appropriately in civil cases beyond its present limits. Criminal actions are not the only category of cases at which critical interests are at stake. At present, the range of civil cases in which court-appointed counsel can be applied for is fairly limited in most jurisdictions.[2] Counsel should be available in a broad range of matters in which critical interests are at stake. Some litigants typically have the determination to litigate frequently. Some develop the ability to represent themselves, (*pro se*), and others have resources to secure legal representation. Access to courts can be impeded when judges and other court personnel must give an inappropriate amount of their attention to repetitious or frivolous litigation. Courts should not hesitate to develop efficient methods of dealing with such matters expeditiously.

Court systems need to work at maximizing access to courts and education of the public concerning judicial procedures. The following features may require accommodation in order to maximize the value of legal decisions while minimizing the drawbacks.

Idiom of the Law

The problem of the overreaching effect of law, when issues are translated, permanently, into legal language even when considered in other institutional settings, can be countered by carefully restrained legal decisions accompanied by recognition of nonlegal issues that may remain to be dealt with in other forums.

Adversarial Process

Although this problem-solving process is anathema for some kinds of issues that arise out of bioethics, it is well suited for others, where legal issues are at stake. So long as the legal process does not purport to speak in broad, sweeping terms that undermine ethical resolutions, adversarial process is workable in this field.

Finality, Closure, and the Retrospective View

These aspects of legal decision-making work well in ordinary disputes. They tend to insure that a decision will result from the process, unlike many other types of problem-solving. Mediation of ethical issues may or may not produce a firm result. Bringing a legal action guarantees a final result under most circumstances. That feature is a benefit and a detriment, depending on the purpose of undertaking problem-solving. These features are designed to insure that a decision will be made, since they establish rules that move the process along toward resolution. The over-simplification of issues is a necessary corollary of the process which is geared toward concrete decision-making.

Institutional Biases

This aspect of litigation needs attention. Some biases, such as the favoring of maintaining life, arise out of the nature of litigation, itself, and are healthy features. The bias in favor of individualism grows out of our political system and founding documents, which lean toward individual rights as opposed to public interests. Others, such as the bias toward economic interests or naturalizing new developments, arise partly because of the nature of litigation and partly because of convenience. Economic interests are easier to define than ethical or moral interests and obviously easier to quantify.

Impact on future controversies

Decisions of appellate courts do have a restrictive effect on future litigants who were not involved in the earlier cases. While future litigants are not strictly bound by the earlier ruling (as in the case of other doctrines of finality, such as res judicata), prior decisions serve as precedent—the principle of *stare decisis*. In addition, I have noted that courts have a boundary-defining function, which impacts the institutional role of the courts as they compete with the other branches. Courts typically reaffirm their own authority while restricting the scope of legislative deliberation. Courts tend to place themselves at the center of the controversy and the decision process.

To the extent that courts are not specifically charged with establishing public policy, as legislatures are, the consequences of court decisions are not uniform. Often, we observe that current issues are first litigated in court and then developed further by legislatures. Legislatures, surprisingly, may be more risk-averse than courts. Courts, especially federal courts, are far more willing to venture into controversial issues than legislatures because they are insulated from the democratic process, by which legislators can be voted out of office. Courts can unwittingly discourage legislative action when they fail to signal that policy decisions are needed. Legislators also respond on their own initiative based on the consequences of judicial decisions.

For decades, science has been allowed to proceed on its own with no more accountability than technical review and quality control by peer review. The increasingly dramatic developments in science and biotechnology have created a demand for more accountability. In the absence of other forums for discussion, those who wanted more oversight looked to the established branches of government as the primary sources of normative policymaking and guidance. In the United States, a combination of factors including federalism, a presidential election system focused on celebrity rather than substance, a powerful judiciary, a vigorous science lobby, and development of the divisive politics of abortion, have made sweeping and effective legislation difficult. Courts, therefore, have been given latitude to rule on normative issues at the borders of science and biotechnology.

In our law-conscious society, the language of judicial decision-making often has a persuasive impact beyond the expected scope of its authority. As I have noted, legal reconstructions of issues often have normative power beyond the legal forum, and subsequent ethical decision-making usually adopts legal concepts and standards. For these reasons, courts need to consider carefully the consequences of decisions. While that process may not produce a different result from the one originally intended, the contours of the decision—the scope, reasoning, and applicability—may be framed differently. In the field of bioethics, this consideration is especially important since court decisions serve to guide extensive private and public decision-making. Judicial accountability demands nothing less. It is fair to ask whether court decisions on public policy matters illuminate the underlying ethical and social issues, whether they unduly elevate consideration of rights over responsibilities, whether they provide adequate access to affected parties, even those lacking the means of seeking effective access, whether they acknowledge uncertainty and ambiguity, and whether they consider fairly all positions. When court decisions are likely to have normative impact beyond the reach of legal decisions, courts must accept special responsibility to weigh the potential consequences.

Toqueville's observation that virtually all political questions in American society eventually become legal and judicial questions has proven true. As history has developed, many critical questions have started out as legal issues and, later, after court decisions, they have been dealt with in the political realm. Court rulings have often inspired legislatures to act rather than the reverse, a process that attests to the powerful influence of courts in American society. The existence of that important influence demands special attention to insure proper accountability and broad public access.

Notes

CHAPTER 1

1. Alexis de Tocqueville, "Causes Which Mitigate the Tyranny of the Majority in the United States," in *Democracy in America,* vol. 1 (1835).

2. William Shakespeare, *The Tempest,* Act V, Scene 1, lines 183–84 in *Shakespeare, The Complete Works,* ed. G. B. Harrison (New York: Harcourt, Brace and Company, 1952).

3. The President's Council on Bioethics, *Beyond Therapy: Biotechnology and the Pursuit of Happiness,* October, 2003, http://www.bioethics.gov/reports/beyondtherapy/beyond_therapy_final_webcorrected.pdf.

4. Ibid., 2. The Council added importantly that "[o]verarching the processes and products it brings forth, biotechnology is also a *conceptual and ethical outlook,* informed by progressive aspirations. In this sense, it appears as a most recent and vibrant expression of the technological spirit, a desire and disposition rationally to understand, order, predict, and (ultimately) control the events and workings of nature, all pursued for the sake of human benefit."

5. *Cambridge Dictionary Online,* s.v. "biotechnology," http://dictionary.cambridge.org/define.asp?key=7596&dict=CALD.

6. President's Council, *Beyond Therapy,* 1.

7. Ibid.

8. Legal standards that apply to jury decisions in criminal cases, for example, have found their way into the popular culture. People in everyday life readily apply concepts like the presumption of innocence and proof beyond a reasonable doubt as though they had general application to ordinary discussion of criminal

allegations or investigations. This applies to other areas of the law as well. See Carl E. Schneider, "Bioethics in the Language of the Law," *Hastings Center Report* 24, no. 4 (July–August 1994): 16–22.

9. National Center for Policy Analysis, "The Role of Economics and Ethics in Public Policy Debates," http://www.ncpa.org/pi/health/pd061599e.html.

10. Associated Press, "Clinton to Apologize for Tuskegee Syphilis Experiment," *CNN.com*, April 8. 1997. See chap. 3.

11. See G. Edsall, "Experiments at Willowbrook," *Lancet* 2, no. 7715 (1971): 95.

12. See Robert D. Mulford, *Experimentation on Human Beings,* 20 Stan. L. Rev. 99 (1967).

11. See Nuremberg Code, *British Medical Journal* 313, no. 7070 (1996): 1448–49.

12. See World Medical Organization, Declaration of Helsinki, *British Medical Journal* 313, no. 7070 (1996): 1448–49.

13. See Van Rensselaer Potter, *Bioethics: Bridge to the Future* (Englewood Cliffs, NJ: Prentice Hall, 1971).

14. Arthur B. LaFrance, *Bioethics: Health Care, Human Rights and the Law* (Matthew Bender & Co., 2006).

15. See Susan M. Wolf, *Shifting Paradigms in Bioethics and Health Law: The Rise of a New Pragmatism,* 20 Am. J.L. & Med. 395, 395–415 (1994).

16. Ibid.

17. See *Opentopia Online,* s.v. "Roman Catholic Church," http://encycl.opentopia.com/term/Roman_Catholic_Church.

CHAPTER 2

1. William Shakespeare, *Measure for Measure,* Act 2, Scene 2, lines 117–22 in *Shakespeare, The Complete Works,* ed. G.B. Harrison (New York: Harcourt, Brace and Company, 1952).

2. Sheila Jasanoff, "The Life Sciences and the Rule of Law," *Journal of Molecular Biology* 319, no. 4 (2002): 891–92.

3. Ibid., 892.

4. Ibid., 893.

5. Barry R. Schaller, *A Vision of American Law: Judging Law, Literature, and the Stories We Tell* (Westport, CT: Praeger Publishers, 2001), 1.

6. Jasanoff, "Life Sciences," 893.

7. See Charles S. Lopeman, *The Activist Advocate: Policy Making in State Supreme Courts* (Westport, CT: Praeger Publishers, 1999; Edmund M.Y. Leong, *The Hawaii Supreme Court's Role in Public Policy-Making* (New York: LFB Scholarly Publishing LLC, 2002).

8. Tom L. Beauchamps and James F. Childress, *Principles of Biomedical Ethics* (Oxford University Press, 1994). See chap. 1.

9. See Lawrence M. Friedman, *Total Justice* (New York: Russell Sage Foundation, 1985).

10. Schaller, "Shaking the Foundations: Problems of Legal Authority," in *A Vision of American Law.*

11. Schaller, "Taking Responsibility: Societal Change and Judicial Decision Making," in *A Vision of American Law.*

12. See President's Council, *Beyond Therapy.*

13. Sheila Jasanoff, "The Law's Construction of Expertise," in *Science at the Bar: Law, Science, and Technology in America* (Cambridge, MA: Harvard University Press, 1995).

14. Ibid.

15. Alan Meisel, "The Role of Litigation in End of Life Care: A Reappraisal," *Improving End of Life Care: Why Has It Been so Difficult? Hastings Center Report Special Report* 35, no. 6 (2005): S47–S51.

16. Marc Wortman, "Two Alternatives, Each a Little Wrong," *Yale Medicine* (Spring 2004): 30–37.

17. Jay Wolfson, "Erring on the Side of Theresa Schiavo: Reflections of the Special Guardian ad Litem," *The Hastings Center Report* 35, no. 3 (May–June 2005): 17.

18. Ibid.

CHAPTER 3

1. Sally Lehrman, "The Gelsinger Story," *Gene Saga,* May 1, 2000; Ronald Munson, *Intervention and Reflection,* 7th ed. (Belmont, CA: Wadsworth/Thomson, 2004).

2. Rick Weiss and Deborah Nelson, "Penn Settles Gene Therapy Suit," *Washington Post,* November 4, 2000, A4.

3. Nuremberg Code, *British Medical Journal* 313, no. 7070 (1996): 1448–49.

4. Bonnie Steinbock, John D. Arras, and Alex John London, *Ethical Issues in Modern Medicine,* Sixth ed. (New York: McGraw-Hill, 2003), 730

5. Cynthia McGuire Dunn and Gary L. Chadwich, *Protecting Study Volunteers in Research: A Manual for Investigative Sites* (Boston: Thomson/CenterWatch, 2004), 20–21.

6. Ibid.

7. World Medical Organization, Declaration of Helsinki, *British Medical Journal* 313, no. 7070 (1996): 1448–49.

8. Henry K. Beecher, "Ethics and Clinical Research," *New England Journal of Medicine* 274 (1966): 1354–60.

9. Protection of Human Subjects, *Code of Federal Regulations,* title 45, part 46 (2005).

10. Eileen Welsome, *The Plutonium Files: America's Secret Medical Experiments in the Cold War* (Delta, 2000).

11. Robert J. Levine, *Ethics and Regulation of Clinical Research*, 2nd ed. (New Haven, CT: Yale University Press, 1988), 70.

12. University of New Hampshire, Responsible Conduct of Research, "Chronology of Cases Involving Unethical Treatment of Human Subjects," http://www.unh.edu/rcr/HumSubj-GoToChronology.htm.

13. Levine, *Ethics and Regulation*, 71.

14. Philip Zimbardo, *The Lucifer Effect: Understanding How Good People Turn Evil* (New York: Random House, 2007).

15. Levine, *Ethics and Regulation*, 71.

16. *Aderman v. The Trustees of the University of Pennsylvania*, No. 3285 (Ct. Com. Pl.). The defendants are roughly the same as Gelsinger and the claims by this plaintiff are based on the FDA violations. They take the form of a wide variety of legal claims, including a generic breach of the right to be treated with dignity. Although this plaintiff does not appear to have sustained death or physical injury, her lawyers appear to have framed the case with that in mind, having alleged causes of action that do not depend on physical injury or death.

17. *Wright v. Fred Hutchinson Cancer Research Center*, 269 F. Supp. 2d 1286 (W.D. Wash. 2002).

18. *Lett v. The Ohio State University, et al.*, C2-02-0006 (S.D. Ohio 2002).

19. Robertson *ex rel. Robertson v. McGee*, 2002 WL 535045 (N.D. Okla. 2002).

20. E. Haavi Morreim, "Medical Research Litigation and Malpractice Tort Doctrines: Courts on a Learning Curve," *Houston Journal of Health Law and Policy* 4, 2003, 2.

21. Ibid.

22. Ibid.

23. Ibid., 3.

24. Ibid.

25. Ibid. Research is regulated whether or not supported by federal funds.

26. Ibid., 5.

27. "Settlement Reached in Gelsinger Death," *IRB Advisor*, April 2005.

28. Ibid.

29. Dale Keiger and Sue De Pasquale, "Trials & Tribulations," *Johns Hopkins Magazine* (2002), http://www.jhu.edu/~jhumag/0202web/trials.html.

30. United States National Library of Medicine, National Institutes of Health, "FAQ: Clinical Trial Phases," http://www.nlm.nih.gov/services/ctphases.html.

31. Morreim, "Medical Research Litigation," 5.

32. Ibid., 11; *Mink v. University of Chicago*, 460 F. Supp. 713 (N.D. Ill. 1978).

33. *Grimes v. Kennedy Krieger Institute, Inc.*, 782 A. 2d 807 (Md. 2001). This case was first a Maryland Court of Appeals decision followed by a Maryland Supreme Court decision.

34. Ibid.

35. Weiss, "Penn Settles Gene Therapy Suit."

36. Julia Zhou, "Four Years Later, Gelsinger Case Still Has Lasting Implications," *The Daily Pennsylvanian,* November 6, 2003.

37. Ibid.

38. Susan Fitzgerald and Virginia A. Smith, "Penn to Pay $517,000 in Gene Therapy Death," *Philadelphia Inquirer,* February 10, 2005.

39. Ibid.

40. "Settlement Reached," *IRB Advisor,* 44-45.

41. Ibid.

42. Action by the University of Pennsylvania in Response to the "Report of the Independent Panel Reviewing the Institute for Human Gene Therapy," May 24, 2000, http://www.upenn.edu/almanac/v46/n34/OR-IHGT-actions.html.

43. Christy Feig and Sandra Young, "Death Suspends Johns Hopkins Study," *CNN.com,* June 15, 2001, http://archives.cnn.com/2001/HEALTH/06/15/study.death/index.html.

44. Ibid.

45. Ibid.

46. Christine Cassel et al., Report of Johns Hopkins University External Review Committee, 1, http://www.hopkinsmedicine.org/external.pdf.

47. Johns Hopkins Responds to OHRP Suspension of Research, Johns Hopkins Medical Institutions, July 19, 2001, http://www.hopkinsmedicine.org/press/2001/JULY/010719.htm.

48. Cassel et al., Report, 6.

49. Roche Settlement, Hopkins Medical News, Winter 2002.

50. H.B. 917, 2002 Reg. Sess., (Md. 2002), http://biotech.law.lsu.edu/research/ma/ma_hb0917t.htm.

51. *Abney v. Amgen, Inc.,* 443 F.3d 540 (6th Cir. 2006).

52. *Suthers v. Amgen, Inc.,* 441 F. Supp. 2d 478 (S.D.N.Y. 2006).

53. *Suthers v. Amgen, Inc., 372* F. Supp. 2d 416, 418 (S.D.N.Y. 2005).

54. *Abney,* 443 F. 3d at 543.

55. *Abney v. Amgen, Inc.,* 2005 WL 1630154, *12 (E.D. Ky. 2005).

56. See *Mathews v. Eldridge,* 424 U.S. 319 (1976).

57. *Abney,* 2005 WL 1630154 at *12.

58. *Wright v. Fred Hutchinson Cancer Research Center,* 269 F. Supp. 2d 1286 (W.D. Wash. 2002).

59. Another case, *Berman v. Fred Hutchinson Cancer Research Center,* was also brought in the District Court for the Western District of Washington, against the Fred Hutchinson Cancer Research Center after four women died after being treated with a drug to protect them against the effects of high-dose chemotherapy. See order granting partial summary judgment for the plaintiffs at http://biotech.law.lsu.edu/research/wa/Berman_v_Hutchinson.pdf.

60. The Civil Rights Act, U.S. Code 42 (1996), § 1983.

61. Current Good Manufacturing Practice in Manufacturing, Processing, Packing, or Holding of Drugs: General, *Code of Federal Regulations,* title 21, sec.

210–11 (2005); Food and Drug Administration, Department of Health and Human Services, Biologics, *Code of Federal Regulations,* title 21, sec. 610, 610; Protection of Human Subjects, *Code of Federal Regulations,* title 45, part 46 (2005).

62. *United States v. Stanley,* 483 U.S. 669 (1987).

63. *Heinrich v. Sweet,* 62 F. Supp. 2d 282 (D. Mass. 1999).

64. *Stadt v. University of Rochester,* 921 F. Supp. 1023 (W.D.N.Y. 1996).

65. See Jonathan D. Moreno, *Undue Risk: Secret State Experiments on Humans* (New York: Routledge, 2001), 9; Advisory Committee on Human Radiation Experiments, Minutes of June 21–23, 1995 meeting, http://www.gwu.edu/~nsarchiv/radiation/dir/mstreet/commeet/meet15/minute15.txt; Brief of Amicus Curiae Trial Lawyers for the Public Justice, P.C., in Support of the Objectors to the Proposed Settlement, *In re* Cincinnati Radiation Litigation, C-1-94-126 (S.D Ohio January 20, 1998), http://www.tlpj.org/briefs/034-Cincinnati.htm.

66. *Wright v. Fred Hutchinson Cancer Research Center,* 269 F. Supp. 2d 1286, 1295 (W.D. Wash. 2002).

67. Other potentially significant cases are pending without court rulings to this point. In addition to the cases mentioned in passing earlier, there is *Guckin v. Nagle,* 259 F. Supp. 2d 406 (E.D. Pa. 2003) in which the defendants include the individual IRB members who passed on the study in question. In another case pending in the same court, *Scheer v. Burke,* the chairperson of the IRB is a defendant. In *Hamlet v. Fradin,* 03 CVS 1161 (2003) in the North Carolina state court, the plaintiff claimed that he suffered the effects of psoriasis because he was receiving placebos, rather than an existing treatment while he was in the study. See complaint at http://www.sskrplaw.com/gene/hamletcomplaint.pdf; In *Beth Wade v. Oregon Health & Science University,* 02-CV-877-KI (2002), a class action from Oregon, the plaintiff students asserted that they were forced to participate in a study concerning drug use by high-school students who were involved in extracurricular activities, as a condition of participating in those activities. See complaint at http://www.sskrplaw.com/gene/cordy.html.

68. Doctrines, such as comparative negligence, exist to apportion liability but that is strictly confined by the rules and does not apply to our discussion.

69. Present circumstances count occasionally in court such as for determining technical matters such as injunctive relief or mootness.

CHAPTER 4

1. *Paretta v. Medical Offices for Human Reproduction,* 760 N.Y.S.2d 639, 642 (2003).

2. *Roe v. Wade,* 410 U.S. 113 (1973); *Planned Parenthood of Southeastern Pa. v. Casey,* 505 U.S. 833 (1992); *Stenberg v. Carhart,* 550 U.S. 914 (2000); *Cruzan v. Director, Missouri Department of Health,* 497 U.S. 261 (1990); *Washington v. Glucksberg,* 521 U.S. 702 (1997); *Vacco v. Quill,* 521 U.S. 793 (1997).

3. Down Syndrome is a congenital disorder caused by the presence of an extra 21st chromosome. Anencephaly involves the congenital absence of all or a major part of the brain. Tay-Sachs disease is a hereditary disorder of lipid metabolism typically affecting persons of Eastern Jewish ancestry.

4. Wendy F. Hensel, *The Disabling Impact of Wrongful Birth and Wrongful Life Actions,* 45 Harv. C.R.-C.L. L. Rev. 141–42 (2005).

5. I recognize that the U.S. Supreme Court has so far declined to recognize such a right in cases such as *Cruzan, Glucksberg,* and *Vacco.* See Schneider, "Bioethics in the Language of the Law," , 16–22.

6. Adam A. Milani, *Better Off Dead Than Disabled?: Should Courts Recognize a "Wrongful Living" Cause of Action When Doctors Fail to Honor Patients' Advanced Directives?,* 54 Wash. & Lee L. Rev. 149, 151 (1997).

7. Ibid., 153.

8. Ibid.

9. Ibid.

10. *Zepeda v. Zepeda,* 190 N.E.2d 849 (1963).

11. Ibid., 857.

12. Ibid., 859.

13. *Gleitman v. Cosgrove,* 227 A.2d 689 (N.J. 1967).

14. Ibid., 692.

15. See *Roe v. Wade,* 410 U.S. 113 (1973) and *Planned Parenthood of Southeastern Pa. v. Casey,* 505 U.S. 833 (1992).

16. *Gleitman,* 227 A.2d at 693.

17. Hensel, *The Disabling Impact,* 142.

18. *Becker v. Swartz,* 386 N.E.2d 807 (N.Y. 1978)

19. Ibid., 810.

20. Ibid., 812 (quoting *Park v. Chessin,* 400 N.Y.S.2d 110, 114 (1977)).

21. Ibid.

22. *Curlender v. Bio-Science Laboratories,* 106 Cal. App. 3d 811 (1980).

23. *Willis v. Wu,* 362 S.C. 146 (2004).

24. Ibid.

25. See S.C. Code Ann. §§ 44-41-10 – 44-41-85 (2002) (prohibiting abortions after the twenty-fourth week of gestation unless two unrelated physicians certify in writing it is necessary to preserve the life or health of the mother).

26. *Willis,* 362 S.C. at 162.

27. Ibid.

28. *Grubbs v. Barbourville Family Health Center,* 120 S.W.3d 682 (Ky. 2003) (*Bogan v. Altman & McGuire,* P.S.C. was consolidated with Grubbs and the two consolidated cases went to the court of appeals prior to this action before the Kentucky Supreme Court).

29. Ibid., 685.

30. Ibid.

31. Ibid., 686.

32. Ibid., 687.

33. Ibid., 690.

34. Ibid., 691.

35. *Paretta v. Medical Offices for Human Reproduction*, 760 N.Y.S.2d 639 (2003).

36. *Becker v. Swartz*, 386 N.E.2d 807 (N.Y. 1978).

37. *Taylor v. Kurapati*, 236 Mich. App. 315 (1999).

38. Ibid., 320.

39. *Proffitt v. Bartolo*, 162 Mich. App. 35 (1987).

40. Ibid., 57–58.

41. *Taylor*, 236 Mich. App. at 340.

42. Ibid., 349.

43. Ibid.

44. Ibid.

45. *Buck v. Bell*, 274 U.S. 200 (1927).

46. Ibid., 207.

47. *Taylor*, 236 Mich. App. at 354.

48. Ibid., 355.

49. *Curlender v. Bio-Science Laboratories*, 106 Cal. App. 3d 811, 815 (1980).

50. Ibid., 826.

51. Ibid.

52. Ibid.

53. Ibid., 827, 826.

54. Ibid., 829.

55. *Turpin v. Sortini*, 31 Cal.3d 220 (1981).

56. Ibid., 223.

57. Ibid.

58. Cal. Health & Safety Code Ann. § 7186 (West 2000).

59. *Turpin*, 31 Cal.3d at 233.

60. *Harbeson v. Parke Davis*, 98 Wash.2d 460 (1983).

61. *Procanik by Procanik v. Cillo*, 97 N.J. 339 (1984).

62. Lori B. Andrews, *Torts and the Double Helix: Malpractice Liability for Failure to Warn of Genetic Risk*, 29 Hous. L. Rev. 149, 152 (1992).

63. Ibid., 153.

64. *Roe v. Wade*, 410 U.S. 113 (1973).

65. *Gildiner v. Thomas Jefferson Univ. Hosp.*, 451 F. Supp. 692, 695 (E.D. Pa. 1978)

66. Andrews, *Torts and the Double Helix*, 154.

67. Andrews, *Torts and the Double Helix*, 156 (see n. 27 citing *Siemieniec v. Lutheran Gen. Hosp.*, 480 N.E.2d 1227, 1232 (Ill. App. Ct. 1985)).

68. The following states preclude wrongful life actions by statute: Indiana, Idaho, Maine, Michigan, Minnesota, Missouri, North Dakota, Pennsylvania,

South Dakota, and Utah. See Catherine Palo, *Causes of Action for Wrongful Birth and Wrongful Life*, 23 COA 2d 55 (2006).

69. *Wrongful Birth Actions: The Case Against Legislative Curtailment*, 100 Harv. L. Rev. 2017 (1987); Andrews, *Torts and the Double Helix*, 59–60, n. 50.

70. Andrews, *Torts and the Double Helix*, 162.

71. Ibid.

72. Oregon Rev. Stat. Ann.§§ 127.800 – 127.897 (2005).

73. *Gonzales v. Oregon*, 546 U.S. 243 (2006).

74. Milani, *Better off Dead*, 151.

75. See Grayson Barber, "Privacy and the New Jersey State Constitution," http://graysonbarber.com/pdf/PrivacyandtheNJConstitution.pdf

76. In re Quinlan, 355 A.2d 647 (N.J. 1976)

77. Milani, *Better off Dead*, 155.

78. Ibid., 156.

79. Ibid., 167.

80. Ibid., 168.

81. Ibid., 169.

82. *Anderson v. St. Francis-St. George Hospital, Inc.*, 614 N.E.2d 841 (Ohio App. 1992).

83. See Milani, *Better off Dead*, 184.

84. *Estate of Leach v. Shapiro*, 13 Ohio App.3d 393 (1984).

85. *Anderson*, 614 N.E.2d at 845.

86. Ibid., 846.

87. *Anderson v. St. Francis-St. George Hospital*, 1995 WL 109128, *3 (Ohio App. 1995).

88. *Anderson*, 614 N.E.2d at 228. (citation omitted).

89. See Milani, *Better off Dead*, 184; *McGuinness v. Barnes*, No. A-3457-94T5, slip op. (N.J. Super. Ct. App. Div. 1996).

90. See Milani, *Better off Dead*, 187.

91. *Willis v. Wu*, 362 S.C. 146 (2004).

92. *Taylor v. Kurapati*, 236 Mich. App. 315 (1999).

93. *Turpin v. Sortini*, 31 Cal.3d 220 (1981).

94. *Procanik by Procanik v. Cillo*, 97 N.J. 339 (1984).

95. *Willis*, 362 S.C. at 155.

96. Ibid., 159.

97. Hensel, *The Disabling Impact*, 194.

CHAPTER 5

1. Arthur Caplan, "Cutting in Line for Organ Transplants," *MSNBC*, August 25, 2004, http://www.msnbc.msn.com/id/5810779/print/1/displaymode/1098/; Associated Press, "Man Who Advertised for Liver Dies," KGBT 4 News, April 26, 2005, .

2. Raymond J. Devettere, "Transplantation," in *Practical Decision Making in Health Care Ethics* (Washington, D.C.: Georgetown University Press, 2000), 513–51.

3. Ibid.

4. Ibid.

5. Lawrence K. Altman, "The Ultimate Gift: 50 Years of Organ Transplants," *New York Times*, December 21, 2004.

6. Devettere, *Practical Decision Making*, 162–97, 513–51.

7. Robert Steinbrook, "Public Solicitation of Organ Donors," *New England Journal of Medicine* 353, no. 5 (August 4, 2005): 441–44.

8. Ibid.

9. United Network for Organ Sharing, http://www.unos.org/.

10. James F. Childress, "The First of Life: Ethical Issues in Organ Transplantation," American College of Surgeons. Committee on Ethics, http://www.facs.org/education/ethics/childresslect.html.

11. Devettere, *Practical Decision Making*, 521–23.

12. Steinbrook, "Public Solicitation," n.3.

13. The Organ Procurement and Transplantation Network, "OPTN/UNOS Board Opposes Solicitation for Deceased Organ Donation," http://www.optn.org/news/newsDetail.asp?id=374.

14. Ibid.

15. Steinbrook, "Public Solicitation," 443.

16. Ibid., 442.

17. Ibid, n.1.

18. Final Rule, Organ Procurement and Transplantation Network, *Federal Register* 64 no. 56650-01 (October 20, 1999).

19. Donald Joralemon and Phil Cox, "Body Values: The Case Against Compensating for Transplant Organs," *Hastings Center Report* 33, no. 1 (2003): 27–33.

20. Ibid., 31.

21. Ibid., 32.

22. Ibid., 31–32.

23. Ibid., 31. While U.S. common law has no "duty to rescue," one who "voluntarily assumes to assist a sick, injured or imperiled person . . . is charged with the duty of common or ordinary humanity to provide proper care and attention." See 57A Am. Jur. 2d Negligence § 106. Unlike the United States, most European countries have passed laws creating a duty to rescue. In the United States, only five states had enacted such states. In four of these states, the "duty to rescue" means a "duty to report a crime," if such can be done without risk to the person reporting. Only Vermont requires a person to provide "reasonable assistance" to another person if they are exposed to "grave physical harm," but again, only in the case where the rescuer can go so without danger or peril to their self or others.

24. Childress, "The First of Life," 3. "[F]ewer than 50 percent of American adults are very or somewhat likely to donate their organs after their deaths, and even fewer actually sign donor cards or other documents of gifts." Contrast this with 1968 figures where approximately 70 percent indicated a willingness to donate. Ibid.

25. United States Attorney Northern District of Illinois, Press Release, "UIC Medical Center Pays $2 Million to United States and State of Illinois to Settle Liver Transplant Fraud Suit" (November 17, 2003).

26. Chris Rauber, "Kaiser Whistleblower Files Lawsuit, Raises Concerns," *East Bay Business Times* (July 21, 2006), http://bizjournals.com/eastbay/stories/2006/07/17/daily40.html?t=printable.

27. Ibid.

28. Ibid.

29. Ibid.

30. Ibid.

31. Ibid.

32. "Kaiser Permanente Fined $5M for Poor Management of Kidney Transplant Program," *Medical News Today,* (August 15, 2006), http://www.medicalnewstoday.com/printerfriendlynews.php?newsid=49532.

33. Associated Press, "HMO Fined Over Kidney Transplant Program," *CBS News* (August 11, 2006), http://www.cbsnews.com/stories/2006/08/11/ap/health/printableD8JDUS2G1.shtml.

34. "Kaiser Permanente's Kidney Transplant Program: Kaiser Mismanagement Under Investigation," *Free Advice, Insurance Law, Health Insurance, Current Lawsuit: Kaiser of Northern California Kidney Transplant,* http://law.freeadvice.com/insurance_law/health_insurnace/kaiser-permanente-kidney-transplant.htm.

35. Associated Press, "Kaiser Sued Over Kidney Transplant Program," *ABC News,* (2006), http://abcnews.go.com/Business/print?id=1957005.

36. Rauber, "Kaiser Whistleblower Files Lawsuit."

37. "Lawsuit Alleges Negligence at UCIMC Liver Transplant Program," *California Healthline,* California Healthcare Foundation (November 16, 2005), http://www.californiahealthline.org/index.cfm?Action=dspItem&itemID=116007&classcd=CL350.

38. Ibid.

39. Ibid.

40. Tracy Weber and Charles Ornstein, "20% of U.S. Transplant Centers Are Found to Be Substandard," *Los Angeles Times* (June 29, 2006), http://www.latimes.com/news/printedition/la-me-transplant29jun29,1,7236975.story.

41. Ibid.

42. Emily Ramshaw, "After Transplant Tragedy, Parents Want Safeguards," *Dallas Morning News* (March 26, 2006).

43. "Anatomy of a Mistake," *CBS News* (September 7, 2003), http://www.cbsnews.com/stories/2003/03/16/60minutes/printable544162.shtml. See Barron H. Lerner, "From Libby Zion to Jesica Santillan," in *A Death Retold: Jesica Santillan, the Bungled Transplant, and Paradoxes of Medical Citizenship,* eds. Keith Wailoo, Julie Livingston, and Peter Guarnaccia (Chapel Hill: The University of North Carolina Press, 2006).

44. Cedars-Sinai's Live Donor Liver Transplant Program Receives "Unos-approved" Designation," *Eurek Alert* (July 7, 2005), http://www.eurekalert.org/pub_releases/2005-07/cmc-cld070705.php.

45. Ibid.

46. Associated Press, "Report Sheds Light on Absence of Data About Living Donors," *Columbia Daily Tribune,* (May 9, 2005), http://archive.columbiatribune.com/2005/may/20050509news005.asp.

47. Ibid.

48. Ibid.

49. Ibid.

50. Ibid.

51. Steinbrook, "Public Solicitation," 443.

52. Ibid.

53. United Press International, "Analysis: Sweetening the Deal for Donors," *Science Daily* (July 26, 2006).

CHAPTER 6

1. John A. Robertson, *Causative vs. Beneficial Complicity in the Embryonic Stem Cell Debate,* 36 Conn. L. Rev. 4, 1099 (2004).

2. Ibid., 1099–1100.

3. Robert S. Schwartz, "The Politics and Promise of Stem-Cell Research," *The New England Journal of Medicine* 355, no. 12 (2006): 1189.

4. "Bush Vetoes Stem Cell Legislation," *Washington Post.com*(June 21, 2007), http://www.washingtonpost.com/wp-dyn/content/article/2007/06/20/AR2007062000180.html; "President Bush Vetoes Another Stem Cell Bill: Congress and States Respond," American Institute of Biological Sciences (July 9, 2007), http://www.aibs.org/public-policy-reports/2007_07_09.html#003796; "Shea-Porter Votes to Support Life-Saving Research," *Nhpols.com* (June 7, 2007), http://www.aibs.org/public-policy-reports/2007_07_09.html#003796.

5. Abigail Leonard, "Stem Cell Treatment Could Save Patients with Heart Failure," *ABCNews.com* (March 26, 2007), http://abcnews.go.com/GMA/OnCall/story?id=2980927&page=1.

6. Ann A. Kiessling, *What Is an Embryo?* 36 Conn. L. Rev. 4, 1051 (2004).

7. The President's Council on Bioethics, *Monitoring Stem Cell Research* (Washington D.C.: January 2004).

8. Ibid., 3.

9. Ibid., 4.

10. Ibid., 5.

11. Ibid., 4–5.

12. Ibid., 5.

13. Stephen S. Hall, "Stem Cells: A Status Report," *The Hastings Center Report* 36, no. 1 (2006): 18.

14. Mark Silk, "Church State Entanglement," http://www.trincoll.edu/depts/csrpl/RINVol5No2/entanglement.htm.

15. Roger Williams, "Mr. Cotton's Letter Lately Printed, Examined, and Answered," in *The Complete Writings of Roger Williams,* ed. J. Hammond Trumball (New York: Russell & Russell, 1963), 108.

16. James Hutson, "'A Wall of Separation' FBI Helps Restore Jefferson's Obliterated Draft," *The Library of Congress,* http://www.loc.gov/loc/lcib/9806/danbury.html.

17. *Reynolds v. United States,* 98 U.S. 145 (1878).

18. "Founders Designed Establishment Clause to Protect Religion, McConnell Says," Virginia Law, http://www.law.virginia.edu/html/news/2005_fall/mcconnell.htm.

19. Barak Obama, "Call to Renewal," (keynote speech presented at Call to Renewal's Building a Covenant for a New America Conference, Washington D.C., June 28, 2006), http://obama.senate.gov/speech/060628-call_to_renewal_keynote_address/index.html.

20. *Roe v. Wade,* 410 U.S. 113 (1973); Susan L. Crockin, *'What Is an Embryo?' A Legal Perspective,* 36 Conn. L. Rev.4, 1179 (2004).

21. *Roe,* 410 U.S. at 158.

22. See *Moore v. Regents* of the University of California, 793 P.2d 479 (Cal. 1990); *Davis v. Davis,* 842 S.W.2d 588 (Tenn. 1992); *Hecht v. Superior Court,* 20 Cal. Rptr. 2d 275 (Cal. CT. App. 1993); *McFall v. Shimp,* 10 Pa. D. & C.3d (1978).

23. National Conference of Legislatures, "State Embryonic and Fetal Research Laws," www.ncsl.org/programs/health/genetics/embfet.htm.

24. Ibid.

25. Russell Korobkin, "An Abusive Stem-Cell Lawsuit," *San Francisco Gate,* March 13, 2006, B5.

26. Andrew Pollack, "Trial Over California Stem Cells Research Ends," *New York Times,* March 3, 2006, A1.

27. *California Family Bioethics Council v. California Institute for Regenerative Medicine et al.;* 147 Cal.App.4th 1319, 55 Cal.Rptr.3d 272 (2007).

28. Ibid.

29. David Magnus, "Stem Cell Research: The California Experience," *The Hastings Center Report* 36, no. 1 (2006): 27.

30. "Judge Dismisses Stem Cell Lawsuit," *Sacramento Bee,* October 25, 2005, A4.

31. See "Appeals Court Hears Stem Cell Institute Case," *Los Angeles Times,* February 15, 2007.

32. Magnus, "Stem Cell Research," 27.

33. Committee on Guidelines for Human Embryonic Stem Cell Research, National Research Council, *Guideline for Human Embryonic Stem Cell Research* (National Academies Press 2005).

34. Magnus, "Stem Cell Research," 27.

35. Josephine Johnston, "Paying Egg Donors: Exploring the Arguments," *The Hastings Report* 36, no. 1 (2006): 28.

36. Roger G. Noll, "The Politics and Economics of Implementing State-Sponsored Embryonic Stem Cell Research," http://siepr.stanford.edu/ Papers/pdf/04-28.pdf; http://www.nyas.org/ebriefreps/ebrief/000440/pdfs/ Noll.pdf.

37. Ibid., 1054–64.

38. Crockin, 'What Is an Embryo?', 1178.

39. I will use the term "pre-embryo" to refer to sperm-fertilized eggs prior to the blastocyst stage. The term "pre-implantation embryo" could be used as well. The choice of term, however, is not as important as the fact that whatever terminology is used should accurately reflect the variety of genetic material and stages of development known to exist as scientific research continues. Crockin, 'What Is an Embryo?', 1179.

40. *Roe v. Wade,* 410 U.S. 113, 158 (1973); Crockin, 'What Is an Embryo?', 1179.

41. Ibid., 1179–80.

42. *Davis v. Davis,* 842 S.W. 2d 588 (Tenn. 1992).

43. Crockin, *What' Is an Embryo?',* 1180.

44. Ibid., 1181.

45. Ibid.; *A.Z. v. B.Z.,* 725 N.E. 2d 1051, 1057–58 (Mass. 2000).

46. *A.Z.,* 725 N.E. 2d at 1057.

47. Ibid.; Shirin Movahed, "The Legal Status of Embryos in the United States," http://stemcellsclub.com/stemcellsclub/articlemovahed.html; *Santana v. Zilog,* 878 F. Supp. 1373 (D. Idaho 1995); *York v. Jones,* 717 F. Supp. 421 (D. Va. 1989); *Kass v. Kass,* 696 N.E.2d 174 (N.Y. 1998); *Cahill v. Cahill,* 757 So.2d 465 (Ala. 2000).

48. See Kiessling, *What Is an Embryo?*

49. William P. Cheshire, "Human Embryo Research and the Language of Moral Uncertainty," *American Journal of Bioethics* 4, no. 1 (2004): 1–5.

50. *Moore v. Regents,* 793 P. 2d 479 (Cal. 1990).

51. Ibid.

52. R. Alta Charo, "Body of Research—Ownership and Use of Human Tissue," *The New England Journal of Medicine* 355, no. 15 (October 12, 2006): 1517–19.

53. See "Founders Designed Establishment Clause."

54. Monica Davey, "South Dakota Bans Abortion, Setting Up a Battle," *New York Times* (March 7, 2006), http://www.nytimes.com/2006/03/07/national/07

abortion.html?ex=1299387600&en=bc436021a5de3fd9&ei=5088&partner=rssny
t&emc=rss.

55. Crystal Phend, "ACC: Stem Cell Therapies Hint at Promise for Old and New Heart Attacks," *MedPage Today,* Conference Report (March 29, 2007), http://www.medpagetoday.com/MeetingCoverage/ACCMeeting/tb/5352.

56. See Susan L. Crockin, "How Do You 'Adopt' a Frozen Egg," *Boston.com,* News (December 4,2005), http://www.boston.com/news/globe/editorial_opin ion/oped/articles/2005/12/04/how_do_you_adopt_a_frozen_egg/.

57. Sina A. Muscati, *Defining a New Ethical Standard for Human In Vitro Embryo in the Context of Stem Cell Research,* Duke L. & Tech. L. Rev. 26, 37 (2002).

58. See Andrea-Romana Prusa et al., "Oct-4-Expressing Cells in Human Amniotic Fluid: A New Source for Stem Cell Research?" *Human Reproduction* 18, no. 7 (2003): 1489–93; Shaoni Bhattacharya, "Amniotic Fluid May Hold 'Ethical' Stem Cells," *NewScientist.com* (June 30, 2003), http://www.new scientist.com/article.ns?id=dn3886; Mary Carmichael, "A New Era Begins: Stem Cells Derived from Amniotic Fluid Show Great Promise in the Lab and May End the Divisive Ethical Debate Once and for All," *Newsweek* on *MSNBC.com* (January 7, 2007), http://www.msnbc.msn.com/id/16513279/site/newsweek/.

CHAPTER 7

1. Gregory E. Pence, *The Elements of Bioethics* (New York: McGraw-Hill, 2006), 139.

2. Ibid., 137–39.

3. Christopher Hook and Paul S. Mueller, "The Terri Schiavo Saga: The Making of a Tragedy and Lessons Learned," *Mayo Clinic Proceedings* 2005, 80 (11) (2005): 1449–60.

4. Bruce Jennings, "The Long Dying of Terri Schiavo—Private Tragedy, Public Danger" (lecture, The Hastings Center, Garrison, NY, May 20, 2005).

5. Hook and Mueller, "The Terri Schiavo Saga."

6. Pence, *The Elements of Bioethics,* 137.

7. O. Carter Snead, *Dynamic Complementarity: Terri's Law and Separation of Powers Principles in the End-of-Life Context,* 57 Fla. L. Rev. 53 (2005).

8. Jay Wolfson, "Erring on the Side of Theresa Schiavo: Reflections of the Special Guardian ad Litem," *Hastings Center Report,* 35, no. 3 (2005): 17.

9. *In re* Quinlan, 355 A.2d 647 (N.J.1976).

10. Carl E. Schneider, "Hard Cases and the Politics of Righteousness," *Hastings Center Report* 35, no. 3 (2005): 24–27.

11. Snead, *Dynamic Complementarity.*

12. Jennings, "The Long Dying."

13. "A Definition of Irreversible Coma," Report of the Ad Hoc Committee of the Harvard Medical School to Examine the Definition of Brain Death, *The Journal of the American Medical Association* 205, no. 6 (1968): 337–40.

14. *Quinlan,* 355 A.2d at 647.

15. Barry R. Schaller, *A Legal Prescription for Bioethical Ills,* 21 Quinnipiac L. Rev. 183 (2002).

16. *Quinlan,* 355 A.2d at 653–54.

17. Ibid., 658.

18. M.L. Tina Stevens, *The Quinlan Case Revised: A History of the Cultural Politics of Medicine and the Law,* 21 J. Health Pol. Pol'y & L. 347, 348 (1996).

19. *Quinlan,* 355 A.2d at 666.

20. Ibid., 666–67.

21. Ibid., 670.

22. Stevens, *The Quinlan Case Revised,* 353.

23. Ibid., 353–54.

24. Ibid.,354–55.

25. Ibid., 355–56.

26. Ibid., 358.

27. Ibid.

28. Ibid., 359.

29. Ibid.

30. *In re* Quinlan, 355 A.2d 647, 660 (N.J.1976).

31. Ibid.

32. *Eisenstadt v. Baird,* 405 U.S. 438 (1972).

33. *Stanley v. Georgia,* 394 U.S. 557 (1969).

34. *Griswold v. Connecticut,* 381 U.S. 479 (1965).

35. *Quinlan,* 355 A.2d at 671–72.

36. Stevens, "The Quinlan Case Revisited," 362.

37. Ibid., 363.

38. Jennings, "The Long Dying."

39. Hook, "The Terri Schiavo Saga."

40. Snead, *Dynamic Complementarity.*

41. A living will is a document in which a person expresses in advance his or her wish not to receive life sustaining treatment in that event of later incapacity.

42. A durable power of attorney is used to designate a person to act on another's behalf.

43. Snead, *Dynamic Complementarity.*

44. Ibid.; Fla. Stat. § 765.101(12) (2003).

45. Guardian ad litem literally means "guardian for the suit." The guardian provides independent advice to the court to bring balance to the decision making progress. A guardian ad litem is often appointed in divorce cases to represent the interest of minor children. As with the *Schiavo* case, a guardian ad litem may be appointed in situations in which the person whose interests are being represented lacks capacity.

46. *In re* Guardianship of Browning, 568 So.2d 4 (Fla. 1990).

47. Snead, *Dynamic Complementarity.*

48. Hook, "The Terri Schiavo Saga," 4.

49. Ibid.

50. Ibid.

51. Ibid., 5.

52. Snead, *Dynamic Complementarity,* 68.

53. H.B. 35-E, 2003-E S. Spec. Sess. (Fla. 2003).

54. Wolfson, "Erring on the Side."

55. Jay Wolfson, "A Report to Governor Jeb Bush in the Matter of Theresa Marie Schiavo," 13 (2003).

56. *Schiavo v. Bush,* 2004 WL 980028 (Fla. Cir. Ct. 2004).

57. Hook, "The Terri Schiavo Saga."

58. Ibid., 6.

59. *Bouvia v. Superior Ct.,* 225 Cal. Rptr. 297 (1986).

60. *In re* Martin, 538 N.W.2d 399 (Mich. 1995).

61. Robert A. Burt, "The End of Autonomy," in "Improving End of Life Care: Why Has It Been so Difficult?" *Hastings Center Special Report* 35, no. 6 (2005), S9–S13.

62. Schneider, "Hard Cases."

63. Julia Duin, "Judge in Schiavo Case Faces Death Threats," *Washington Times* (March 30, 2005), http://www.washingtontimes.com/national/20050330-125345-6451r.htm.

64. John A. Robertson, *Schiavo and Its (In)Significance,* 35 Stetson L. Rev. 101 (2005).

65. Fla. Const. art. II §3.

66. *Chiles v. Children,* 589 So.2d 260, 263 (Fla.1991); Snead, *Dynamic Complementarity.*

CHAPTER 8

1. Michael D. Fox, "A Defined Right to Counsel: An Idea Whose Time Has Come?" *Connecticut Lawyer* 16, no. 7 (2006): 14.

2. In Connecticut, for example, "[a]mong those who have a statutory right to counsel in civil cases are petitioners in habeas corpus proceedings arising from criminal matters, General Statutes § 51-296 (a); litigants in termination of parental rights cases, General Statutes § 45a-717 (b), and proceedings on behalf of neglected, uncared for or dependent children or youths, General Statutes § 46b-135(b); and persons who might be involuntarily confined due to mental condition or for purposes of quarantine, e.g., General Statutes §§ 17a-498 and 19a-221." Connecticut Practice Series: Connecticut Rules of Appellate Procedure (2007 ed.) § 63-6, official commentary to 2006 amendments, 145.

Selected Bibliography

I list here only books and articles that are cited in *Understanding Bioethics and Law*. This bibliography is by no means a complete record of all the works and sources that I have consulted. It does indicate, however, the substance and range of research upon which my ideas are based.

Andrews, Lori B. "Torts and the Double Helix: Malpractice Liability for Failure to Warn of Genetic Risk." *Houston Law Review* 29 (1992): 149.

Beauchamps, Tom L., and Childress, James F. *Principles of Biomedical Ethics.* New York: Oxford University Press, 1994.

Burt, Robert A. "The End of Autonomy" in "Improving End of Life Care: Why Has it Been So Difficult?" *Hastings Center Special Report* 35, no. 6 (2005): S9.

Cheshire, William L. "Human Embryo Research and the Language of Moral Uncertainty." *American Journal of Bioethics* 4, no. 1 (2004): 1.

Crockin, Susan L. "What is an Embryo?: A Legal Perspective." *Connecticut Law Review* 36, no. 4 (2004): 1178.

Evans, R.W. "How Dangerous Are Financial Incentives to Obtain Organs?" *Transplantation Proceedings* 31 (1999): 1337.

Friedman, Lawrence. *Total Justice.* New York: Russell Sage Foundation, 1985.

Hall, Stephen S. "Stem Cells: A Status Report." *Hastings Center Report* 36 (2006): 18.

Hensel, Wendy F. "The Disabling Impact of Wrongful Birth and Wrongful Life Actions." *Harvard Civil Rights-Civil Liberties Law Review* 45, (2005).

Hook, Christopher, and Mueller, Paul S. "The Terri Schiavo Saga: The Making of a Tragedy and Lessons Learned." *Mayo Clinic Proceedings* 80, no. 11 (2005): 1449.

Jasanoff, Sheila. *Science at the Bar: Law, Science, and Technology in America.* Cambridge, MA: Harvard University Press, 1995.

———. "The Life Sciences and the Rule of Law." *Journal of Molecular Biology* 319, no. 4 (2002): 891–92.

Jennings, Bruce. "The Long Dying of Terri Schiavo—Private Tragedy, Public Danger." (Lecture, The Hastings Center, May 20, 2005).

Kiessling, Ann A. "What is an Embryo?" *Connecticut Law Review* 36, no. 4 (2004): 1051.

LaFrance, Arthur B. *Bioethics: Health Care, Human Rights and the Law.* New York: Matthew Bender & Co., 1999.

Leong, Edmund M.Y. *The Hawaii Supreme Court's Role in Public Policy-Making.* New York: LFB Scholarly Publishing LLC, 2002.

Levine, Robert J. *Ethics and Regulation of Clinical Research.* New Haven: Yale University Press, 1988.

Lopeman, Charles S. *The Activist Advocate: Policy Making in State Supreme Courts.* Westport, CT: Praeger, 1999.

Magnus, David. "Stem Cell Research: The California Experience." *Hastings Center Report* 36, no. 1 (2006): 27.

Meisel, Alan. "The Role of the Litigation in End of Life Care: A Reappraisal." *Hastings Center Report* 35, no. 6 (2005).

Milani, Adam A. "Better Off Dead Than Disabled?: Should Courts Recognize a "Wrongful Living" Cause of Action When Doctors Fail to Honor Patients' Advanced Directives?" *Washington and Lee Law Review* 54 (1997): 149.

Morreim, E. Haavi. "Medical Research Litigation and Malpractice Tort Doctrines: Courts on a Learning Curve." *Houston Journal of Health Law and Policy* 4 (2003).

Muscati, Sina A. "Defining a New Ethical Standard for Human in Vitro Embryo in the context of Stem Cell Research." *Duke Law and Technology Review* 26 (2002): 37.

Pence, Gregory E. *The Elements of Bioethics.* New York: McGraw-Hill, 2006.

Potter, Van Rensselear. *Bioethics: Bridge to the Future.* Englewood Cliffs, NJ: Prentice-Hall, 1971.

President's Council on Bioethics. *Beyond Therapy: Biotechnology and the Pursuit of Happiness.* October, 2003.

———. *Monitoring Stem Cell Research.* October, 2004.

Schneider, Carl E. "Bioethics in the Language of the Law." *Hastings Center Report* 24, no. 4 (1994).

———. "Hard Cases and the Politics of Righteousness." *Hastings Center Report* 35, no. 3 (2005): 24.

Snead, O. Carter. "Dynamic Complementarity: Terri's Law and Separation of Powers Principles in the End-of-Life Context." *Florida Law Review* 57, no. 53 (2005).

Stevens, M.L. Tina. "The Quinlan Case Revised: A History of the Cultural Politics of Medicine and the Law." *Journal of Health Politics and Policy and Law* 21 (1996): 347.

Tocqueville, Alexis de. *Democracy in America.* Vol. 1 (1835).

Wolf, Susan M. "Shifting Paradigms in Bioethics and Health Law: The Rise of a New Pragmatism." *American Journal of Law and Medicine* 20 (1994): 395–415.

Wolfson, Jay. "Erring on the Side of Theresa Schiavo: Reflections of the Special Guardian ad Litem." *Hastings Center Report* 35, no. 3 (May–June 2005).

Index

About the Author

BARRY R. SCHALLER is a Connecticut Supreme Court Justice. He is an instructor of trial advocacy at Yale Law School and has recently held visiting lecturer appointments at Trinity College, Wesleyan University, and the University of Connecticut's School of Public Health.